The role legislatures play in the public policy-making process is of central concern to political scientists. Conventional wisdom claims that all legislatures except perhaps the US Congress are either marginal to the policy-making process or becoming increasingly so. In *Legislatures in the policy process* leading specialists in comparative government reassess this view and significantly advance research on the influence of legislatures.

In the opening chapter, David Olson and Michael Mezey identify three categories of variables – external influences, internal influences and policy attributes – which can affect the policy-making role of legislatures. They specify sixteen hypotheses that describe the relationship between these variables and the policy participation of legislatures. In subsequent chapters, these hypotheses are examined through a series of individual and comparative country studies which focus upon the role of the legislatures in various aspects of economic policy making. These include the influence of the French, German, British and US legislatures on monetary policy; the role of the Brazilian Congress and Indian Parliament in computer and electronics policy and the part played by the Polish Sejm in labor policy.

This volume is distinguished by its hypothetical framework and by the breadth of cases it examines. It makes an original contribution to our understanding of the role of legislatures in the policy-making process and as such will be of interest to specialists and students of politics and economic policy making.

Advances in Political Science
Legislatures in the policy process

Advances in Political Science: An International Series reflects the aims and intellectual traditions of the International Political Science Association: the generation and dissemination of rigorous political inquiry free of any subdisciplinary or other orthodoxy. Along with its quarterly companion publication, the *International Political Science Review*, the series seeks to present the best work being done today (1) on the central and critical controversial themes of politics and/or (2) in new areas of inquiry where political scientists, along or in conjunction with other scholars, are shaping innovative concepts and methodologies of political analysis.

Political science as an intellectual discipline has burgeoned in recent decades. With the enormous growth in the number of publications and papers and their increasing sophistication, however, has also come a tendency toward parochialism along national, subdisciplinary, and other lines. It was to counteract these tendencies that political scientists from a handful of countries created IPSA in 1949. Through roundtables organized by its research committees and study groups, its triennial world congresses (the next of which takes place in July 1991 in Buenos Aires, Argentina), and through its organizational work, IPSA has sought to encourage the creation of both an international-minded science of politics and a body of scholars from many nations (now from more than forty regional associations), who approach their research and interactions with other scholars from an international perspective.

Legislatures in the Policy Process: The Dilemmas of Economic Policy, edited by David M. Olson and Michael L. Mezey, is the eighth volume in *Advances in Political Science: An International Series*. Like its predecessors, it comprises original papers which focus in an integrated manner on a single important topic – in this case, how national legislatures form economic policy. It asks what legislatures do in western, socialist, and Third World countries, and how they function regarding such issues as economic development, industrial policy, and monetary policy. The papers in the volume were originally presented at sessions organized by the IPSA Research Committee of Legislature Specialists at the 13th World Congress of the International Political Science Association, held in Paris, France in July 1985.

Richard L. Merritt

Legislatures in the policy process

The dilemmas of economic policy

EDITED BY

DAVID M. OLSON

The University of North Carolina at Greensboro

AND

MICHAEL L. MEZEY

De Paul University, Chicago

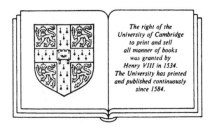

The right of the
University of Cambridge
to print and sell
all manner of books
was granted by
Henry VIII in 1534.
The University has printed
and published continuously
since 1584.

CAMBRIDGE UNIVERSITY PRESS

Cambridge

New York   Port Chester   Melbourne   Sydney

CAMBRIDGE UNIVERSITY PRESS
Cambridge, New York, Melbourne, Madrid, Cape Town, Singapore, São Paulo

Cambridge University Press
The Edinburgh Building, Cambridge CB2 8RU, UK

Published in the United States of America by Cambridge University Press, New York

www.cambridge.org
Information on this title: www.cambridge.org/9780521381031

First published 1991
This digitally printed version 2008

A catalogue record for this publication is available from the British Library

ISBN 978-0-521-38103-1 hardback
ISBN 978-0-521-06402-6 paperback

Contents

Contributors

Abdo I. Baaklini, Associate Professor in the Department of Public Administration and Policy at The State University of New York at Albany, is at work on *The Brazilian Congress: Transformation, Adaptation and Resurgence, 1964–1988.*

Roger H. Davidson is Professor of Government and Politics at the University of Maryland, College Park, and is author of *The Role of the Congressman* (1969).

Dennis Ippolito is Eugene McElvaney Professor of Political Science at Southern Methodist University in Dallas, and author of *Uncertain Legacies: Federal Budget Policy from Roosevelt to Reagan* (1990).

R. B. Jain, Head and Professor of Political Science at The University of Delhi, is author of *Comparative Legislative Behaviour* (1980).

W. Thomas Kephart was in the Congressional Research Service of the Library of Congress at the time he worked on his chapter, and is now a graduate student in Political Science at Ohio State University.

Lance T. LeLoup is Director of the Public Policy Research Centers, and Professor of Political Science, at the University of Missouri, St. Louis. He is author of *Politics in America* (1989).

David S. Mason is Associate Professor of Political Science at Butler University, Indianapolis, and author of *Public Opinion and Political Change in Poland* (1985).

Michael L. Mezey is Professor of Political Science and Dean of the College of Arts and Science at DePaul University in Chicago. He is author of *Congress, the President and Public Policy* (1990).

David M. Olson is Professor in the Department of Political Science at the University of North Carolina at Greensboro. He is organizer of the "Policy and Parliaments" research group, and is author of the *Legislative Process: A Comparative Approach* (1980).

Antonio Carlos Pojo do Rego, formerly an Assessor Legislativo with the Chamber of Deputies, is now an advisor to the Brazilian Ministry of Justice.

David M. Wood, the Frederick A. Middlebush Professor of Political Science at the University of Missouri, Columbia, has written extensively on both the British Parliament and the French National Assembly.

John T. Woolley is Associate Professor of Political Science at the University of California, Santa Barbara, and author of *Monetary Politics: The Federal Reserve and the Politics of Monetary Policy* (1984).

Preface

In the 1960s and 1970s, democracies failed around the world and legislatures either were abolished or subordinated, leading to the thesis of the "decline of parliaments." By 1990, however, as democracy returned to Latin America and the Mediterranean region, and as Communist systems of Eastern Europe were transformed into coalitional and elective regimes, we might be tempted to assert the rhetorically opposite thesis, the resurgence of legislatures.

We do not succumb to that temptation in this book. We do, rather, closely examine the conditions under which legislatures are autonomously active in setting public policy.

We include countries around the world in a variety of political systems. Our chapters on Brazil and Poland provide a snapshot of institutions in evolution, showing how they became more active and assertive than under previously rigid military and Communist regimes, respectively.

But our chapters on more stable democratic systems raise cautionary flags in our thinking about legislatures – be they in advanced industrial states as in Europe and the United States, or newly industrializing former colonies such as India. In these democracies, legislatures face formidable obstacles in even defining, much less asserting, policy preferences independently of and in opposition to their chief executives.

We do not look at legislatures as inert impersonal structures, but as organizations and politicians in action as they attempt to shape their respective countries' policy on economic issues. We examine economic issues both as important in themselves and as providing a clear view of legislatures and legislators in motion.

It is important to clarify the policy-making role of legislatures because the strength of a nation's legislature is often viewed as directly related to the strength of that nation's commitment to democratic procedures. The connection, though simplistic, is understandable because the legislature, more than any other political institution, stands at the confluence between democratic theory and democratic practice. This understanding of the role of legislatures, however, is premised upon a set of often unexamined assumptions about how legislatures and their members influence public policy. Our goal in this volume is to examine some of these assumptions so that we, as scholars, practitioners, or simply as interested citizens, can more clearly understand the implications of resurgent or declining legislative institutions for political systems and for the public policies they produce.

Acknowledgments

This volume is a collaborative multinational project. We include over a dozen authors who, in turn, have relied upon the comments and advice of countless colleagues as specialists in and about their respective countries and parliaments.

In addition, we are proud to include this volume in the International Political Science Association's "Advances in Political Sciences" series. Our chapters were initially presented at the IPSA World Congress in Paris, 1985, as part of the program of the Research Committee of Legislative Specialists. We have greatly relied upon the support and encouragement of the Legislative Specialists' Research Committee and the counsel of the IPSA series editors throughout the entire process of developing the present volume.

Both as editors and contributing authors, we have special expressions of appreciation to our immediate sources of support and assistance. Olson has been assisted by the secretarial staff and graduate research assistants of the Political Science Department, and also by grants from Graduate School's Research Council at the University of North Carolina – Greensboro. Mezey wishes to acknowledge with gratitude the support of Dean Richard Meister of DePaul University's College of Liberal Arts and Sciences as well as the secretarial staff of the College office.

This volume is the result of almost a decade of collaboration and conferences among the authors. Our collaborative and multinational research has been supported financially by many of the authors' home universities, by research groups within individual countries, and by the National Endowment for the Humanities in the United States. We are grateful to our host universities for conferences at The University of North Carolina – Greensboro and Duke University in the United States, Lunds University in Sweden, and Jagiellonian University in Poland.

PART I
INTRODUCTION

1

Parliaments and public policy

DAVID M. OLSON AND MICHAEL L. MEZEY

At one time there was among American political scientists something of a consensus about the role of the world's legislatures in the policy-making process. The United States Congress, so the conventional wisdom went, was a legislature with a central policy-making role. Even while many observed and lamented what seemed to be an increasing tendency toward presidential domination of congressional decision-making, they found the rest of the world's legislatures even more deficient as policy-making bodies. The policy-making role of European legislatures was viewed either as permanently subordinated to political parties, cabinets, and bureaucracies or at best in decline relative to these institutions. As for legislatures in Third World and in Marxist political systems, the issue for these institutions was neither their centrality nor their decline, but rather their political irrelevance. Not only did these legislatures play less of a policy-making role than the modal European case, they often were blatantly manipulated and intimidated by military, civilian and partisan bureaucracies. The consensual view was that these legislatures existed for the primary purpose of providing a democratic facade for authoritarian political systems (see Packenham, 1970).

Beginning in the late 1960s, however, students of legislative behavior began to develop a more sophisticated sense of what legislatures did and how they affected public policy. While admitting that most legislatures seldom made the major policy decisions and usually followed the lead of other institutions, more subtle ways by which legislatures influenced public policy were detected. Through public debates, the private interactions of their members with the executive, the linkage activities that they performed on behalf of their constituents, and their activities in regard to oversight, legislatures as collective bodies and their members individually seemed to have a greater impact on the contours of public policy than had been perceived by the earlier generation of scholars.

1

While this more refined image of the legislature emerged first in the study of the minimal legislatures of the Third World (see Mezey, 1985) those studying European legislatures soon began to utilize this expanded policy framework (see Blondel, 1969; 1973). Thus, instead of beginning and ending discussions of the British House of Commons by noting the prevalence of straight party-line votes, studies began to look at the lobbying activities that British MPs conducted on behalf of their constituents, the nature of the questions asked on the floor, and the impact of public parliamentary debate on the plans of the executive (see Leonard and Herman, 1972). And even in the United States, where the constitutional claim of the Congress for a central policy-making role was beyond dispute, attention began to shift toward the linkage activities that legislators performed for their constituencies (Mayhew, 1974; Fiorina, 1977) and toward their oversight activities (Saloma, 1969).

While it would be too much to say that we have witnessed a convergence of scholarly opinion on the policy-making role of the legislature, it is probably accurate to say that most political scientists now look at legislative policy-making activity with fewer and less rigid preconceptions about what the proper policy-making role of legislatures should be, and are willing to consider the impact of a variety of legislative activities on public policy.

PARLIAMENTS AND ECONOMIC POLICY

This expanded perspective on the legislature's policy-making role is particularly important to assessments of the legislature's influence in economic policy-making because the legislature's role in this area, although fundamental to the history of the institution, has seemed in recent years to be eroding, at least by conventional standards. The principle that the power of the purse was at the heart of legislative power was made clear at Runnymede when King John agreed to share power with his barons in return for their willingness to supply him with funds. Ensuing events established the notion that the power to raise governmental revenue was related to the consent of the governed and the connection was made between such consent and the right to have something to say, either directly or through representatives, about how the money was spent.

In later years, as mass publics sought to gain access to representative institutions, they were motivated in large measure by a desire to gain control of the economic decisions that most affected their lives. The parliamentary history of nineteenth-century Europe is marked by debate over land, agriculture, the rights of workers, social security, and other economic class issues which, along with religion, determined the partisan cleavages of the time.

Despite this historic claim of the legislature for an active role in economic policy-making, legislative involvement in this area has become increasingly problematic. During this century, the principle of the executive budget was accepted along with the more subtle and more significant claim that legislature should defer to these proposed budgetary figures. Another factor, at least in the West, that diminished legislative involvement in economic policy-making was the Keynesian revolution in economic thinking. The principle that governmental budgetary policies could be the engine for economic growth as well as the cause of economic stagnation, and the apparent emergence of the economic well-being of the society as the major criterion on which the success or failure of the executive would be judged, further enhanced arguments for executive budgetary control.

In many countries, Keynesianism moved a step further toward national planning approaches in which the executive took responsibility for developing overarching economic strategies. Whether these were Soviet-style five-year plans or more modest exercises in economic goal setting, whether they were motivated by a partisan ideology or a technocratic mindset, all of these approaches meant a greater bureaucratic role in the development and implementation of economic policies. While planning took the form of a state dominated undertaking in some countries, the corporatist model integrating the public and the private sectors became the preferred method in non-Marxist countries such as Germany and Japan. No matter what economic planning process was chosen, however, the legislature's role was usually a marginal one.

In some countries the logic of the planning model was extended to a more general movement toward the de-politicizing of economic policy-making. The establishment and empowerment of central banks insulated from the political processes meant that major economic decisions would be made not just without legislative input but often with only minimal direction by political executives. In other policy areas, a disposition to establish independent commissions to which significant economic decision-making authority was delegated constituted an additional step toward reducing political influences, legislative and executive alike, on economic decision-making.

Thus, as a result of action taken by others and sometimes as a result of their own actions, control of economic policy moved away from the legislature, usually in the direction of the executive, but occasionally away from both. As this shift in institutional control took place and often after it happened, several justifications or rationalizations were offered.

It was claimed that economic policy-making was too complex and too important to be left to legislators many of whom had neither the expertise nor the talent to deal with these issues. It was claimed that these matters were not really political, that there were right and wrong answers to economic questions, and that experts resident in Treasury Departments, Budget Bureaus, Central Banks, and National Planning Commissions were the people best situated to find those answers. When the politicians in the legislature intervened, local and regional concerns rather than the national interest would be advanced, political criteria would be substituted for technical criteria, and poor public policy would result. This view is well summarized in the statement by former United States Federal Reserve Chairman Paul Volker with which Lance LeLoup and John Woolley begin their chapter in this volume: "these decisions should emerge from a dispassionate, professional, deliberative process and be shielded from partisan pressures."

In recent years these arguments coincided with and were reinforced by the emergence of a truly international economy. As national banking systems became increasingly interdependent, changes in credit and monetary policies, particularly those of economic superpowers such as the United States, Japan, and West Germany, had significant impacts on the economies of other nations. Leaders of these countries convened at economic summits so that such policy changes could be negotiated and coordinated. The impact of these international decisions was often felt through trade, and trade policy came to be understood not simply as a vehicle of economic intercourse among nations but, in many cases, as the most important dimension of bilateral relations. An additional international dimension of economic policy came from the increased importance of multinational economic organizations such as the European Economic Community, OPEC, the World Bank and the International Monetary Fund. The cumulative impact of all of this was that economic policy, once viewed as a purely domestic set of issues, came to be an integral part of foreign policy. And this internationalizing of economic policy meant that not only could the executive claim greater expertise in economic policy matters, it also could claim that the international dimensions and implications of these issues further justified their dominant role, given the traditional preeminence of the executive in the international arena.

It would be a mistake to view these arguments as simply the fabrication of self-aggrandizing presidents, ministers, and bureaucrats. Legislatures often did exhibit marked deficiencies in dealing with complex economic issues. In regard to the American Congress, a strong literature developed questioning the Congress' capacity to generate coherent public policies, to move with dispatch, and to act effectively even in areas less complex than economic policy (Huntington, 1965; Sundquist, 1981; Mezey, 1986). While such weaknesses could be tolerated on "less important" issues such as the criminal code and the environment, in the case of economic issues, particularly those with a global dimension, the stakes were too high and, therefore, the executive needed to be the dominant player. In the Third World, where economic change was for many the highest priority, proponents of change often became opponents of legislative involvement. A "conservative legislature" hypothesis emerged in the literature arguing that legislatures in these countries typically obstructed necessary economic reforms because they were manipulated and controlled by more conservative monied interests, and that civilian and even military bureaucracies were often more progressive (Huntington, 1968).

Against these strong arguments for executive dominance, or legislative subordination, was the obvious fact that certain types of economic policies affected the people of a nation in an immediate and critical manner. The nature of trade policies affected the level of inflation, the unemployment rate, and the availability of a variety of products. Failed monetary policies or government austerity plans meant economic stagnation, unemployment, stress on the national budget, and, in some cases, mass political discontent. Choosing economic winners and losers as one implemented an industrial policy strategy could mean the life and death of communities and sometimes whole regions. Because they did not depend on popular support for their tenure in office, bureaucrats might well be less sensitive than legislators to the human consequences of technically correct economic policy choices.

Therefore, while arguments for minimizing legislative involvement in these issues seemed persuasive to elites – legislators and technocrats alike – they proved less persuasive to the citizens and interest groups who constituted a legislator's constituency. Legislators would be judged on their success or failure in advancing the economic interests of those whom they represented and localized interest groups make increasingly strong demands on their representatives for action on their behalf. All of this meant that even if many legislators preferred not to be involved, some degree of involvement would be unavoidable. Thus, legislatures and their members approach economic policy-making in a rather uncertain manner, aware of their limitations in this area, aware as well that their involvement is expected and even desirable, yet confronted by substantial political and sometimes legal barriers to their participation.

EXPLAINING THE POLICY-MAKING ROLE OF LEGISLATURES

Exactly what role a legislature and its members will have in economic policy-making will be subject to a great deal of variation across nations. The stage of economic development that a nation has reached, its prevailing political ideology, its constitutional and political history, and the nature of the policy challenges that it confronts are contextual variables that, when combined, will create a somewhat unique environment within which each of the world's legislative bodies operates. Therefore, the policy-making role that any one legislature assumes, as the various country studies contained in this volume will amply demonstrate, will have certain idiosyncratic features that will resist attempts at cross-national explanation. However, while some of the variance will, because of the context, go unexplained, the field of comparative legislative research is committed to the search for variables that can account for at least a portion of the cross-national political variation. Such an enterprise, it is hoped, can move political scientists toward a more general explanation for why some legislatures are more active and others less active in the policy-making process. It is to this task that we now turn.

We begin from the premise that to understand the legislature's role in economic policy-making we must first understand the legislature's general policy-making role. That is, the factors which explain the salience of the legislature as a policy-making body will also explain its salience in economic policy-making. The policy-making role of a legislature is in the first instance dependent upon its relationship with other political institutions and actors, most notably executive-centered elites in the civilian and military bureaucracy, chief executives in presidential systems, cabinet members in parliamentary systems, and party elites in those systems characterized by strong political parties. To the extent that legislatures are subordinate to these institutions – to the extent that the members of the legislature are constrained from acting autonomously by political actors situated in these external institutions – the legislature's policy-making role will be restricted. On the other hand, the legislator's claim to a significant policy-making role may be bolstered by its relationship with broader public outside government. That is, the strength of the legislature's connection with the constituencies and groups that its members represent may be directly related to its capacity to achieve a strong policy-making role.

A second category of variables has to do with the internal structure of the legislature. While a legislature's relationship with external institutions and actors may endow it with a potentially strong policy-making role, it may not be able to realize that potential if it has no efficient way of dealing with policy questions and if it has no professional staff to assist it. And if the policy-making activities of individual legislators are tightly controlled by highly disciplined political party organizations, then their members will be less able to play an active policy-making role than they would under more collegial partisan arrangements. So the condition of a legislature's committee and staff system as well as the organization of its legislative parties will significantly affect the manner and degree to which the legislature can participate in the policy-making process.

Having defined the general capacity of the legislature to participate in public policy-making, we are now in a position to assess its capacity to act in more specific policy areas. Put differently, at any general level of policy-making capacity, a legislature may be more capable of acting on some policy proposals than on others, and it may be more capable of action at some stages of the policy-making process that at others. Thus, the particular characteristics of a policy will affect the legislature's capacity to participate in that area.

From this discussion, and from the existing literature on legislative behavior,[1] specific variables can be identified and incorporated into hypotheses that link them with cross-national variations in the policy-making role of legislatures. These hypotheses can be grouped into three categories, differentiated from each other by the specific independent variables that they include. One category of hypotheses includes variables having to do with the nature of the political institutions and actors external to the legislature, their role in the policy-making process, and their connection with the legislature. These institutions and actors include executive elites, political parties, constituencies, and interest groups. The second category of hypotheses deal with the two key elements that characterize a legislature's internal structure – its parliamentary parties and its committee system. The third category of hypotheses includes variables associated with differences in the public policies with which legislatures must deal. These hypotheses suggest that the policy-making role of the legislature will vary across policy areas and policy stages as well as across nations.

EXTERNAL INFLUENCES ON THE LEGISLATURE'S POLICY-MAKING ROLE

Legislatures are not isolated entities. Rather they are connected to a set of external forces, including the executive, the larger electorate to which its members are responsible, and, in most political systems, organized interest groups. These external elements can either constrain or enhance the policy-making role of the legislature.

The executive. The strength of the legislature's policy-making role is most frequently connected to its capacity to resist or modify policy initiatives emanating from the executive branch (see Polsby, 1975: 277; Mezey, 1979: 26–27). When the legislature has no such capacity, its policy-making role is obviously weak; in contrast, legislatures with strong policy-making roles can say no to the executive and make it stick.

In most nations, the bulk of the legislation with which legislatures deal is proposed by the executive branch, and most of what the executive proposes is adopted (see Olson, 1980: 174). In this respect, the United States Congress is the major deviant case. However, even legislatures other than the Congress have demonstrated a capacity to resist executive initiatives, to force modifications upon the executive and even on occasion to defeat executive proposals. The growing ability of the Bundestag to amend and reject government legislation (Braunthal, 1972), the increasing frequency of government defeats on amendments in Great Britain (Norton, 1981), and even the ability of the Polish Sejm to thwart certain of the government's legislative objectives (Olson and Simon, 1982) suggest a potential for independent legislative action, even in legislatures where one is unaccustomed to seeing it.

In this connection, the most common generalization concerning the capacity of the legislature for independent policy-making action has to do with the differences between parliamentary and presidential systems. In the former, prime ministers and cabinets, because of their selection by the parliament and their control of a partisan majority, are quite likely to see their policy initiatives pass the parliament. Separately elected presidents, in contrast, usually have a more tenuous relationship with legislative majorities, and therefore encounter more difficulty in gaining parliamentary approval for what they propose. One reason usually cited for this difference between parliamentary and presidential systems is that the consequences of a government defeat in the former may be quite severe – resignation of the cabinet or dissolution of the legislature – whereas in the latter, this cannot occur. Also, parliamentary systems are more likely than presidential systems to be characterized by disciplined political parties that serve as links between the executive and a reliable legislative majority. Thus:

Hypothesis 1. The policy activity of legislatures will be greater in presidential than in parliamentary systems.

The policy-making role of legislatures may be affected also by the degree to which the executive branch is centralized. Some countries, such as the United Kingdom and Canada, are characterized by "closed" or highly centralized bureaucracies, whereas other countries, such as the United States and Switzerland are more decentralized or "open" systems (see Campbell and Garrand, 1981). The emphasis on hierarchy and on collective cabinet decisions in the former greatly limits the latitude of individual legislators for independent action, whereas in more open systems, the latitude for legislative action is greater. Thus:

Hypothesis 2. The policy activity of legislatures will be greater if the executive branch is more "open" than "closed," and decentralized rather than centralized.

Similarly, the level at which executive decisions are typically made may reduce or increase the possibility of legislative action. To the extent that issues are resolved at the highest levels of the executive, such as the cabinet or the president, the opportunity for legislative action will be reduced. As high level executives become committed to decisions, the political price of rejection goes up and the likelihood of rejection declines accordingly. On the other hand, if decisions are taken by people occupying lower level positions in the executive branch, it may be politically easier for the legislature to act. In the United States, for example, the president's position on a legislative proposal may be unclear or simply unstated, and in such instances a much greater range of legislative activity is possible. In parliamentary systems, however, nearly all legislation is government legislation and clearly identified as such, so legislators are deprived of the latitude for action that the frequent ambiguity of executive positions in the United States provides for American legislators.

Hypothesis 3. The policy activity of legislatures will increase as issues are handled by operating agencies rather than by high level executives.

The electorate. Legislatures and what they are capable of doing are profoundly influenced by their connection with the mass public from which they draw their legitimacy. Through the electoral process, citizens can change the composition of the legislature, the party that controls it, and the public policy agenda that parliamentary and executive elites will pursue. The implications of this "electoral connection" for the legislature's policy-making role is largely mediated by political parties and the role that they play in the electoral process.

In those political systems where parties dominate the process by which members of the legislature are elected – where parties nominate candidates and finance and organize their election – the policy-making activities of legislators is likely to be controlled by party elites and legislators will, as a result, have less latitude for action. But in those political systems where elections are largely decentralized and candidate-centered – where candidates can be nominated over the opposition of party leaders or even without their consultation, and where candidates organize and fund their own election – they will arrive in the legislature with few if any obligations to party leaders and therefore with a great deal of latitude for independent policy action. Between these two extremes, there are, of course, gradations. For example, there is some evidence of an increasingly candidate-centered electoral system in Great Britain. However, the parties continue to play a much more dominant role there than they do in the United States, but they play a less dominant role than, for example, the parties in Italy (see Ragsdale, 1985). To the extent then that elections are party dominated, executives will be able to rely on party organizations as they try to control the role that legislators seek to play in the policy-making process. However, if the electoral system tends to be candidate-centered, parties normally will be unable to perform this service for the executive. Thus:

Hypothesis 4. Legislative policy activity will be greater in decentralized and candidate-centered electoral systems than in party-centered and centralized electoral systems.

The connection between mass public opinion and legislative action is problematic, primarily because on most of the issues that policy-makers confront, public attitudes are at best ambiguous (see Wahlke, 1971). In these instances, legislators find themselves relatively unconstrained by constituency opinion and therefore more vulnerable to the entreaties of partisan leaders or executive elites. However, there are issues that are more salient to mass publics and about which public opinion is likely to be quite clear. Matters involving the regional allocation of government expenditures or the regulation of private behavior are the types of issues on which public opinion is likely to be heard most clearly. Thus, the effect of public opinion on the policy-making role of the legislature is likely to be conditional on the clarity of the opinions held and on the direction of the opinion: if opinion is clear and clearly opposed to the executive, the chances of legislative activity are enhanced, whereas if opinion is ambiguous or if it clearly favors the executive, the chances of legislative activity are reduced. Thus:

Hypothesis 5. The clearer the policy preferences of the electorate and the more they disagree with the chief executive, the greater will be the policy activity of legislatures.

Interest groups. While on most issues the policy preferences of mass publics are likely to be ambiguous, the policy preferences of organized interests are likely to be quite clear. And to the extent that such groups focus their demands on the legislature, they may succeed in encouraging legislators to act independently of the executive. Party and executive elites, in whose interest it is to minimize legislative influence, in turn will work to insulate legislators from interest groups.

The effect of interest group activity on the nature of the legislature's participation in the policy-making process depends in part upon the characteristics of the group or groups involved in the policy area, in part upon the political institutions with which these involved groups typically interact, and in part upon the degree of consensus or desensus that characterizes the groups that are activated by the particular policy.

Some interest groups are functionally specialized. That is, they have a relatively homogeneous membership and they focus on a relatively narrow set of issues of specific concern to most of the members. Farm organizations, trade associations, and professional groups are examples of such functionally specialized interest groups. Other interest groups, sometimes referred to as "peak associations" are characterized by a more diverse membership and by a more sweeping and comprehensive public policy agenda. National labor federations and business councils are examples of these groups.

Functionally specific groups usually tend to focus their attention in the first instance on administrative agencies whose jurisdictions match the groups' policy concerns (LaPalombara, 1974: 33). However, if they fail to get what they want from such agencies, they often will turn to the legislature. In those legislatures where committee systems are strong, they will direct their efforts especially towards the committees whose jurisdictions match their interests, and they will do so as frequently as they involve themselves with relevant administrative agencies. The larger more heterogeneous groups, in contrast, are likely to concentrate their efforts first on national political party organizations and on top executive branch personnel. However, as the level of controversy on a particular policy question increases, more interest groups will be drawn into the fray – perhaps including some groups that are new to the particular policy area – and the level of inter-group conflict will intensify. In such circumstances, even these larger, more established, organizations will seek legislative support on the argument that on big issues one should look for supporters wherever one can find them. Newer, less established organizations will typically have no other recourse but to seek support from legislative precincts.

On the same reasoning, the legislature is less likely to be drawn into an issue if it is characterized by consensus among established groups and therefore little or no controversy. Such issues are unlikely to pose a challenge to established patterns of decision-making, nor will they disrupt ongoing relationships between executive elites and agencies on the one hand and established interest groups on the other. However, when new groups are drawn into the issue and when the level of controversy rises, these established patterns and relationships may well be challenged and the likelihood of legislative involvement will increase. All of this suggests:

Hypothesis 6. Parliamentary policy participation will increase as interest groups are functionally specialized and homogeneous in composition.

Hypothesis 7. Parliamentary policy activity will increase as interest groups disagree with operating bureaus.

Hypothesis 8. Parliamentary policy activity will increase as interest groups disagree among themselves.

Hypothesis 9. Policy participation by legislatures will increase as new interest groups become active on policy matters.

INTERNAL CHARACTERISTICS OF PARLIAMENTS

In addition to the variance in the legislature's policy role explained by its relationship with external political institutions and actors, the internal characteristics of the legislature – its organizations, procedures, and the resources that it employs as it goes about its policy-making activities – will affect the degree to which it participates in the policy-making process. The two major internal characteristics that distinguish one legislature from another are the role of political parties in their operation and the nature of their committee systems.

Political parties. Political parties function in nearly every legislature to group and unite individual legislators behind common policy goals. They also play a role in organizing the agenda of the legislature and determining its procedures. While all legislative parties perform these same functions, there is a great deal of cross-national variation in what they do and how they do it, variation that has consequences for the legislature's policy-making role (see Brady and Bullick, 1985).

First, legislative parties vary in regard to their connection with the executive. In parliamentary systems, members of the governing cabinet are also members of parliament and share the same party allegiance as the legislative party or coalition of parties that holds a majority. In presidential systems, legislative parties typically have a more tenuous relationship with the executive; while they may share a party label with the chief executive, they often act independently of executive wishes (see King, 1976).

Second, legislative parties vary in terms of their connection with party leaders external to the parliament. Parliamentarians belonging to certain parties, typically those on the Left, are officially subordinate to the party's extra-parliamentary leadership (see Duverger, 1954: 190–202; Epstein, 1980). Such arrangements are associated with high levels of voting cohesion among legislators who must toe the policy line laid down by the party organization. This, in turn, leads to a reduced policy-making role for the legislature because policy decisions are in effect taken by party leaders. In situations in which the parliamentary party is more autonomous from its national party leadership, cohesion within the legislative party is usually lower and the role of the legislature in the policy-making process concomitantly greater.

Third, quite apart from the influence of external party organizations, legislative parties differ in regard to their internal structure and the degree of discipline that they impose on their members. Some legislative parties are characterized by hierarchical structures and cohesive voting patterns (France and Italy are examples). Such situations usually mean a greater policy-making role for the legislature. Other legislative parties are able to combine party discipline with a more collegial internal structure (West Germany and Sweden for example). In such instances, the legislative party may have some degree of autonomy from national party leaders, but individual legislators have relatively little policy-making autonomy. Finally, some legislative parties, such as those operating in the United States Congress, have collegial structures and relatively low levels of voting cohesion, structural conditions that allow for a maximum degree of policy-making autonomy for the legislature collectively as well as for individual legislators.

Fourth, the party system that obtains within a legislature will vary, from those in which only a single party is represented in the legislature to those in which several parties have significant legislative strength. In general, systems with single legislative parties are likely to be characterized by reduced levels of policy influence for both individual legislators and legislative committees. But as the number of political parties increases, so too will the latitude accorded to individual legislators, and the committee system also will become stronger.

The internal structure of the parliamentary parties and the number of parties represented have a joint impact on the policy-making role of the legislature. These two dimensions are combined in Table 1.1 and legislative systems are suggested that exemplify each of the categories. Generally, in nations toward the upper right of the table, parties tend to control the policy process of their parliaments because they combine majority or dominant status with high levels of internal cohesion. In systems toward the lower left, parties are unlikely to dominate policy-making either

Table 1.1 *Characteristics of parliamentary parties*

Party systems	Internal organization of parties	
	Decentralized	Hierarchical
One	Tanzania	USSR
Hegemonic		Poland
Dominant	Mexico	Japan
	India	
Two	United States	United Kingdom
		West Germany
Multiple	French 4th Republic	Italy
		Israel

because they are internally weak, or because, given the multiplicity of parties in the legislature, they are not able to form a stable, working majority. These considerations lead to the following hypotheses:

Hypothesis 10. The policy activity of parliaments will be greater in party systems in which parties are numerous and in which no one party or coalition is dominant, rather than in systems in which there are few parties and in which one party or coalition is dominant.

Hypothesis 11. The policy activity of parliaments will be greater if the parliamentary parties are weakly organized or fragmented, rather than hierarchically organized and cohesive.

And, based on the connection between parliamentary parties and party elites external to the parliament, either in the executive or in national party organizations:

Hypothesis 12. The policy activity of parliaments will be greater if parliamentary parties are autonomous from external units, rather than subordinate to party leaders in the executive or in external national headquarters.

Committees. Legislatures also vary in regard to their committee structures (see Shaw, 1979). In many modern parliaments, committees have become vital components of the policy-making process, sometimes as structures for encouraging policy expertise in the legislature through a division of labor, sometimes as instruments for allowing the legislature to supervise the policy implementation activities of the bureaucracy, and sometimes in both capacities.

Committee systems vary in several respects and this variation has consequences for the legislature's policy-making role. First, in some legislatures committees are permanent, while in others they are temporary. Permanent committees that continue from one legislature to the next are typically characterized by relatively slow membership turnover and by a fixed and defined policy area jurisdiction. Temporary committees in contrast are usually re-formed with each new legislative session, have a relatively transient membership, and have at best an ambiguously defined jurisdiction. Because a permanent committee structure provides members with the opportunity to acquire expertise in specific policy areas, and because permanent committees tend to become to some degree autonomous, such committee systems are usually associated with a more active policy-making role for the legislature. Temporary committees are unlikely to support an active legislative policy-making role.

Secondly, committee systems vary in the extent to which their structure parallels that of the bureaucracy. When committee systems are organized in such a fashion that each administrative agency has a specific committee that legislates in and oversees its policy area, committees are more likely to become sources of expertise for the legislature and the activities of the bureaucracy are likely to be subjected to more careful scrutiny. But when committee structures bear no relationship to the structure of the administrative agencies, policy expertise and administrative oversight tend to be reduced and, it follows, the policy-making role of the legislature is likely to be less.

When the factors of permanence and bureaucratic parallelism are combined, the conditions for strong committee systems with strong policy-making roles are established. Permanent committees that parallel the bureaucracy, such as those that function in the United States Congress, suggest a strong committee system and a strong policy-making role for the legislature. *Ad hoc* committees with non-continuing jurisdictions and greater membership turnover rates, such as those that operate in the British House of Commons, are weaker and the legislatures in which they operate are unlikely to have a significant policy-making role. The implications of the condition of the committee system for the strength of the legislature can be summarized as follows:

Hypothesis 13. The policy activity of parliaments will be greater if committees are permanent and parallel the structure of administrative agencies, rather than if they are temporary and cross-cut the administrative structure.

Parties, committees, and public policy. While there is some evidence that the strength of legislative parties varies inversely with the strength of committees, there are also examples of political systems in which both parties and committees are strong (West Germany) and in which both are weak (Thailand). Nonetheless, the burden of hypotheses 10 to 13 is that strong committees are associated with a strong legislative policy-making role while strong political parties are associated with a more constrained legislative policy-making role. But it should be kept in mind that the absence of both strong parties and strong committees may suggest a legislature so weak internally that it is capable of playing only the most minimal policy-making role.

POLICY ATTRIBUTES

Now that the external and internal factors that influence the legislature's policy-making role have been specified, we can turn to that portion of the variation attributable to the nature of the policy being considered and the circumstances under which it is being considered. These policy attributes refer to the content of the policy, to the characteristics of that policy when compared with other policies, and to the stage of the policy-making process.

Policy content. Policies can be divided into four categories according to their content, with each category implying a different role for the legislature.[2] The category of policies treated in the chapters in this volume deal with the nation's economy. Included within this category are the traditional budgetary issues of expenditures and revenues, along with the more modern issues of planning and economic growth. A second category of issues, also carrying economic implications, are those that involve allocative and regulatory decisions. These include the distribution of government benefits to individuals and groups, and the regulation of behavior to enhance the public good – for example, policies that are designed to protect public health or the environment. A third category involves matters of domestic and international security, matters connected with the state's use of physical force. A fourth category of issues involves the propagation of values. Policies involving the rights of citizens, questions of religion and race, issues involving the approach toward (as compared with funds for) education, and matters having to do with the mass media fall into this broad category.

Our experience with legislatures leads us to expect greater legislative participation in some of these policy areas than in others. For example, as suggested earlier in this chapter, legislatures have tended to be less involved than the executive in matters of foreign policy-making, and in the resolution of crucial economic questions. This leads us to hypothesize that:

Hypothesis 14. The policy activity of legislatures will be greater on issues involving the distribution of benefits to society, the regulation of behavior, and the propagation of values, and it will be less on issues of internal and external security and on macroeconomic financial issues.

Policy circumstances. Issues arise under different circumstances which in turn affect the manner and means of their resolution. For example, issues vary in their salience, with some issues highly visible to large segments of the public while others are less visible to most people. Issues also vary in terms of the size and composition of the public whose interest they arouse. Certain issues arouse publics that are numerous, heterogeneous, and therefore divided against one another; others arouse publics that are few, homogeneous, and therefore more unified. A third distinction relates to the newness of the issue. While "old" issues are likely to be handled in a more or less routine fashion, "new" issues are likely to be dealt with in a less predictable manner, in part because they may activate interests which have not been previously involved in governmental affairs. For this reason, new issues may be more controversial than old issues.

Because legislatures are representative bodies, we expect that they are more likely to be involved with issues that are controversial and that are high on the agendas of significant segments of the population. Thus:

Hypothesis 15. The policy activity of parliaments will be greater on issues that are new rather than old, more rather than less salient, and which activate numerous and diverse publics rather than small and homogeneous publics.

Stages of policy development. It has long been recognized that the policy-making process goes through a number of stages from the time that an idea is placed on the public agenda to the actual implementation of a policy to which the relevant governmental actors have agreed. While any number of stages can be identified (see Price, 1972; Mezey, 1979: 47–48), we will use four.

Policy proposals begin at the *gestation* stage. This stage of the process may be of indeterminate length, for to the extent that we view public policies as responses to societal problems, it may take years and even decades for such a problem to move on to the public agenda. Health care, for example, has been a societal concern for centuries, but did not move on to the public agenda in the United States until well into the twentieth century. Atomic energy, in contrast, was an issue that moved on to the public agenda almost as soon as it was recognized as a problem. Legislators may be instrumental in bringing the gestation phase to a close by talking publicly about problems to the point that the issue moves on to the public agenda. However, other factors also may be critical. For example, it is often suggested that in the United States the president is the key actor in setting the nation's policy agenda, while in Europe, political parties and their leaders are likely to be the primary movers.

When a policy problem moves on to the public agenda it reaches the *proposal preparation* stage at which specific policy recommendations are formulated. These policy options can be generated by private citizens, by semi-public bodies such as commissions of inquiry, by office holders such as presidents or legislators, or by public bodies such as bureaucracies and legislative committees. Thus, legislators and their members are among a number of potential participants in this stage of the policy-making process.

Once proposals are prepared, they move to the *deliberation and decision* stage where authoritative decisions are made that bind the polity to a particular course of action. To call this a single stage of the policy-making process is to some extent misleading because the deliberation and decision process can be extraordinarily complex. It can involve the interaction of legislative and executive personnel, various formal groups such as inter-agency committees, various forums for discussion such as legislative committees or the floor of the parliament, and various informal processes such as lobbying and bargaining among the interested parties. While legislatures gathered in plenary session often have the formal final say on public policy decisions, informally these decisions to an increasing extent are made in non-legislative arenas, such as bureaucracies, cabinets, or party leadership councils.

Once proposals are approved at the deliberative and decision stage, they move to the *implementation* stage where administrative rules are designed that turn the words of the law into the real policy actions that govern people's lives. The implementation stage, like the gestation stage, will be of indeterminate length, for once a policy is approved, it will need to be administered as long as it is in force. And as specific problems are encountered, administrative policies and rules will need to be altered. While primarily the responsibility of executive agencies, implementation is also a stage of the policy process that has attracted increasing legislative concern. Through committees and on the floor, legislators have sought to influence the decisions that administrators make and to supervise their actions in order to detect inefficiency, unfairness, and corruption. And through their efforts to respond to the complaints of individual constituents and to the collective needs of their constituencies, legislators continually encounter the bureaucracy, often in the role of lobbyist for their constituents.

Table 1.2 *Factors relating to the policy participation of parliaments*

Hypothesis number	Variable	Policy participation of parliament	
		High	Low
External influences			
1	constitutional structure	presidential	parliamentary
2	executive structure	decentralized, open	centralized, closed
3	executive decision-making level	operating bureaus	high-level executives
4	electoral systems	candidate-centered	party-centered
5	constituency opinion	clear and contrary to executive	ambiguous and congruent with executive
6	interest group type	specialized and homogeneous	comprehensive and diverse
7	group-agency relationship	disagreement	agreement
8	inter-group relationship	dissensus	consensus
9	group involvement	new groups	old groups
Internal influences			
10	party system	multiple and unstable majority	few and stable majority
11	organization	collegial	hierarchical
12	relationship with external party organization	autonomous	subordinate
13	committee system	permanent and parallel to bureaucracy	temporary and cross-cutting bureaucracy
Policy attributes			
14	content	distributive and regulative	security and finance
15	circumstances	new, salient, broad publics	old, non-salient, homogeneous publics
16	stage	implementation	proposal

The recent literature on legislative behavior argues that the enhanced role of the executive in the policy-making process has been most apparent at the early stages of the policy-making process and that legislatures have shifted their focus to the latter stages of the process. Thus:

Hypothesis 16. The policy activity of parliaments will be most extensive at the implementation stage, intermediate at the stages of gestation and deliberation and decision, and least at the proposal stage.

SUMMARY

The various hypotheses that have been identified in the preceding discussion are summarized in Table 1.2. In the chapters that follow, we will seek to explore these hypotheses through a series of case studies focusing on legislative policy-making activity in several different national settings. None of these individual studies will address all of the hypotheses that we have specified here, but each hypothesis will be addressed by at least one of the studies. In the last chapter, the evidence generated in these chapters on each hypothesis will be summarized and assessed.

While all of the chapters deal with economic issues, a wide variety of specific issues within this broad category are included. Chapters drawing on data from the United States, Germany, France, and Great Britain deal with macroeconomic issues such as credit and monetary policy, and industrial policy. Economic issues which affect specific segments of the economy or the society are also addressed. Thus, chapters on India and Brazil deal with the development of the computer and electronics industries, a chapter on Great Britain deals with economic development of depressed regions, and a chapter on Poland examines labor legislation during the 1980–81 period of liberalization in that political system.

As we move ahead in this analysis, we understand all too well the limitations of this approach. To gain breadth of coverage, we have included nations with widely dissimilar political and economic conditions. Studies from advanced industrial countries as well as from newly industrializing ones are included, as well as studies drawing on information from democratic, Marxist, and Third World nations. This breadth has come at least in part at the expense of strict comparability, for despite the fact that each of the country studies deals with some dimension of economic policy-making, the diversity of the political systems that we have included combined with the small number of cases significantly reduces the likelihood of definitive findings.

Finally, these studies exhibit the usual weaknesses of comparative legislative research: a broad range of methods are employed, and a variety of data are collected by a variety of different means. This too is part of the price that must be paid for a truly global sample of case studies executed by scholars who are intimately familiar with the nations about which they are writing. So, while we cannot hope to test in a definitive manner the various hypotheses that we have enumerated here, our cases can help us to explore these hypotheses with a view toward identifying those that hold out the greatest promise for moving us toward more reliable generalizations about the role of legislatures in the policy-making process.

Notes

1. The literature on comparative legislative behavior is extensive. Our discussion draws heavily upon Blondel, 1973; Lees and Shaw, 1979; Loewenberg and Patterson, 1979; Mezey, 1979; Olson, 1980; Loewenberg, Patterson, and Jewell, 1985.
2. For the most commonly cited policy classifications, see Lowi, 1964; Clausen, 1973; Ripley and Franklin, 1987.

References

Blondel, Jean (1973) *Comparative Legislatures* (Englewood Cliffs, New Jersey: Prentice-Hall).

Blondel, Jean, *et al.* (1969–70) "Comparative Legislative Behaviour," *Government and Opposition*, 5 (Winter), 67–85.

Brady, David W. and Charles S. Bullock, III (1985) "Parties and factions within legislatures," in Gerhard Loewenberg, Samuel C. Patterson, and Malcolm E. Jewell, eds. *Handbook of Legislative Research* (Cambridge, Mass: Harvard University Press).

Braunthal, Gerard (1972) *The West German Legislative Process: A Case Study of Two Transportation Bills* (Ithaca, New York: Cornell University Press).

Campbell, Colin and Ted Garrand (1981) "Bureaucracy and legislative democracy in Canada, the U.K., the U.S., and Switzerland: from turtle syndrome to collegiality," prepared for delivery at the Annual Meeting of the American Political Science Association, September.

Clausen, Aage R. (1973) *How Congressmen Decide: A Policy Focus* (New York: St. Martin's Press).

Duverger, Maurice (1954) *Political Parties: Their Organization and Activity in the Modern State* (New York: Wiley).

Epstein, Leon (1980) "What happened to the British party model?" *American Political Science Review*, 74 (March), 9–22.

Fiorina, Morris P. (1977) *Congress: The Keystone of the Washington Establishment* (New Haven: Yale University Press).

Huntington, Samuel P. (1965) "Congressional response to the twentieth century," in David B. Truman, ed., *Congress and America's Future* (Englewood Cliffs, New Jersey: Prentice-Hall).

Huntington, Samuel P. (1968) *Political Order in Changing Societies* (New Haven: Yale University Press).

King, Anthony (1976) "Modes of executive-legislative relations: Great Britain, France and West Germany," *Legislative Studies Quarterly*, 1 (February), 11–36.

LaPalombara, Joseph (1974) *Politics Within Nations* (Englewood Cliffs, New Jersey: Prentice-Hall).

Lees, John D. and Malcolm Shaw, eds. (1979) *Committees in Legislatures: A Comparative Analysis* (Durham: Duke University Press).

Leonard, Dick and Valentine Herman (1972) *The Backbencher and Parliament* (London: St. Martin's Press).

Loewenberg, Gerhard and Samuel C. Patterson (1979) *Comparing Legislatures* (Boston: Little, Brown).

Loewenberg, Gerhard, Samuel C. Patterson, and Malcolm E. Jewell, eds. (1985) *Handbook of Legislative Research* (Cambridge, Mass: Harvard University Press.

Lowi, Theodore J. (1964) "American business, public policy, case studies and political theory," *World Politics*, 16 (July), 677–715.

Mayhew, David E. (1974) *Congress: The Electoral Connection* (New Haven: Yale University Press).

Mezey, Michael L. (1979) *Comparative Legislatures* (Durham: Duke University Press).

Mezey, Michael L. (1985) "The functions of legislatures in the Third World," in Gerhard Loewenberg, Samuel C. Patterson, and Malcolm E. Jewell, eds., *Handbook of Legislative Research* (Cambridge, Mass: Harvard University Press).

Mezey, Michael L. (1986) "The legislature, the executive and public policy: the futile quest for Congressional power," *Congress and The Presidency*, 13:1 (Spring), 1–20.

Norton, Philip (1981) *The Commons in Perspective* (New York: Longman).

Olson, David M. (1980) *The Legislative Process: A Comparative Perspective* (New York: Harper and Row).

Olson, David M. and Maurice Simon (1982) "The institutional development of a minimal parliament: the case of the Polish Sejm," in Daniel Nelson and Stephen White, eds. (1982) *Communist Legislatures in Comparative Perspective* (Albany: State University of New York Press).

Packenham, Robert A. (1970) "Legislatures and political development," in Allan Kornberg and Lloyd Musolf, eds., *Legislatures in Developmental Perspective* (Durham: Duke University Press).

Polsby, Nelson W. (1975) "Legislatures" in Fred I. Greenstein and Nelson W. Polsby, eds., *Handbook of Political Science* vol. 5 (Reading, Mass: Addison-Wesley).

Price, David (1972) *Who Makes the Laws: Creativity and Power in Senate Committees* (Cambridge, Mass: Schenkman).

Ragsdale, Lyn (1985) "Legislative elections and electoral responsiveness," in Gerhard Loewenberg, Samuel C. Patterson, and Malcolm E. Jewell, eds., *Handbook of Legislative Research* (Cambridge, Mass: Harvard University Press).

Ripley, Randall and Grace A. Franklin (1987) *Congress, the Bureaucracy, and Public Policy* 4th edn (Homewood, Ill.: The Dorsey Press).

Saloma, John S. (1969) *Congress and the New Politics* (Boston: Little, Brown and Company).

Shaw, Malcolm (1979) "Committees in legislatures," in John Lees and Malcolm Shaw, eds., *Comparative Committees* (Durham: Duke University Press).

Sundquist, James L. (1981) *The Decline and Resurgence of Congress* (Washington, D.C.: The Brookings Institution).

Wahlke, John C. (1971) "Policy demands and system support: the role of the represented," *British Journal of Political Science*, 1 (July), 271–90.

PART II
MACROECONOMIC POLICY

2

Legislative oversight of monetary policy in France, Germany, Great Britain, and the United States

LANCE T. LELOUP AND JOHN T. WOOLLEY

A legislative approach – even one with some built-in leeway – would raise the basic question as to whether the Congress would want to inject itself so directly into these (monetary) judgements, filled with technical complexity and doctrinal controversy. It does not seem to be consistent with the approach taken by Congress in establishing the Federal Reserve System 65 years ago, and consistently adhered to since, that these decisions should emerge from a dispassionate, professional, deliberative process and be shielded from partisan pressures.

Federal Reserve Chairman, Paul Volker (1979)[1]

INTRODUCTION

Even the US Congress, the national legislature with probably the greatest independent impact on the formation of economic policy, faces formidable obstacles in its attempt to influence monetary policy. Confronting central bankers, the financial community, economists, presidents, prime ministers, and treasury ministers, legislatures seem far removed from monetary decision-making. Yet with the resurgence of monetary policy in the 1970s and 1980s – its greater visibility and perceived viability in the arsenal of government economic weapons – legislators, too, have taken notice.

Keynesian fiscal policy centering on demand management, viewed by governments as so efficacious in the 1960s, was badly tarnished as an approach to an economic policy by the 1970s. Governments increasingly turned to monetary policy to deal with chronic inflation, sluggish growth, and high unemployment. The four nations included in our study all adopted some form of targeting the growth of the money supply: West Germany in 1974, Britain and France in 1976, and the United States in

1979.[2] As these policies began to affect the economic and political systems, legislative and parliamentary concern was aroused.

Like the legislators themselves, political scientists' interest in the politics of monetary policy is relatively recent. Little published research exists on the relationship between legislatures and monetary policy. Even the most basic questions have not been systematically posed for most political systems. Is there any evidence of the regular and systematic influence of legislatures on monetary policy? Is there legislative action that intermittently has some effect on monetary actions? What factors or conditions promote legislative action? Our study explores legislative participation in monetary policy in Britain, France, Germany, and the US guided by the parliaments and policy hypotheses used as a framework for this volume. The relationship between legislatures and monetary policy must be understood by considering the constraints imposed by the broader context of political economy and policy-making. We believe that three groups of factors and a number of the hypotheses help explain low participation and differences between nations.

(1) *The nature of policy.* Hypotheses concerning policy content and attributes are of particular concern because of policy related barriers to legislative influence. The technical nature of monetary policy affects legislative incentives to act. Policy goals, the complexity and coordination of monetary instruments, and their linkage to other economic policies differ significantly between countries. Central bankers have used the technical nature of monetary policy to shield themselves from legislative scrutiny and from other potential competitors for power. The hypotheses to be tested are:

Hypothesis 14: Content. The policy activity of parliaments is greater on issues of societal regulations and benefits, and on propagation of values, than on questions of security and of finance.

Hypothesis 15: Circumstances. The policy activity of parliaments is greater on issues which are new, rather than old, controversial rather than accepted, salient rather than quiet, and which involve diverse and numerous publics rather than a small and homogeneous public.

Hypothesis 16: Stage. The policy activity of parliaments is greater at the implementation stage, intermediate at the stages of gestation and enactment, and least in proposal formulation.

(2) *Constitutional structure.* Differences between presidential and parliamentary systems as well as the legal basis of the central bank affect the potential role a legislature may play. Potent legal barriers often hamper legislative participation: statutory and constitutional arrangements between the central bank, the financial community, and govern-

ment. The main political equation of monetary policy in Western democracies is between the central bank and the government, not the central bank and the legislature. Explanations of legislative participation must account for the differences between countries in the autonomy of the central bank and the statutory relationship between political and monetary systems. The hypothesis to be tested is:

Hypothesis 1. Constitutional structure. The policy activity of legislatures is greater in presidential than in prime ministerial systems.

(3) *Legislative incentives and reward systems.* The incentives of legislators are related to institutionalization and environment: the nature of candidate-centered versus party-centered elections, the varying powers of the legislatures, the party and committee structures within legislatures, and the role and importance of interest groups. The hypotheses to be tested are:

Hypothesis 10. Party system. The policy activity of parliaments is greater in party systems in which parties are numerous and in which no one party or coalition is dominant, rather than in a system in which there are few parties and in which one party or coalition is dominant.

Hypothesis 13. Committees. The policy activity of parliaments is greater if committees are permanent and parallel the structure of administrative agencies, rather than *ad hoc* and cross-cut the administrative structure.

Hypothesis 4. Elections. Legislative policy activity is greater in decentralized and candidate-centered electoral systems than in party-centralized electoral campaigns.

Hypothesis 8. Inter-group relationship. Parliamentary policy activity increases as interest groups disagree among themselves.

This analysis is a first step in comparing and attempting to explain legislatures' role in monetary policy. Since the level of legislative participation and available information varies considerably between countries, coverage of these four cases is necessarily unequal. Because of the differences in data availability, our analysis is organized case by case rather than comparatively by analytic dimension. Our study draws on previously published sources and on original data on legislative activity including hearings, legislation, published committee reports, elite interviews, and direct observation. In this study, space does not permit us to go into detail about the constitutional and statutory relationships or the goals and instruments of monetary policy.[3] Attention here is devoted to the legislatures themselves in an attempt to analyze their concerns, institutional arrangements, and actions relative to monetary policy. Finally, the conclusions based on our findings to the hypotheses proposed by Professors Olson and Mezey allow us to make some general observations concerning the policy activities of legislatures and their impact on monetary policy.

No central bank is autonomous from the larger political and economic systems in which it operates. Some, however, make decisions on money and credit with greater legal autonomy than others. Central banks in the four nations we are comparing differ in the ownership of bank capital, control of the appointment of top officials, budget control, and the major constitutional and statutory provisions concerning the bank. Central bank autonomy is also a function of the practices and politics that have evolved around the legal structure.[4]

The US Federal Reserve (Fed), the Bank of England, the Banque de France, and the German Bundesbank all enjoy budgetary independence and with the exception of the US Federal Reserve, bank capital is publicly owned. The governors and presidents who head the banks are generally appointed by the government. Concerning the legal autonomy and specification of bank roles, however, more significant variation exists. Of the four, the Bundesbank appears to be the most independent from government, the Banque de France the most subordinate. Yet, from the perspective of legislatures, statutory arrangements favor the US Congress over the three parliaments. The creation of the Fed as a congressional agency in a presidential system gives American legislators greater potential control over monetary policy.

Legal arrangements provide only part of the basis for legislative influence. The *way* monetary policy is conducted also affects the potential for legislative influence. A wide array of monetary tools are available to central banks. Some involve a high degree of selectivity in impact and a high degree of direct control by authorities. Others are more general in effect. The greater the number and selectivity of monetary instruments – i.e., the greater the complexity of instrumentation – the greater the precision in targeting monetary actions at certain groups. This should make it easier for groups and legislators to calculate the distributive consequences of policies. In such settings, monetary policy is more politicized almost by definition.

Monetary policy consists of actions taken to affect the supply and cost of money and credit. The most common instruments are the purchase and sale of securities in the money market (open market operations), setting rates at which the central bank lends money to commercial banks (discount policy), establishing the proportion of assets that banks must hold in cash (reserve requirements), and administrative requirements concerning the quantity and type of loans banks may make (direct credit controls). The more monetary instruments available to a monetary authority, the more selective and discriminating it may be in choosing policy actions. But complexity of instrumentation also demands greater coordination and involves higher administrative costs. More specific policy actions tend to increase the salience of policies for interest groups by clarifying their distributive consequences. General, economy-wide policy, acting more indirectly on the economy (through "simpler" instrumentation) makes it more difficult to link policy action and specific effects. We suggest that relative simplicity in instrumentation increases bank autonomy by lowering interest group mobilization and increasing the ability of the bank to use technical sophistication to shield itself from scrutiny.[5]

By most measures, the United States has the least complex instrumentation, followed by Great Britain, West Germany, and France. French monetary policy instrumentation is distinctly more complex than that of the other three nations. The French have an elaborate system of credit controls and direct allocations of credit to various economic sectors. It is a more planned and statist approach to monetary policy that relies less on market forces and more on administrative action. Despite the transition in France to targeting the growth of monetary aggregates in the 1970s, the complex system of administrative credit controls was essentially unchanged.

What impact does the complexity of instrumentation and the legal authority of the central bank have on potential for legislative control? We hypothesize that legal subordination directs the attention of would-be policy makers to the government, not the central bank. Thus, in a system with significant legal subordination, the correct strategy for influencing policy would be to focus attention on trying to influence the government. We expect that complexity has the effect of directing more political attention to monetary policy, especially to its distributive effects. In general we expect that the distributive consequences more than the macroeconomic aspect of monetary policy are likely to attract legislative attention. Thus, we have two hypotheses about the institutional and substantive focuses of legislative attention. The lower the level of legal subordination, the more likely it is that legislative attention will focus on the central bank. The higher the level of complexity of instrumentation, the more likely it is that attention will be directed to monetary policy – and that attention will be motivated by distributive concerns. We

Table 2.1 *Complexity and subordination of Central Banks*

Complexity	Subordination	Examples
Low	Low	US, Germany
Low	High	Britain
High	High	France
High	Low	—

summarize these, with appropriate expectations for each country, in Table 2.1.

The French system, with a subordinate central bank is one in which legislators may attribute responsibility for particular actions to the government rather than the bank. On the other hand, the highly differentiated policy actions should make it easier to identify the specific effects of policies and should encourage legislative participation. The Federal Reserve and the Bundesbank present the case of a very strong central bank with relatively simple instrumentation. While political responsibility for monetary decisions is clear in a formal sense, the decisions themselves are difficult to link to specific distributional consequences or credit problems. While political conflict should focus directly on the bank, the simplicity of instruments suggests that the policy debate will be restricted to technically skilled observers. Legislative participation should be discouraged, and relatively simple instrumentation should enhance central bank autonomy. In the case of the Bank of England, relatively simple instrumentation combined with a relatively subordinate central bank status would seem to be a combination especially likely to produce low levels of legislative interest in monetary policy. Interest that exists, if this scheme is correct, would be focused on influencing government policy rather than the central bank.

The legal status of the central bank and the general patterns of complexity of monetary instruments provide a preliminary framework for examining possible legislative influence on monetary policy. In addition to legal and policy characteristics, parliamentary participation in policy-making depends on a host of constitutional, political, and institutional variables. The importance of these characteristics is, as we shall see, substantial. We turn to these in subsequent sections as we examine evidence of legislative efforts to monitor and affect monetary policy.

THE US CONGRESS AND THE FEDERAL RESERVE

Although the legal independence and relatively simple instrumentation of monetary policy in the United States favor central bank autonomy, no other legislative body has such clear legal authority to influence monetary policy as the US Congress. Throughout its seventy-year history, members have tried to remind Fed Chairmen of their ultimate responsibilities to Congress. Former Fed Chairman William McChesney Martin was once handed a slip of paper on which was written, "The Federal Reserve is an agency of Congress," and asked to tape it to his mirror so he could read it every morning while he shaved.[6] Yet over the years, many legislators remained frustrated at their inability to participate in a meaningful way.

To what degree has congressional participation increased in recent years? The answer reflects on the capabilities of Congress, the motivations of legislators, and the organization of congressional committees. Specific actions taken by Congress in recent years include structural changes to reduce Fed independence, procedural changes to enhance routine oversight, and attempts to directly affect monetary actions.

Congress can affect the conduct of monetary policy in the United States in a number of ways. In the broadest context, congressional decisions on the federal budget have a profound impact on the conduct of monetary policy. In the 1980s, record budget deficits have continually been denounced by Fed Chairman Paul Volker as dangerous and at least partially responsible for continued high real interest rates. Historically, the Fed has often taken action to blunt what it perceived as overstimulative fiscal policy promoted by the president and Congress.

Beyond attempts to urge greater coordination of monetary and fiscal policy, Congress may propose structural changes to reduce the independence of the Fed and foster *post hoc* discipline through a more systematic oversight process. This has been the most dominant approach. Hearings and investigations are an opportunity to seek justifications of Fed decisions, to articulate concerns of particular interest groups such as the housing construction industry, or to vent general frustrations about interest rates and consumer credit. Other possible actions for Congress are to reject or delay appointments to the board, subject the system to the regular budget process, subordinate the Fed to the president, shorten terms of appointment, or reduce the secrecy of the Federal Open Market Committee (FOMC) decision-making.

Finally, Congress can attempt to dictate certain monetary actions directly: monetary aggregate targets, interest rate targets, or GNP growth targets. The more specific and direct the proposed congressional actions, the more difficult it is for Congress to muster the necessary expertise and political support to proceed.

Congressional incentives and capabilities

Research on Congress in the past decade has increasingly focused on the motivations of members and links between individual incentives and collective performance.[7] Much emphasis has been placed on the representation of local concerns to enhance incumbents' chances for reelection. The committee system is a key link in the system of responding to constitutent demands and delivering tangible benefits to the district. The primary committees dealing with monetary policy are the House Banking, Finance, and Urban Affairs Committee and the Senate Banking, Housing, and Urban Affairs Committee. The Joint Economic Committee also periodically holds hearings on the conduct of monetary policy but lacks the institutional status of a House or Senate standing committee. As institutional posts to maximize electoral fortunes by providing pork barrel for the district, a seat on one of the Banking committees has not been seen as being as desirable as a seat on Ways and Means, Appropriations, or other money committees. Recently, however, new members have shown an increasing interest in banking and finance.

Members respond to constituent and group interests, and Banking committee activities are related to how changes in monetary policy affect certain interests. Key groups include realtors, homebuilders, banks, savings and loans, the construction industry, and the consumer finance industry. Members of the Banking committees receive substantial contributions from banking industry political action committees (PACs). This, rather than some burning concern about monetary policy, has undoubtedly contributed to the increased attractiveness of the Banking committees. Compared to divisions over other aspects of economic policy in Congress such as fiscal policy, trade, or labor, monetary disputes tend not to divide members along clear partisan or ideological lines. Liberal members often take pro-banking positions. Legislators seem to respond more on the basis of economic performance, interest group impact, and specific monetary policies themselves, rather than partisanship or ideology.

If the electoral link to monetary policy is less dominant than for other economic policies, other motivations may be more important. In particular, concern for the general institutional capability of Congress in national policy-making seems to have played an important role in recent congressional actions *vis-à-vis* monetary policy. Because of the nature of the Federal Reserve Act, monetary policy is considered an area where congressional participation is at least as legitimate as presidential participation.

Congressional resurgence in the post-Watergate era created an environment conducive to legislative influence and resulted in some important reforms (discussed further below). None the less, efforts at oversight of monetary policy have remained intermittent. Such performance is understandable for a decentralized institution which limited technical capabilities and mixed incentives. Regular oversight has high costs for legislators with uncertain payoffs. Combined with the fact that many members of Congress support continued Fed independence, oversight and policy intervention has been largely spasmodic. Senator William Proxmire describes the problems inherent in congressional participation in monetary policy-making:

Monetary policy is considered to be extremely complicated by most Senators. The influence of policy on the economy is indirect, and the lags are long – and the length of lags is controversial. How surely monetary policy will affect things like unemployment, inflation, economic growth, and so forth is very hard to say...

If things get too extreme, however, there is more of an interest – if, say for instance, tightening monetary policy results in making things very uncomfortable for home building... Congressmen have many other obligations and interests. And other things don't require the preparation and technical analysis that monetary policy does.[8]

Structural changes to enhance oversight

Congressional actions to increase oversight and exert *post hoc* discipline on the Federal Reserve began long before the 1970s. As one expects of bureaucratic actors, the Fed, like other central banks, has actively opposed attempts to limit its autonomy or more closely scrutinize its actions.[9]

GAO Audit proposals. After twenty years of efforts initially begun by Representative Wright Patman (Democrat – Texas), longtime chair of the House Banking Committee, Congress finally passed a bill which required GAO audit of the Fed in 1978. However, the monetary policy functions of the Fed were specifically excluded from the legislation which had been drafted with the "technical assistance of the Fed itself."[10]

The Fed and "sunshine" laws. In the wake of Watergate, legislation to require open meetings ("sunshine" laws) was proposed in 1975, and would have encompassed the FOMC, as well as other Federal Reserve Board regulatory activities. The Fed strongly opposed all attempts to require open meetings or the requirement to produce a transcript, electronic recording, or minutes of meetings. The Fed avoided the intent of the law by issuing a "Record of Policy Actions" rather than an actual

verbatim record. In the face of strong opposition from Fed Chairman
Arthur Burns, two open meeting bills were defeated in the late 1970s.
Despite concerted congressional efforts, the Fed successfully protected the
secrecy of its deliberations either through successful lobbying and
avoidance or delay of release of information until it was harmless.

Reporting monetary targets. As early as 1964, the House Banking
Committee staff proposed that the president set forth guidelines for the
growth of the money supply in the annual Economic Report and that it
be targeted to achieve the goals of the 1946 Employment Act.[11] In the next
twenty years, Congress would attempt on numerous occasions to mandate
such a requirement.[12] In 1975, Congress approved a resolution (House
Concurrent Resolution (HCR) 133) requiring the Federal Reserve to
report monetary targets to Congress. The Fed accepted it as a milder
alternative to several more aggressive bills.[13]

When HCR 133 expired, Congress drafted permanent legislation on
reporting targets for monetary aggregates to replace it. Once again, the
Fed successfully blocked efforts to require some information. The resulting
legislation, the Federal Reserve Reform Act of 1977, mandated that the
Federal Reserve consult with Congress at semi-annual hearings, required
Senate confirmation of nominations to the chairmanship and vice-
chairmanship of the Federal Reserve Board, prohibited discrimination in
the selection of regional bank directors, and required consideration of
broader economic interests in the selection of bank directors representing
the public.[14] Critics noted that the continued ability of the Fed under the
1977 Act to announce multiple targets, "made it possible for the Federal
Reserve to hide its efforts by always, or nearly always, hitting some
target."[15] The ambitious if ill-conceived Humphrey–Hawkins Act (the
Full Employment and Balanced Growth Act of 1978), which attempted to
mandate specific inflation and employment targets, further refined
requirements for Federal Reserve reporting of monetary aggregate
targets.[16]

Although Congress successfully increased both the amount and
regularity of information it receives from the system, congressional
oversight continues to provide minimal constraints on the Fed. In fall of
1982, the Fed decided to temporarily ignore its stated targets for the
growth of M1 – the sum of currency and demand deposits. Citing
technical factors, the Fed did not feel compelled to report this change to
Congress at the time. Many observers felt the Fed was concealing a major
policy shift.[17]

Attempts to directly shape monetary policy

Congressional activities in recent years have not been limited to reforms to reduce the independence of the Federal Reserve or improve oversight. In a number of instances, the House and Senate have attempted to mandate specific monetary actions by the Fed. Compared to other steps, the direct approach has been perhaps the least successful tactic, meeting strong opposition from the system. None the less, such attempts demonstrate the legal authority of Congress and the relatively high potential it possesses for meaningful influence.

Congressional efforts to instruct the Federal Reserve have come primarily in the areas of credit allocations, the specification of target ranges for monetary aggregates, and the specification of other targets such as interest rates and GNP/GDP growth. Congressional attempts to directly influence policy have been closely tied to increases in interest rates and slumps in the housing industry.[18] Since the mid-1960s, housing starts bottomed out in early 1970, early 1975, and late 1981.[19] These dates correspond closely to surges in congressional action.

The process which eventually resulted in the passage of HCR 133 in 1975 began as a more direct attempt to dictate monetary policy. In the House, Banking chair Reuss offered HR (House of Representatives) 212 specifying a 6 per cent annual growth rate in the money supply and mandating credit allocations to "national priority uses."[20] Fed Chairman Burns, the only witness at the hearing, successfully blocked the aggressive measure.

In the 1980–82 period, Congress produced an array of bills and resolutions concerning monetary policy after interest rates hit historic highs of over 20 per cent. SJR (Senate Joint Resolution) 120, cosponsored by 35 of the 100 senators, required the president to assure an adequate flow of affordable credit to small borrowers. In 1981, one House member introduced a resolution to impeach Fed Chairman Paul Volker.[21] In July of 1981, the House approved a resolution condemning interest rates as "needlessly and destructively high."[22] Scores of bills to restructure the system were introduced but no action was taken. In 1982, Democrats in both houses introduced the Balanced Monetary Policy Act to force the Federal Reserve to abandon its policy of controlling the money supply and, instead, to establish long-term targets for interest rates. The version of a continuing spending resolution passed by the House instructed the Fed to set targets for interest rates. While frustration and legislative activity were high, no major policy instructions or revolutionary overhauls of the system came close to passage. The decline in interest rates in late

Table 2.2. *Legislative actions concerning the Federal Reserve, 1970–80*[a]

Year	Structural reforms					Credit allocation					Conduct of monetary policy				
	0	1	2	3	4[b]	0	1	2	3	4	0	1	2	3	4
1970	—	—	—	—	—	—	—	—	—	—	—	X	—	—	—
1971	X	—	—	—	—	—	X	—	—	X	X	—	—	—	—
1972	—	—	X	—	—	—	—	—	—	—	—	—	—	—	—
1973	—	—	X	—	—	—	—	—	—	—	X	—	X	—	—
1974	—	—	—	X	—	—	—	—	—	—	X	—	—	—	—
1975	X	X	X	—	—	—	X	X	—	—	—	X	—	—	X
1976	—	X	—	X	X	—	—	—	—	—	—	X	—	—	—
1977	—	—	—	X	X	—	—	—	—	—	—	—	—	—	—
1978	—	X	—	—	X	X	—	—	—	—	—	X	—	—	X
1979	—	—	X	X	—	—	X	—	—	—	X	X	—	—	—
1980	—	X	—	—	—	X	—	—	—	—	—	X	—	—	—

Notes: [a] Both House and Senate Banking Committees and Banking Sub-committees and, in 1977, the Government Operations Committee. See also Appendix B.
[b] Key to entries
  (0) Investigatory hearings other than routine oversight (i.e., after 1975); no bill considered.
  (1) Hearings on proposed legislation.
  (2) Legislation reported out by committee.
  (3) One house passes legislation.
  (4) Both houses pass legislation.

1982 may have been partially influenced by complaints from Congress and the administration, but there is little hard evidence to support this view. The leveling off of interest rates did, however, lead to a decline of legislative interest and activity.

Congress and monetary policy: an assessment

The most significant recent change in Fed policy, the decision to target bank reserves, came in 1979 despite congressional displeasure with its obvious implication for interest rates. Yet the last decade and a half has been one of important changes for congressional participation in monetary politics. Table 2.2 summarizes legislative actions between 1970 and 1980. Although sporadic, congressional concern has resulted in a considerable volume of legislative activity and output.

Congress interacts more frequently, and more combatively, with the

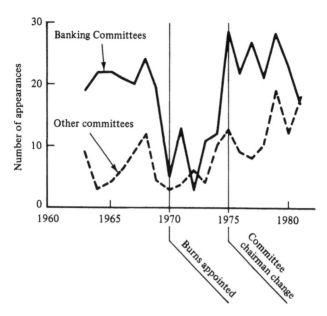

Figure 2.1 Appearances by members of the Board of Governors for testimony
before the Banking Committees and other committees, 1963–81

Federal Reserve than in the past, particularly since 1975. Figure 2.1 charts
the appearances of the Board of Governors before congressional
committees since the early 1960s. Unlike direct attempts to instruct the
Fed, which seem to follow the performance of the economy, oversight
activity appears largely shaped by personal factors. Appearances declined
following the appointment of Arthur Burns despite the economic troubles.
After the change in Banking committee leadership, appearances increased.
There also appears to be a drop-off around election time, reinforcing our
earlier suggestions about the incentives of members. Structural reforms in
the late 1970s institutionalized the reporting of monetary targets providing
for a minimum number of appearances, but variations in frequency seem
to be continuing in the 1980s.

The verdict on congressional impact remains ambiguous. In comparison
with other actors such as professional economists, bankers, and the
administration, Congress does not appear to exert as much influence.
Interest and activity is periodic, costly, and technically difficult. Attempts
to instruct the Fed break down as members head off in contradictory
directions. Yet congressional influence, although limited, is both real and
important. As we shall see in subsequent sections, compared to other

legislatures, Congress is dramatically more influential. Despite the more simple policy instrumentation, congressional interest is sometimes great, and as expected, it is focused quite clearly on the Fed. The Federal Reserve respects the ultimate authority of Congress and may at times actually fear it. Federal Reserve officials are therefore not arrogant in their disregard for Congress, but actively seek to assuage congressional concerns while avoiding closer supervision or guidance. Congressional uncertainty has precluded taking strong, direct action, leaving the Fed with considerable discretion. Yet, in the past decade, members of Congress are more technically equipped to understand and monitor monetary policy. If blatantly unacceptable policy is pursued by the Fed, congressional uncertainty could be forged into resolve. It is this knowledge which sustains some central bank accountability directly to the legislature and makes Congress a potentially important influence on US monetary policy.

THE BRITISH PARLIAMENT AND THE BANK OF ENGLAND

The growing political salience of monetary policy

For many years, monetary policy in Great Britain was nearly invisible. The statistics available to policy-makers were poor or non-existent. Not until after the Radcliffe Report in the late 1950s did the Bank of England begin to monitor British financial institutions and it was 1963 before accurate data on the growth of the money supply was kept.[23]

Monetary politics in Britain in this period seemed limited to a generally predictable ideological perspective by the two major parties. Labour, suspicious of the interests served by the Bank of England, tended to be critical of Bank influence. Conservatives generally seemed more favorable to bank autonomy and influence. Political concern in the early 1970s centered on economic growth and high interest rates as a possible barrier to growth, rather than on changes in the money supply. Only a few members of parliament were concerned about monetary growth.[24]

During the Heath government, economic policy was dominated by conventional Keynesian growth prescriptions subordinating monetary policy to these broader concerns. However, the expansion of M3 at an annual rate of 26 per cent in 1971 and 1972 caused other economic problems, and eventually focused more attention on monetary growth. Lack of monetary control was seen as one of the political consequences of democracy. Next followed the famous U-turn in policy in the pursuit of high employment and growth. Whatever the complete explanation of British political economy in this period, Sir Keith Joseph's call for tighter monetary control in 1974 presaged major policy changes later in the decade and a new emphasis on monetary policy in general. Did the participation of parliament undergo any meaningful changes during this period of economic volatility?

Parliamentary incentives and capabilities

By 1978, a glance at some of the headlines from *The Times* may have suggested considerable parliamentary interest and activity:[25] "Ouster of Bank of England Governor called for by Labour left-winger." "Conservative Shadow Chancellor proposes Bank of England Independence." "Labour working party report calls for reform of Bank of England." "Labour to accuse government of losing control of Bank of England." Yet behind the headlines, discussions on the conduct of monetary policy rarely mention parliament.[26]

Moving from the presidential system of the United States to parliamentary systems in Europe demands some alterations in the yardstick of legislative influence. Only in the US does the national legislature have the authority and political resources to even attempt to instruct the central bank. Constraints on legislative participation are much greater in parliamentary democracies such as Great Britain. In Britain, where the central bank is subordinate to the government, the House of Commons has been less directly concerned with the Bank of England than with the Treasury and the conduct of monetary policy in general.

Opportunities for MPs to influence policy are relatively limited. Of course, their ultimate power is the negative power to topple a government through a no-confidence vote – the analog to Congress's power to rewrite the Fed's charter whenever it wants to. Although its likelihood is remote, such an eventuality remains possible in the face of a devastating sterling or balance of payments crisis. The impact of MPs on legislation through standing committees is highly restricted because of the more limited role of parliament in the wider political system. Bernard Crick provided a useful description of legislative control in Britain when he noted that, "control means influence, not direct power; advice, not command; criticism, not obstruction; scrutiny, not initiation; and publicity, not secrecy."[27] While ministers have the most direct impact on policy, backbench MPs have some opportunity to influence policy through oversight inquiries of select committees, and by criticism and direct inquiry of the government in parliamentary questions.

The party-centered elections of Great Britain create a different set of incentives from the candidate-centered elections of the United States. The most obvious career path in parliament is through the party. An MP can work his way down from the back-benches within the party eventually becoming a junior minister and finally a minister. Party loyalty, even on non-confidence votes, is important to the MP taking this career path.[28]

Yet years spent on the back-benches can be long and relatively unproductive. Recent parliamentary reforms have provided MPs with a different, if somewhat risky, alternative career path. The select committee report of 1979 was issued in response to back-benchers who wanted parliament to be stronger in its dealings with the government.[29]

Strengthening parliamentary committees particularly for oversight activities may frequently clash with traditional party discipline in the House. Government MPs face a conflict in attempting to develop a meaningful legislative role through independent inquiry. It often aligns them with members of the opposition party whose motives, although overlapping in the desire for oversight, are fundamentally different.[30]

Government back-benchers, then, are caught in a dilemma. Desire for greater impact on policy through committee oversight conflicts with powerful incentives for career advancement. In contrast to the US Congress, there is no well-established role of an independent, influential MP. MPs are more likely to take venturesome policy positions if they have a secure electoral base. While this does not provide the policy autonomy enjoyed by members of Congress, members from safe seats have slightly more freedom to bring pressure on the government on non-confidence issues.

The incentives of MPs are very important in explaining parliament's role in monetary policy. MPs from constituencies with large proportions of owner-occupied housing may find that high interest rates put them at odds with government monetary policy. The result of these factors in recent years has been sporadic increases in parliamentary attention to monetary policy related to interest rates and the housing industry, greater overweight through select committees, and somewhat more public back-bench dissension over government policy.

Select Committee oversight of monetary policy

From 1956 to 1979, the Bank of England fell under the purview of the Select Committee on Nationalized Industries. During this period, the committee had from thirteen to eighteen members and was always chaired by a government supporter. Authority was granted to the committee: "to examine the reports and accounts of the nationalized industries established by statute, whose controlling boards are wholly appointed by Ministers of the Crown and whose annual receipts are not wholly or mainly derived from moneys provided by Parliament or advanced by the Exchequer."[31] While the Bank of England was subject to committee review, monetary activities were largely exempt from oversight. The authorizing statute specifically prevented the Nationalized Industries Committee from looking into:[32]

(1) The formulation and execution of monetary and financial policy, including the responsibilities for management of gilt-edged, money, and foreign exchange markets.
(2) The Bank as agents of the Treasury in managing the exchange equalization account and administering exchange controls.
(3) Activities as a banker to other banks and private customers.

Despite such limitations, the committee managed to find enough to review to issue two reports (May 1970 and October 1976) on the Bank of England in its twenty-three-year history. Despite Bank resentment at such intrusions, little meaningful oversight took place; the Bank's most crucial activities in the formulation and execution of monetary policy were out of bounds. Not until the select committee reform of 1979 did a select parliamentary committee conduct a penetrating substantive investigation into the conduct of monetary policy.

The fourteen new select committees created in 1979 have some advantages over their predecessors and over the subcommittees of the Expenditure committee. In particular, their jurisdiction is broader; each committee is charged with "the examination of all aspects of expenditure, administration and policy" of the department it oversees.[33] Under the new system, oversight of the Bank of England became the responsibility of the Select Committee for Treasury and Civil Service. The Committee consists of eleven members and includes a subcommittee. Data show that the committee compares favorably with the other newly created select committees in terms of attendance, sessions, and reports. George and Evans report that average attendance between 1979 and 1982 at Treasury and Civil Service Committee sessions was significantly higher than the all-committee average (88 per cent vs. 75 per cent).[34] The Treasury and Civil Service Committee (and its subcommittee) met 59 times, including 29 formal evidence sessions, printed 1,103 pages of testimony, and issued 8 reports. All of these measures of activity place the committee near the top of all select committees. George and Evans conclude that both the workload and the member's commitment has increased since the 1979 change in the authority and the status of the committees.

Treasury and Civil Service is notable in particular for its specific investigations. Its investigation into the Thatcher government's monetary

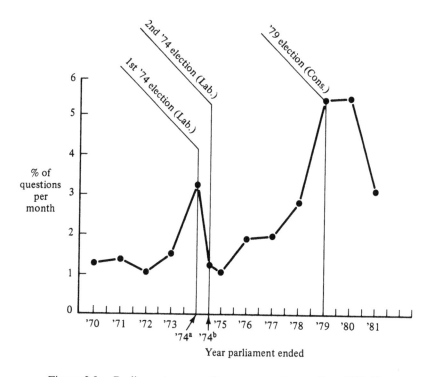

Figure 2.2.   Parliamentary questions on monetary policy, 1970–81

policy was one of the most controversial and important subjects of any select committee investigation. The inquiry was long and detailed, and despite the raging public controversy surrounding the government's medium-term financial strategy (MTFS), the multiparty committee issued a unanimous report in 1981.

The three volumes of the 1981 report on monetary policy represent a marked change in the quality and sophistication of parliamentary oversight of monetary policy. The report is a comprehensive review of the government's monetary policy, not merely a limited review of the Bank of England. Included in the report is extensive evidence, much of it technical, and a set of specific conclusions viewed by most as a partial indictment of the government's monetary policy. The report in part concluded:

We believe that there are risks attached to such a subordination of fiscal policy to monetary targets. In a recession caused by a fall in private domestic demand, built-in automatic stabilizers tend to raise the PSBR [public sector borrowing requirement] which in turn, with unchanged interest rates, may lead to an increase in monetary growth above the target. Meeting MTFS targets may then require either a rise in interest rates or a tightening of fiscal stance. Either of these would tend to counterbalance the moderating effect the automatic stabilizers have on the recession. In these conditions, additional sacrifices of output may be made to meet anti-inflationary monetary targets...

We discuss the view that monetary policy can work directly, through expectations, to reduce inflation without significantly affecting output. We conclude that in the light of experience this view is not valid.[35]

The real test of parliamentary impact is not to be found in parliamentary reports, but in the responses they produce. Despite the bipartisan criticism of government policy in the report, its impact on government actions was limited. The Commons did not debate the report.[36] Even by Crick's criteria, parliamentary control in this key area was slight at best. The power of select committees is not the power to legislate, it is rather the "power of publicity."[37] Despite a marked change in the quality and expertise of the committee's review, the committee lacks the power to act on or even demand an appropriate response to its recommendations. To date, it has not been able to muster the support to lobby for action on its own reports in the House.

In an interesting twist on the issue of parliamentary control of monetary policy, the increase in parliamentary oversight appears to provide the Bank of England with greater scope to criticize the government openly. Instead of back-benchers finding a means to more effectively influence the Bank and government policy, parliament seems, in fact, to have become an additional form for the Bank and the government to lobby one another – in public.

Parliamentary questions on monetary policy and the Bank of England

Despite the constraints confronting MPs, interest and concern with the conduct of monetary policy has increased in the past decade. This is evident in the frequency of parliamentary questions dealing with monetary policy for the period 1970 to 1981. Based on entries in Hansard's index,[38] calculated on a per-month basis to correct for the different lengths of parliamentary sessions, we found the interesting pattern plotted in Figure 2.2.

The data confirm our expectations about when legislative concern about monetary policy should increase. In general, the state of the economy and the terms of government policy discussion appear to stimulate parliamentary interest. Prior to the first 1974 election (entered on the chart as '74ᵃ), a period marked by rapid inflation, bitter industrial strife, and generally deteriorating economic circumstances, we note roughly a tripling of interest in issues of monetary policy. The interval prior to the second 1974 election (marked on chart as '74[b]), showed a return to the "normal" level of parliamentary interest in monetary policy. Beginning around 1976, following the crisis of the pound, protracted IMF negotiations, and the announcement of monetary targets, the average number of questions concerning monetary policy began a steady rise to an approximate peak in 1979 – coincident with further economic crisis, inflation, and industrial strife. The level of parliamentary interest increased slightly in the first year of the Thatcher government. The fact that interest did not rise more is perhaps remarkable given the much more explicit monetarism of the Thatcher government. Even more remarkable, however, is the observed *fall* in parliamentary interest during the devastating recession of the second Thatcher year. Perhaps this was due to the attention being given to monetary policy in the Treasury and Civil Service Committee where much more effective questioning of government policy was then taking place. As with the United States experience, legislative interest in monetary matters is uneven and sporadic, although its salience appears to have permanently increased since the mid-1970s. Recent governments have been increasingly called upon to answer for their monetary actions. Once again, however, the gap between questioning and more meaningful input is often a large one.

Parliament and monetary policy: an assessment

The House of Commons has directed its attention regarding monetary policy more to the government than the Bank of England, unlike the United States, where Congress focuses directly on the Federal Reserve. The major differences are the result of the nature of parliamentary government, however, not the nature or structure of monetary policy. The interest of back-bench MPs has been manifested through select committee inquiries and an increase in parliamentary questions. Some have argued that the increased activity of the select committees represents a shift in power from government to parliament.[39] Others, however, note that, "until back-bench members of parliament would rather be a chairman of a select committee than part of the executive, the reforms...are not going to make much real difference."[40]

The recent experience of parliamentary participation in monetary policy does suggest some notable changes in the British political system. Important developments have occurred in parliament in terms of staff, committee structure, and access to technical expertise. Yet, parliamentary policy-making still lags far behind Congress, Treasury and Civil Service Committee hearings are held in a small, if dignified, hearing room; thirty-five or forty people are a standing-room audience. Television cameras are absent, and press coverage is minimal. Influence on government policy is no more evident. One former Labour junior Treasury minister suggested that in his experience while governments were alert to parliamentary concern about movements in mortgage rates, the committee themselves had limited influence. A conservative back-bencher with similar government experience disagreed somewhat. In his view, the committee had some influence on policy but only with a time lag of six to eight months. This MP suggested that the publicity of hearing evidence – not the report – was important. Indeed, by this account, the hearings on monetary policy had been an important factor propelling the Thatcher government away from the "mechanical monetarism" that had characterized the first few years.

Like members of Congress, MPs investigating monetary policy face obstacles such as technical complexity and central bank evasion, but they do so in an institutional setting that even more severely limits their prospects for influence. Efforts to increase their influence through bipartisan select committee investigations may threaten an MP's opportunities to move up the ministerial ladder. Despite these limitations, in recent years the House of Commons has clearly made measurable progress in increasing Treasury and Bank accountability.

THE FRENCH NATIONAL ASSEMBLY AND THE BANQUE DE FRANCE

French monetary policy and the politics that surround it can be distinguished in several ways from Britain, Germany, and the United States. The Banque de France is less independent and autonomous than the other central banks and the government has more direct control. While the bank is prominent in monetary policy, it lacks the freedom to act counter to government wishes as have, upon occasion, the Federal Reserve and the Bundesbank. Despite the generally rising importance of monetary policy in economic management, monetary policy is accorded less significance as an element in macroeconomic management in France than in the other three countries. Although French monetary authorities did begin announcing targets for the growth of the money supply in 1976, controlling monetary growth has been subordinate to other goals such as stable interest rates and credit availability.[41]

Parliamentary capabilities and incentives

The technical inaccessibility of monetary policy is only a minor addition to the factors that leave the National Assembly with little meaningful impact on monetary policy. Like almost all parliaments, French legislators have the ultimate weapon of censure or no-confidence vote at their disposal. This might appear to enhance influence over monetary policy because the Banque de France is so clearly responsible to the government. However, real parliamentary influence remains but a remote abstraction to legislators more likely to be concerned with highly specific and particularized issues involving the cost and distribution of credit to their constituents.

Given an independently elected president and the requirement that cabinet members resign their seat in the Assembly when they become part of the government, legislative and executive branches are more separate in France than in Britain, but not as separate as in the United States. However, the party system creates incentives for legislators much more like that in Britain than the United States. Even though cabinet members may not be part of the Assembly, more than half of the cabinet has typically been drawn from the legislature. In the Fifth Republic, party cohesion in voting among the governing party has been high, and advancement to higher office has been based to a large extent on loyalty to the national party.[42] As in Britain, the most capable, career-oriented parliamentarians imperil their political future by taking an active role in criticizing their national party or government.

Independent parliamentary influence on legislation is limited by a number of constitutional and political factors. While the National Assembly is empowered to consider economic policies, there are many constraints, both *de jure* and *de facto*, on their freedom to do so. The government controls the legislative agenda. It is nearly impossible for a private member bill not accepted by the government to receive a debate, let alone be enacted into law. The National Assembly of the Fifth French Republic is weak – indeed, the president may bypass the Assembly by emergency decree. However, observers conclude that, in general, a president or a government cannot afford to ignore the Assembly. The government must consult with the Assembly and must maintain majority support. One observer notes that, "many reforms are not undertaken because prior consultation reveals the lack of a majority, while some projects are presented in diluted form to make them palatable to the majority on which the president counts."[43] Yet this does not often translate into influence on specific policy questions, particularly monetary policy.

Committee legislation and oversight

Committees in the Assembly are limited and generally ineffective in shaping policy. Floor debate takes place on the basis of the government's original legislation, not a committee's amended version. The government may request a package vote on a bill, including only amendments proposed or accepted by the government.[44] The Assembly has only six rather large (60–120 members) standing committees with broad jurisdictions. The Finance Committee considers a wide array of budget and economic matters including monetary policy.

Limitations on the Finance Committee's powers over the national budget, which is considered annually, almost certainly would hold true in any consideration of monetary policy as well. The only difference is that the conduct of monetary policy in France, as elsewhere, needs no action from the Assembly. When the government presents its budget, the Finance Committee and the Assembly have seventy days to consider it. The Finance Committee lacks professional staff and other resources. No amendments that increase spending are in order, and the government may demand a vote on the original version of the budget regardless of the amendments added by the committee. If the Assembly does not pass a budget within seventy days, the government's version automatically becomes law. We have found no evidence of either regular or periodic participation of the Finance Committee on monetary policy, except indirectly through consideration of the government's proposed budget deficit which relates to monetary growth.

Investigatory committees actively examined financial management and government policy during the Fourth Republic, but such committees were purposely limited in the Fifth Republic. An investigation may not extend longer than four months and publication of testimony or findings is restricted.[45] In addition, membership on the investigating committees is determined by the majority party in the Assembly. Unlike the select committee in Britain, opposition party participation is restricted. As a result, few special committees have been formed and those that have been formed deal largely with noncontroversial, non-partisan issues.[46] We have found no evidence of special investigatory committees empowered to examine either the Banque de France or monetary policy in general.

Legislative reauthorization of the Banque de France, 1972

An interesting case that demonstrates both French monetary politics and the limited influence of the National Assembly concerned the revision of the statute authorizing the Banque de France in 1972. Oliver Wormser was appointed governor of the Banque de France in 1969 by Prime Minister Couve de Murville at the same time that Giscard d'Estaing became Minister of Finance. Wormser felt that the statute authorizing the bank, which dated from Napoleonic days, needed revision. In 1972, he persuaded Prime Minister Pompidou and Giscard d'Estaing to propose revamping the bank's authorization.

The ultimate result of these proposals was perhaps the most important parliamentary debate about the structure and conduct of monetary policy in two decades. All the decisive moves were made prior to parliamentary consideration, and the major conflict was between the Ministry of Finance and the Banque de France. It is possible that some of the changes prior to cabinet adoption were made to enhance parliamentary support, but once submitted, only minor changes were made by the Assembly. The debate gave the opposition a chance to attack the government and some government deputies a chance to express reservations. Neither affected the outcome. Wormser in 1974 publicly criticized the government's policies at the time of Giscard d'Estaing's election to the presidency. He was forced to resign, leaving little doubt about the subordinate position of the Banque de France and the continued ability of the government to dominate monetary policy.

Parliamentary questions

Limited in other avenues of influence, members of the National Assembly have an opportunity to question the government on the conduct of monetary policy. We present some fragmentary data on parliamentary questions in an attempt to duplicate the data on Britain. Because of differences in indexing practices, and because comprehensive indexes have only recently become available in the case of the Assembly, strict comparability with the British case is not possible. Table 2.3 presents figures for 1979, 1980, and 1981, the period immediately before and after the election of François Mitterand.

Clearly, the number of questions directly concerning monetary policy and the Banque de France is extremely small. Questions on monetary policy did increase immediately after the election of Mitterand (second half of 1981), but for the two-and-one-half year period, most parliamentary questions related to the details of the administration of the French economy and credit allocations. The questions about credit controls came frequently from the right on behalf of interests such as small and medium enterprises, the Chamber of Commerce of Paris, the National Federation of Credit Agricole, and the French Employers Council (the Patronat). Parliamentary questions concerning monetary policy seem to stem from interest group activities and constituent concerns rather than the overall conduct of policy. This might be expected given monetary policy instrumentation that emphasizes distributional consequence.

Table 2.3 *Parliamentary inquiries in the French National Assembly. Questions on monetary policy, the Banque de France, credit, economic conditions, and the administration of economic policy*

Parliamentary questions, 1979

number of questions	topic
7	credit controls and allocations
63	administration of the economy
0	monetary policy
0	Banque de France
4	economic conditions (inflation, unemployment)

Parliamentary questions, 1980

number of questions	topic
105	credit controls and allocations
33	administration of the economy
1	monetary policy
2	Banque de France (personnel, strikes)
6	economic conditions (inflation, unemployment)

Parliamentary questions, 1981 (June to December only)

number of questions	topic
6	credit controls and allocations
24	administration of the economy
6	monetary policy
1	Banque de France
n.a.	economic conditions

Source: Based on the indexes of the French National Assembly. Drawn from, with rearrangement, the general categories, "Banques et etablissements financiere"; "Economie (ministere)"; and "Politique economique et social."

The Assembly and monetary policy: an assessment

In France we find a weak legislature, extraordinarily limited in dealing with complex, technical policy issues. In the case of monetary policy, we encounter an issue that is only rarely even brought before parliament. Interview evidence tends to confirm that the Assembly's influence on reviewing monetary policy is less than that of the British parliaments. In discussions about monetary politics with French officials, parliament simply did not come up unless mentioned first by the interviewer. Only the distributive aspects of French monetary policy seem to stimulate legislative interest. Even when such interest *is* expressed, French legislators lack the institutional resources to participate meaningfully in the policy debate. It is not even possible for the French legislator to hope, as his British counterpart can, that he may shape the course of debate by providing a forum for a protracted public dialogue between extra-parliamentary policy makers.

While the information available to us in the German case is the most limited of the four, there is enough to create a fairly clear picture. Legislative influence on monetary policy in Germany is dwarfed not so much by restrictions on legislative capabilities, as in the case of France, but by the singular autonomy and political strength of the central bank. Since its creation in 1957, the Bundesbank has played a dominant role in monetary policy and an influential role in overall economic management. Its position of strength is a result not only of its legal authority, which is considerable, but its performance and clarity of purpose which has allowed it to maintain broad support inside and outside of government.[47]

That is not to say that the Bundesbank is invincible. On occasions, such as prior to the passage of the 1967 Economic Growth and Stability Law, its wishes have not been adopted by the government or parliament. Yet the more common pattern is one of negotiation and cooperation with the government, avoiding public battles altogether. With the government and the bank acting in concert, legislative opposition or public debate rarely occurs. On those rare occasions when the government has opposed specific monetary decisions of the Bundesbank, the bank has usually prevailed.

Unlike the highly differentiated instrumentation of French monetary policy, the Bundesbank's operations rely much more on market intervention designed to guarantee price stability above all other goals. Such instrumentation, we have noted, obscures the impact of monetary policy on particular interests, and serves to diffuse potential criticism and political opposition. In the face of a powerful central bank and a political system where the key political relationships seem to be between the government and the bank, has the Bundestag managed to have any influence on the content or the conduct of monetary policy?

Legislative capabilities and incentives

With the exception of the legal authority of the central bank, the West German political system shares more characteristics with its European neighbors than with the United States. The Chancellor is responsible to the Bundestag, but in a slightly more circumscribed way because of the no-confidence provisions of the German constitution. None the less, legislators' influence on policy comes primarily through the parliamentary parties. The legal independence of the Bundesbank means, however, that not even a change in government would necessarily cause a change in monetary policy.

Legislative parties in Germany are less cohesive than in Britain or France. Party loyalty appears to have been less essential to career advancement and less a guarantee of renomination than in the other two ' parliaments.[48] None the less, there seems to be little advantage for back-benchers to attempt to influence policy outside their parliamentary parties. This would be particularly true for monetary policy given the broad-based political support enjoyed by the Bundesbank.

Standing committees in the Bundestag have greater influence on legislation than in the House of Commons or the National Assembly, but much less than in the US Congress. While policy formulation is executive-centered, meaningful changes are often made by legislative committees. Independent members bills are adopted more frequently than in France or Britain, but committee amendments often fail for lack of government support. Standing committees actively scrutinize ministers and policy, including matters of expenditures and budget. It is a cautious oversight, however, managed by members of the governing party who know full-well that the life of the government could be imperiled by overzealous criticism.

Special investigatory committees have not been important. Such committees may be created by a vote of only one-fourth of the members of the Bundestag, but the governing parties still name a majority of the committee members and, thus, can prevent it from being vigorous. We have found no evidence of investigatory committees actively examining monetary policy.

Question period, by the 1970s, occasioned some 3,000 inquiries of the government per year, both by governing and opposition parties. While parliamentary questions are used by the Bundestag as a device to oversee the government, this does not appear to be important for overseeing monetary policy. While we do not have systematic data on parliamentary inquiries on monetary policy, our impression is that very few concern the Bundesbank or the conduct of monetary policy. This impression is reinforced by the comments of informants suggesting that open criticism of the Bundesbank is both useless and potentially dangerous for politicians because of the Bundesbank's public, especially media, support.

The Bundestag's Committee on Economic Affairs holds hearings on economic policy several times per year, and the president of the Bundesbank personally testifies at these hearings. Committee oversight of the bank seems quite different than the work of either the US banking

LANCE T. LELOUP AND JOHN T. WOOLLEY

committees or the Commons Treasury and Civil Service Committee. Few critical questions are asked, and the forum is more informational than supervisory. Little publicity results. As with the other legislatures, no legislation requiring Bundestag approval is needed in the ordinary conduct of monetary policy. Key negotiations over monetary issues take place prior to any presentation to the Bundestag. Committee hearings are little more than an opportunity for the bank to inform legislators of monetary policy and its relationship to other economic policies.

Back-bench dissatisfaction with the Bundesbank

Despite the lack of meaningful legislative participation in German monetary policy, we have found some evidence of legislative dissatisfaction with the bank. In 1974, labor unions were highly critical of bank actions and urged greater concern with unemployment. More recently, some back-bench SPD members were disgruntled by the close relationship between the Schmidt government and the bank. This closeness was not merely in terms of agreement on policy. It is reported that former bank president Klassen used to play chess with Schmidt, and it was said that credit policy was decided during those chess games. The current president Poehl, an SPD member, was a former Schmidt assistant. He continues to maintain close relationships to the Kohl government, reinforcing the non-partisan context of monetary politics. As a result, back-bench attempts to influence the government within the parliamentary parties has met with little success.

Perhaps the most interesting case of back-bench dissatisfaction is the exception that proves the rule. One SPD member, Wolfgang Roth, conducted a one-person campaign for changes in Bundesbank policies in the early 1980s. Roth was unusual because he had enough technical expertise to criticize bank officials in technical terms. In contrast, despite the general view that committee staffing in the Bundestag is relatively strong compared to most legislatures, the Committee on Economic Affairs generally lacks the staff, resources, and expertise to confront the bank on a technical level.

The image of a solitary legislator taking on the Bundesbank in extra-parliamentary media hardly suggests meaningful parliamentary participation in monetary policy. Even the power of publicity seems to favor the bank. Press coverage of the bank is highly favorable with most financial reporters enjoying close ties to the bank. Press and legislative critics alike run the risk of being labeled inflationist. One official in the Finance ministry suggested that the bank's strong public support was no accident. "The Bundesbank is very active in reinforcing impressions of their own independence. They issue monthly reports, they hold press conferences, they give speeches. They sell their policy to the public and have been very consistent."

The Bundestag and monetary policy: an assessment

More than anything, legislative influence on monetary policy in West Germany is limited by the extraordinary legal and political strength of the Bundesbank. In terms of decisive impact on policy decisions, the important relationship is between the government and the bank. Little of substance is brought before the Bundestag although the bank actively courts legislative support. A prominent German economist close to the CDU offered this overview in an interview:

Politicians don't fight with the Bundesbank because they will lose. The bank has an important role in shaping public opinion – informed, elite opinion. The bank is very close to the major economic journalists located in Frankfurt. The Bundesbank Directors are very close to the national banking community which is located in Frankfurt. They meet frequently at working dinners and cocktail parties.

While the members of the Bundestag may have more potential within their legislative system to affect policy than do legislators in the French Assembly or the British Commons, to date there has been little opportunity to do so in the case of monetary policy. The continued legal and political strength of the Bundesbank effectively precludes meaningful parliamentary participation in monetary policy.

SUMMARY AND CONCLUSIONS

In terms of legislative influence on monetary policy, we would rank Congress at the top followed by the House of Commons, the Bundestag, and the National Assembly. Congress has significantly more influence than the other three, with the French and German parliaments having virtually no discernable impact on monetary policy. Generalizations about legislative influence on monetary policy and conclusions regarding the common hypotheses can be summarized as follows.

Policy content and circumstances *(Hypotheses 14 and 15)*

Legislative interest in monetary policy has increased in recent years in Britain and the United States. There is less evidence that legislative interest has increased in Germany (where monetary has always had a special prominence and independence) and France (where monetary goals remain subordinate to other economic policies).

Despite the increase in interest, the level of legislative interest remains relatively low and sporadic. Only when it has clear impacts on constituencies or relevant interest groups are legislators activated. That is, the macroeconomic aspects of monetary policy are not a central concern for most legislators.

The nature and content of monetary policy plays a key role in all four countries in shielding it from legislative influence and scrutiny. While more complex, diversified instrumentation makes policy more visible and of higher interest to legislators, these cases clearly show that complexity alone is insufficient to counterbalance the many other factors tending to discourage legislative involvement in monetary policy. (Of course, greater complexity may still result in a generally more politicized monetary policy not involving legislative actors). French monetary policy is characterized by the most complex instrumentation, but the inherent weaknesses in the French National Assembly effectively preclude legislative participation. Even in this case, however, we can see evidence that it is the distributive, not macroeconomic, aspects of monetary policy that motivate legislators.

Policy stage *(Hypothesis 16)*

Legislatures overwhelmingly participate in monetary policy only at the implementation stage, and then solely through attempts to assert *post hoc* discipline. Input at the proposal and enactment stage is rare or nonexistent. Only the US Congress has attempted to instruct the central bank on the formulation of monetary policy – there too with little apparent success. In no case is the central bank or the government required to bring monetary policy before the legislature on a regular basis for review or approval. Therefore, policy participation must be spurred from within the legislature. Only Congress has mandated in law regular reports by the central bank.

Parties and election systems *(Hypotheses 10 and 4)*

Legislators' incentives divide on the basis of presidential or parliamentary systems which produce candidate-centered or party-centered elections. In the US Congress, monetary policy produces relatively few election advantages and participation involves relatively high costs. Incentives relating to institutional power appear to have stimulated congressional action as much as reelection considerations. In parliamentary systems, incentives favoring party loyalty as a means for career advancement penalize those who might try to advance an independent, aggressive examination of policy. None the less, at least in the Commons, back-bench dissatisfaction with a lack of policy participation has created some incentives to strengthen committees and legislative oversight.

The ultimate sanctions of legislatures on policy – censure or no-confidence votes in the parliaments and impeachment or wholesale revision of the Federal Reserve Act in the US – remain remote and abstract possibilities. Yet in a broader context, central banks recognize the importance of maintaining legislative support and actively court that support as much as possible with little sacrifice of independence.

Committees *(Hypothesis 13)*

Committee action is generally more important than floor action as a means to affect monetary policy. In none of the four legislatures is the passage of legislation very important, although several significant bills have passed the Congress. In Congress and the House of Commons, committee oversight has been the most important means of influencing monetary policy.

Constitutional structure *(Hypothesis 1)*

Constitutional and legal foundations remain the main determinants of potential legislative influence on monetary policy. Differences in presidential versus parliamentary systems and the legal autonomy of the central bank are critical in determining the parameters of legislative influence. Only in United States Congress do legislators have the constitutional and statutory authority to exert control on the conduct of monetary policy.

Central banks consistently attempt to block attempts at increased legislative participation and scrutiny of their operations, and attempt to maintain or increase their secrecy, autonomy, and discretion from the legislature. When confronted with a serious challenge, central banks may make small concessions while continuing to oppose more meaningful changes.

Interest group relationship *(Hypothesis 8)*

Interest groups are important in monetary politics and their activities may relate to increases in legislative interest. Bankers, arguably the most important interest group, tend to work directly with the central bank. In parliamentary systems, interest groups such as labor unions, realtors, and the construction industry concentrate efforts more on relevant ministries than the legislature. While some lobbying may be directed at members of parliament, it is a testament to their perceived impotence in monetary policy that interest groups usually concentrate their efforts elsewhere. Only Congress is a serious target of lobbying by financial interest groups, and more than anything, banking interests are covering their bets – bets that will be decided elsewhere.

Notes

Research for this chapter was support in part by a grant from the Social Science Research Council of New York and the Weldon Spring Research Fund of the University of Missouri.

1 US House of Representatives, Committee on Banking, Finance, and Urban Affairs, *Monetary Policy: Goals and Conduct for the 1980s*, Hearings on HR 5476, 96th Congress, 1st session (1979), p. 26.

2 Karen H. Johnson, "Foreign experience with targets for money growth," *Federal Reserve-Bulletin*, 69: 10 (October, 1983) 745–54.

3 See our original paper, "Legislatures and monetary policy: a comparative perspective, presented at the 12th World Congress of Political Science, Paris, July 15–20, 1985, for more detail.

4 For insights into the legal and constitutional foundations as well as the different instruments of monetary policy, see John T. Woolley, *Monetary Politics: The Federal Reserve and the Politics of Monetary Policy* (New York: Cambridge University Press, 1984); Donald R. Hodgman, *National Monetary Policies and International Monetary Cooperation* (Boston: Little Brown, 1974); Geoffrey E. Wood, "The monetary policy decision process in the United Kingdom" in Donald E. Hodgman, ed., *The Political Economy of Monetary Policy: National and International Aspects*, Proceedings of a Conference held at Perugia, Italy, July 1983; Joint Economic Committee, Congress of the United States, "Credit policy and industrial policy in France," in *Monetary policy, Selective Credit Policy, and Industrial Policy in France, Britain, West Germany, and Sweden*, 97th Congress, 1st session, June 26, 1981; Robert Raymond, "The formulation and implementation of monetary policy in France," paper delivered at the Conference on The Political Economy of Monetary Policy in Western Europe, University of Illinois at Urbana-Champaign, November 18–20, 1981; Florin Aftalion, "The political economy of French monetary policy," in Hodgman (1974); Anthony S. Courakis, "Monetary thought and stabilization policy in the Federal Republic of Germany 1960–1976," in S. F. Frowen, A. S. Courakis, and M. H. Miller, *Monetary Policy and Economic Activity in West Germany* (London: Surrey University Press, 1977); Manfred Willms, "The monetary policy decision process in the Federal Republic of Germany," in Hodgman (1984); John T. Woolley, "Monetary policy instrumentation and the relationship of

Central Banks and governments," *Annals of the American Academy of Political and Social Science*, 434 (November, 1977), 162–70.

5 Keith Acheson and John F. Chant, "Mythology and central banking," *Kyklos*, 2 (1973).

6 A. Jerome Clifford, *The Independence of the Federal Reserve System* (Philadelphia: University of Pennsylvania Press, 1965), p. 330.

7 See, Gary Jacobsen, *The Politics of Congressional Elections* (Boston: Little Brown, 1982). Morris Fiorina, *Congress: Keystone of the Washington Establishment* (New Haven: Yale University Press, 1977). David Mayhew, *The Electoral Connection* (New Haven: Yale University Press, 1974), and Lawrence Dodd, "Congress and the quest for power," in Lawrence Dodd and Bruce Oppenheimer, eds, *Congress Reconsidered* (New York: Praeger, 1977).

8 Quoted in Woolley, *Monetary Politics*, p. 137.

9 Neil T. Skaggs, "The Federal Reserve system and Congressional demands for Information," *Social Science Quarterly*, 64: 3 (September, 1983), 566–81.

10 *Congressional Record*, 1977, 49407.

11 US House of Representatives, Committee on Banking and Currency, *Proposals for the Improvement of the Federal Reserve System and Staff Report*, 88th Congress, 2nd session, 1964.

12 Robert E. Weintraub, "Congressional supervision of monetary policy," *Journal of Monetary Economics*, 4 (April 1978), 341.

13 Ibid., p. 344; and, James L. Pierce, "The myth of congressional supervision of monetary policy," *Journal of Monetary Economics*, 4 (April, 1978), 363–70.

14 Public Law 95–188 (HR 9710); 91 Stat 1387, and *Congressional Quarterly Almanac*, 1977, p. 152.

15 Weintraub, "Congressional Supervision," p. 345.

16 Lance T. LeLoup, "Congress and the dilemma of economic policy," in Allen Schick, ed., *Making Economic Policy in Congress* (Washington, D.C.: American Enterprise Institute, 1984), pp. 17–21.

17 Karen W. Anderson, "The Fed takes a risky new path," *New York Times*, 17 October, 1982, sec. 3, pp. 1, 8, 9.

18 Woolley, *Monetary Politics*, p. 146.

19 *Business Conditions Digest*, October 1982, p. 25.

20 Woolley, *Monetary Politics*, p. 146.

21 *Congressional Quarterly Weekly Reports*, November 7, 1981, p. 2159.

22 Ibid.

23 Michael Moran, *The Politics of Banking* (New York: St. Martin's Press, 1984), p. 59.

24 Ibid., pp. 60–61.

25 *The Times*, February 26, 1978, p. 22a; *The Times*, March 10, 1978, p. 1e; *The Times*, September 5, 1978, p. 1g; *The Times*, November 18, 1978, p. 2a.

26 All uncited quotes are from interviews conducted by John T. Woolley with officials and informants in London, Paris, and Frankfurt, 1982.

27 Bernard Crick, *The Reform of Parliament*, 2nd edn (London: Wiedenfeld and Nicolson, 1968), p. 80.

28 Geoffrey Smith, quoted in Norman J. Ornstein, ed., *The Role of the Legislature in Western Democracies* (Washington, D.C.: American Enterprise Institute, 1981), p. 127.

29 Kenneth Baker, quoted in Ornstein, *The Role of the Legislature*, p. 114.
30 Tom McNally, quoted in Ornstein, *The Role of the Legislature*, pp. 124–5.
31 David Butler and Anne Sloman, *British Political Facts* (London: MacMillan, 1980), p. 182.
32 House of Commons, Select Committee on Nationalized Industries, Report, *The Bank of England*, 1976 (Cmdn. no. 672).
33 Bruce George and Barbra Evans, "Parliamentary reform – the internal view," in David Judge, ed., *The Politics of Parliamentary Reform* (Rutherford, New Jersey: Fairleigh Dickinson University Press, 1984), pp. 70–95.
34 Ibid., p. 77.
35 House of Commons, Select Committee on Treasury and Civil Service, session 1980–81, *Monetary Policy*, (February 24, 1981), vol. I, pp. xciii, xcv.
36 George and Evans (1984), p. 76.
37 Smith quoted in Ornstein, *The Role of the Legislature*, p. 113.
38 Questions in Hansard's index included: monetary policy, money, money supply, domestic credit expansion, the Bank of England, bank rate, and minimum lending rate. Subsequently, most questions dealing with the Bank of England were excluded since the questions rarely related to the conduct of monetary policy and instead dealt with the personnel practices of the bank or the likelihood of recognition of union representatives and other peripheral concerns.
39 Lord Groham, "The developing structure of United Kingdom government," *Management Services in Government*, vol. 33, August, 1978, pp. 105–13.
40 David Marquand, quoted in Ornstein, *The Role of the Legislature*, p. 125.
41 Joint Economic Committee (1981), p. 17.
42 John E. Schwarz and L. Earl Shaw, *The United States Congress in Comparative Perspective* (Hinsdale, Ill: Drydan Press, 1976), p. 135.
43 Ezra N. Suleiman and Richard Rose, *Presidents and Prime Ministers* (Washington D.C.: American Enterprise Institute, 1980), p. 102.
44 Schwarz and Shaw, *United States Congress*, p. 84.
45 Maurice Duverger, *The Fifth Republic* (Paris: University Press of France, 1968), p. 118.
46 Phillip M. Williams, *The French Parliament: Politics in the Fifth Republic* (New York: Praeger, 1968), p. 51.
47 Joint Economic Committee (1981), p. 92.
48 Schwarz and Shaw, *United States Congress*, p. 140.

3

The US Congress and credit policy – institutional and policy implications

DENNIS S. IPPOLITO

According to Olson and Mezey, the policy activity of legislatures is affected by policy attributes, by internal party and committee character- istics, and by a constellation of outside factors, such as executive branch and interest group involvement, that define the legislature's political environment.[1] Within these broad categories are numerous, specific variables that appear to be related to the extent and means of parliamentary participation in policy.[2] A central research issue is whether and how these variables affect legislative policy-making.

This chapter addresses this research issue by focusing on the US Congress and credit policy. For over half a century, Congress has played a central role in initiating and expanding federal direct loan and loan guarantee programs serving a broad spectrum of borrowers and economic interests.[3] In recent years, government credit programs have accounted for a "substantial portion of the funds moving through US capital markets," and the "outstanding volume of loans supported by government or government-sponsored agencies [has] exceeded a trillion dollars..."[4]

The long-standing, influential participation by Congress in credit policy-making may provide insights about the salient variables that sustain legislative activity. In addition, the growing controversies over the size and proliferation of credit programs may advance our understanding of the institutional capabilities or competence of legislatures in economic policy-making. Mezey has argued, for example, that the "policy-making performance of the legislature is for the most part determined by characteristics generic to *all* legislatures rather than to the quirks and traits of specific institutions."[5] How Congress handles credit programs, therefore, could speak to legislative capabilities more generally in the economic and budget policy arena.

Among democratic legislatures, the United States Congress stands alone in the ubiquity and independence of its policy-making activity. This distinctiveness is pronounced, moreover, across the several components of budget policy – spending policy, tax policy, and credit policy. As noted by Olson, "The policy activity of parliaments is greater on issues of societal regulation and benefits, and on propagation of values," than on questions of security and finance.[6] Congress, by contrast, devotes a great deal of time and legislative energy solely to "questions...of finance."[7]

The history of congressional participation in credit policy-making suggests other exceptions to issue-based generalizations concerning legislative activity. Congress has been extensively involved in formulating and developing new forms of credit assistance, along with overseeing their implementation.[8] Much of this has occurred under conditions of limited visibility and salience, with relatively small numbers of legislators primarily responsible for credit programs in particular policy areas.[9] Indeed, one of the persistent criticisms of federal credit policy has been its piecemeal evolution and the underlying congressional resistance to the coordination and centralization of credit decision-making. Policy attributes, then, are not very useful in accounting for the nature and extent of congressional activity relating to credit programs.

Institutional and environmental factors, however, appear to be more helpful in explaining important dimensions of congressional activity. Relatively low turnover levels, for example, yield an experienced, stable membership in Congress. Permanent committees with fixed jurisdictions promote the expertise that is essential in such a complex, highly detailed policy area.[10] Finally, the decentralization of power to committees and subcommittees makes it possible for legislators to exercise significant, long-term policy influence.[11]

Environmental factors are at work as well, and indeed may interact with these institutional characteristics. Because credit programs are directed toward specific economic interests and identifiable groups of borrowers, they are of major concern to interest groups. In the dominant credit areas, such as agriculture and housing, the links between congressional committees and what Olson and Mezey term "functionally specialized and homogeneous" interest groups have been close and supportive.[12]

Further, the proliferation of credit programs in other policy areas has often been prompted by new, or newly active, interest groups.

Perhaps the most intriguing explanations, however, involve executive branch decision-making. Two propositions have a particular relevance here. In general, note Olson and Mezey, "The policy activity of legislatures is greater if the executive branch is more 'open' than 'closed,' and decentralized than centralized."[13] Moreover, they suggest that policy activity "increases as issues are handled by operating agencies rather than by high level executives."[14]

A striking feature of credit policy development is the extent to which Congress has deliberately sought to preserve these "conditions." For decades, presidents have called for credit program reform. This has typically consisted of proposals to integrate credit programs into the budget, with justification that this integration would promote coordination and better control. At issue as well, however, has been the centralization that would occur as credit policies were coordinated and the subsequent moving of credit policy determination to upper-level decision makers in the executive branch. A similar caution has been evidenced within Congress, as reform efforts that would increase centralization have been repeatedly frustrated.

In reviewing the more prominent credit policy issues, then, this congressional preference for internal and external decentralization should be kept in mind. Congress has preferred to concentrate on discrete programs, not on broad policies. This is perfectly compatible with the electoral and power ambitions of its members.[15] It nevertheless creates potential problems for the collective institutional goal of responsible decision-making. The seemingly arcane issue of budgetary accounting for credit, therefore, has been a source of direct presidential–congressional conflict for a long period of time, and it is an issue that is far from settled.

CREDIT ACCOUNTING

Direct loans and loan guarantees were first used to assist a variety of economic sectors during the 1930s. The scope and impact of federal credit intervention remained fairly limited for a time, but during the 1960s the growth of direct loan and loan guarantee programs began to create control problems. A presidential Commission on Budget Concepts, whose 1967 report led to the adoption of the unified federal budget, strongly recommended improved budget accounting for credit programs. According to the Commission, inaccurate and improper accounting devices had undermined "public and congressional confidence in the integrity of budget totals..."[16] The Commission also warned that improved accounting for direct loan programs alone might simply lead to "further expansion of guaranteed and insured loans not warranted by program considerations."[17] Its proposed solution was to include the subsidy costs of *all* credit programs in the unified budget since "such subsidies are much more like grants than loans."[18]

These credit controls were not adopted, and credit program accounting continued to be a prominent issue when Congress commenced budget reform deliberations in 1973. Indeed, even as these deliberations progressed, large amounts of direct lending were being shifted off-budget and loan guarantees were proliferating. Specific efforts were therefore undertaken to change the budgetary treatment of guaranteed and direct lending and to eliminate off-budget financing.

The 1974 Budget Act

The Joint Study Committee on Budget Control, which reported the first and most restrictive congressional budget reform proposal, recommended that loan guarantees be treated as budget authority. This would have made loan guarantees subject to the targets and ceilings contained in congressional concurrent budget resolutions, to controls on backdoor spending, and to the general discipline of a comprehensive budget process. The final version of the 1974 Budget Act, however, specifically excluded loan guarantees from the definition of budget authority.[19] The exclusion was explained in the report issued by the Senate Rules and Administration Committee, which amended the original budget reform bill:

Such [insured and guaranteed] loans are not direct obligations of the United States, and a liability is incurred only in the case of default. Thus, it would not be appropriate to regard such contingent liabilities as budget authority for purpose of determining the appropriate levels in the budget resolution. Nor should loan guarantees be subjected to the new procedures for handling backdoor spending authority.[20]

This was a clearcut victory for congressional committees that had jurisdiction over loan guarantee programs and were fearful that such programs might not fare well if forced to compete with direct spending.

The final version of budget reform legislation also sidestepped the problem of off-budget agencies. The Senate Rules and Administration Committee recommended that the off-budget status of some half-dozen agencies be terminated. Instead, the budget act merely called for a study of the off-budget problem.[21].

The Federal Financing Bank

This particular action, moreover, can best be appreciated in the context of preceding congressional decisions about the Federal Financing Bank (FFB). In 1972, the Nixon administration proposed the establishment of the FFB in order to centralize and coordinate federal agency borrowing from the public. In order to resolve debt management problems, the Treasury Department was willing to continue existing practices relating to the budgetary treatment of credit programs. It was also prepared to assign off-budget status to the FFB. What the Treasury Department did want, however, was authority for the secretary of the Treasury to review and approve or disapprove all agency proposals for new securities issues.

While the official justification for Treasury scrutiny was that it would facilitate more orderly federal borrowing, members of the House and Senate objected that such an authorization could be used as a type of impoundment to curtail or eliminate credit programs opposed by the administration. Responding to these objections, the Senate Banking Committee, which had jurisdiction over the FFB legislation, imposed deadlines for Treasury review and specified that no program could be disproportionately affected or curtailed by Treasury financing decision. During debate on the Senate floor, an amendment was added to exempt one of the largest lending agencies, the Farmers Home Administration (FmHA), from requirements for Treasury Department approval. The House Ways and Means Committee added another important modification, exempting all guaranteed obligations. While the Senate Banking Committee had earlier rejected such a blanket exemption, arguing that it could severely undermine efforts to coordinate federal borrowing, the Ways and Means exemption was eventually adopted, as were the review restrictions initiated by the Senate.

There were, then, some rather obvious congressional expectations about the Federal Financing Bank. Most important, its budgetary and programmatic effects were to be "neutral." (According to section 11(a) of the FFB legislation, "Nothing herein shall affect the budget status of the Federal agencies selling obligations to the Bank...or the method of budget accounting for their transactions.") In addition, FFB financing activities would be divorced from programmatic considerations. It would help to finance programs, not exercise discretion about their merit.

Finally, while the Bank's charter provided that it could borrow only up to $15 billion from the public, it was also authorized to borrow directly from the Treasury without limits. The assumption was that this latter form of borrowing authority would be used on an interim basis, allowing the FFB to obtain funds between regular public offerings of its own securities and subsequently repaying the Treasury. Instead, the FFB utilized direct public borrowing only once, and since 1974 it has depended exclusively on Treasury borrowing. The FFB's outstanding borrowing rose to over $150 billion in the mid-1980s, and the Bank was, until recently, the primary vehicle for moving on-budget loans off budget and converting loan guarantees into off-budget direct lending as well.

SPENDING AND CREDIT

From fiscal 1976 (when the Budget Reform Act was first implemented) through 1985, the spending side of the federal budget increased from $375 billion to $950 billion. Spending growth for this period averaged approximately 12 percent annually, well above the rate of growth for the preceding two decades. Spending also outpaced economic growth, rising from an average of less than 21 percent of gross national product during the 1970s to almost 23.5 percent for fiscal years 1980–85. The expansion of federal credit paralleled the remarkable rise in federal spending. This was true for both direct loan and loan guarantee programs, but their budgetary effects were largely hidden through inconsistent and inaccurate accounting practices.

Measuring credit activity

There are various ways to measure federal credit activity, one being the level of outstanding, or unpaid, loans at the end of a fiscal year. In 1970, outstanding direct loans and loan guarantees stood at less than $180 billion, and increases over the next several years were relatively modest. The growth in credit programs then began to accelerate, resulting in annual increases that averaged nearly 11 percent for fiscal years 1976–86 (see table 3.1) The volume of *net credit* extended each year – new direct loans and loan guarantees minus repayments – averaged about $40 billion annually after fiscal 1976, but most of this was in off-budget direct loans and loan guarantees. The budgetary effects of credit growth, therefore, were restricted to the considerably lower net outlays of on-budget agencies. For fiscal year 1983, $41.3 billion in new on-budget direct loans resulted in $4.8 billion of net on-budget outlays. For fiscal year 1984, $37.9 billion in new direct loans produced $−3.9 billion in net on-budget outlays.

The use of net lending figures gives a distorted picture of federal credit activity, as a result of the unusual accounting devices utilized by a number of federal agencies and by the treatment of defaults. Agencies can, for

Table 3.1 *Outstanding federal loans, fiscal years 1970–1986 (in billions of dollars)*

Fiscal year:	Direct loans ($)	Loan guarantees ($)	Total ($)	Percentage increases (%)
1970	51.1	125.1	176.2	
1971	53.1	140.1	193.2	9.6
1972	50.1	158.9	209.0	8.2
1973	43.9	174.1	218.0	4.3
1974	61.5	153.2	214.7	−1.5
1975	74.1	158.7	232.8	8.4
1976	85.9	169.8	255.7	9.8
1977	100.9	183.9	284.8	11.4
1978	120.4	226.1	346.5	21.7
1979	140.5	264.6	405.1	16.9
1980	163.9	298.5	462.4	14.1
1981	185.0	309.0	494.0	6.4
1982	207.8	331.2	539.0	9.1
1983	223.0	363.8	586.8	8.9
1984	229.3	386.7	616.0	5.0
1985	257.4	410.4	667.8	8.4
1986	251.6	449.8	701.4	5.0

Average increase 1970–1975   5.8%
Average increase 1976–1985   10.6%

Source: Special Analysis, Federal Credit Programs, Budget of the United States Government, fiscal years 1972–88.

example, deduct repayments of old loans from new loan commitments and report this net figure as an agency's actual direct lending during a fiscal year. In the past, it was not required that these repayments be made by the private borrowers to whom the loans were originally extended or, indeed, by any private sector institution. Instead, several agencies were allowed to "sell" their direct loan obligations to the Federal Bank and to treat these sales as repayments. In 1985, this loophole was finally closed. The Balanced Budget and Emergency Deficit Control Act now requires that budget authority and outlays incurred by the FFB be attributed to the agency initiating the original loan. Agencies can use regular repayments by borrowers to offset new direct loan disbursements. Additional congressional appropriations are then necessary only when disbursements exceed repayments. In addition, defaults are, in most cases, covered by insurance or reserve accounts, with subsequent transfers to an agency's lending budget. This gives defaults the appearance of repayments in an agency's loan account. The bulk of credit activity, then, is carried on outside the budget reported to the public. The budget is a cash-flow document. For loan guarantees, it does not show their volume or the government's growing liability. Direct loans require outlays, but the level of outlay is often understated because of the procedure for repayments and defaults.

Credit costs

Credit budget formats used during the past several years provide greater information about the extent of federal credit activity, but data on costs (or benefits) remain inadequate. Since similar uncertainties regarding benefits apply to conventional spending programs, the major distinction between spending and lending involves budgetary costs. Spending programs are measured as outlays, allowing comparability between programs. For a variety of reasons, a corresponding measure does not exist for credit programs. Two obvious indicators – defaults and interest subsidies – could be used to assess costs, but data about both are surprisingly incomplete. As one recent study concluded, "Defaults are rarely stated as a percentage of loan volume, interest costs are inadequately tied to interest payments, and losses associated with delinquency are almost indecipherable."[22]

Another important credit cost and therefore subsidy is the lower interest rate charged for government loans compared to interest rates in the private sector or even to the costs of the government's own borrowing. Interest rates and loan maturities vary widely among government credit programs. Depending upon the agency and the program, direct loans may be extended for periods ranging from several months to forty years; interest rates differ as well, but they are typically well below comparable rates in private credit markets. Long loan maturities and relatively low interest rates are also characteristic of loan guarantee programs.

When a federally assisted borrower obtains funds at interest rates below those charged by private lenders, the federal government is providing a subsidy equal to the interest rate differential on the loan principal for each year the loan is outstanding. Despite the importance of interest rate subsidies, there is at this time "no generally accepted method for quantifying the present value interest subsidies in the Federal credit programs."[23] (For certain programs, a comparable private rate cannot be estimated, since federal assistance is extended to borrowers and projects that are riskier than private markets would accept under any terms). Recent Office of Management and Budget (OMB) and Congressional

Table 3.2 *Estimated subsidy cost of federal credit assistance, fiscal years 1970–1983 (in billions of dollars)*

Fiscal year	Direct loan obligations ($)	Primary guarantee commitments ($)	Estimated subsidy cost ($)	On-budget net lending ($)
1970	10.4	27.5	6.9	3.0
1971	10.5	38.5	7.5	2.0
1972	18.6	44.8	12.0	2.7
1973	18.1	36.4	11.2	0.3
1974	19.0	30.9	11.4	1.9
1975	28.7	30.5	16.2	4.3
1976	29.9	26.1	16.5	4.2
1977	38.7	58.8	22.9	2.6
1978	49.6	55.0	28.1	8.6
1979	39.0	86.9	24.7	6.0
1980	44.8	82.2	27.3	9.5
1981	50.1	76.5	29.7	5.2
1982	43.4	53.7	24.9	9.1
1983	41.4	97.2	26.5	4.8

Source: Congressional Budget Office, *New Approaches to the Budgetary Treatment of Federal Credit Assistance* (Washington, D.C.: Congressional Budget Office, March 1984), 67.

Budget Office (CBO) estimates, however, put the annual subsidy costs of federal lending at over $25 billion annually for fiscal years 1977–84 (see table 3.2). There are, of course, potential economic costs associated with the allocative impact of federal credit, but these too are not well understood, in part because the economic effects of lending are more variable than is the case for spending.[24]

Program priorities

While there are parallels between the expansion of federal spending and federal lending, important distinctions have also emerged. The composition of the spending and credit budgets has moved along different tracks. This suggests that the two budgets may reflect different political pressures in the Congress.

The composition of the spending budget has changed markedly since the mid-1950s, reflecting a clear shift in government priorities. In particular, the relative budget shares allocated to defense and social welfare have been reversed. Taken together, social welfare, defense, and interest payments now account for approximately 85 percent of federal outlays, and current projections indicate this aggregate share will increase slightly over the next several years.

The composition of the credit budget presents a sharp contrast to the direct spending budget. It is dominated not by defense and human resources – the largest functions in the spending budget – but by agriculture and housing. Other program areas that are well supported in the credit budget are, in many instances, among the smallest in the spending budget. To an extent, these differences merely reflect the fact that credit assistance is more suitable for certain types of programs than for others, but it is also likely that many credit programs simply could not compete effectively for funding if they were in the form of direct spending. The more visible and centralized budget process that determines spending tends to respond to the demands of mass constituencies, as in the case of social security and other income security programs, and to national public opinion, as in the case of defense. As a result, the spending budget at least approximates the fiscal model of coordinated national policy.

The decision-making process for credit programs has been considerably less demanding. Control over credit allocations has been less centralized. Debates about priorities have been virtually non-existent. The costs of many programs have been difficult to estimate, and loan guarantees in particular often have been treated as cost-free. These factors have made it possible to expand credit assistance programs, while avoiding difficult and politically unattractive tradeoffs with direct spending programs.

The priorities incorporated into the spending budget and the credit budget, then, have been quite different. Long-term trends in direct spending have narrowed substantially the budget allocation available to support a broad range of domestic and international programs. The expansion of credit programs, however, has provided government decision makers with an alternative means of funding. When credit and spending are considered together, there is an important modification in the flow of federal assistance, and in the allocation of resources among competing national needs.

CREDIT PROGRAMS AND CREDIT POLICY

In response to the control problems associated with credit programs and FFB operations, the executive branch and Congress have long debated credit budget mechanisms that would direct and ultimately control the flow of federal credit. Initial efforts, promoted by the Office of Management and Budget, the Congressional Budget Office, and the House and Senate Budget Committees, were primarily informational.

More recent efforts have aimed at formal, full integration of credit programs into the congressional budgetary process.

Executive budget control initiatives

In 1980, the Carter administration provided a credit budget section as part of the president's annual budget. This included estimates of new obligations for direct loans (both on-budget and off-budget), new commitments for loan guarantees, and planned FFB activity levels. Similar credit budget sections have been included in subsequent presidential budgets. The Reagan administration had used this opportunity to propose major reductions in a variety of credit programs. Indeed, the administration used its first budget submission to designate "rigorous control over Federal credit programs, including loans financed off-budget, [as] an important part of the President's budget reform plan."[25] Specific program reductions typically encountered strong opposition in Congress, and four major changes were enacted.

In addition, the Reagan administration repeatedly sponsored plans to change the budgetary treatment of direct loan and loan guarantee programs. It altered budget presentations to attribute FFB activity to originating agencies; to report off-budget lending as on-budget; and to remove agency repurchases of loan assets previously sold to the FFB from direct loan tables.[26] Accounting changes included the reclassification of loan guarantee defaults to reflect non-retrievable losses and loans that did not involve cash disbursements. In 1985, statutory changes were adopted that required charging FFB outlays to agencies and treating loan asset sales to the FFB as borrowing.

Congressional budget control initiatives

Prior to the fiscal 1983 congressional budget resolution, congressional procedures with regard to an annual credit budget could best be described as informal. The House and Senate Budget Committees did propose credit budgets under Sec. 301(a)(6) of the 1974 Budget Act, which provides for the inclusion in budget resolutions of "such other matters relating to the budget as may be appropriate..." Targets were established for aggregate direct loan and loan guarantee levels, but these recommended levels were expressed as a "sense of the Congress" provision and did not provide for functional or programmatic allocations, implementation, or enforcement.

In 1982, the Budget Committee decided to press credit controls a bit more aggressively. Appropriate levels of new credit activity were included in the conference substitute on the fiscal 1983 resolution for new direct loan obligations and for loan guarantee commitments, with the totals allocated by budget function. Amounts subject to annual appropriations limits (approximately three-quarters of the totals for direct loans and loan guarantees) were allocated to the Appropriations Committees and suballocated among appropriations subcommittees. The fiscal 1984 budget resolution was a mixed affair. It established credit targets through fiscal 1986, as well as a reserve to be available for specified programs. Functional allocations were included, and the conference report on the resolution contained aggregate credit levels with accompanying "sense of the Congress" language that these be considered binding. There were, however, no formal provisions comparable to those incorporated in the 1983 resolution to make the credit budget "binding." For fiscal 1985, the budget resolution contained credit targets by function for fiscal years 1984–87. The functional allocations were broken down into direct loan obligations, primary loan guarantee commitments, and secondary loan guarantee commitments. Congress also agreed to include, in appropriation acts, twenty of the administration's twenty-eight requests for program limitations, although subsequent demand fell well below the ceiling for most programs.

The fiscal 1985 budget process, however, was effectively circumvented by a congressional–White House agreement on a deficit reduction measure for fiscal years 1985–87. President Reagan signed this package of spending reductions and revenue increases on July 18, 1984. The first concurrent budget resolution was finally approved on October 1, and it merely reflected the spending and tax measures already passed or programmed for passage. The emphasis in fiscal 1985 and subsequently – at least on the president's part – was on specific credit program reductions and terminations rather than on aggregate controls in budget resolutions.

During the 98th Congress, formal amendments to the 1974 Budget Act that would incorporate credit programs into the budget process were once again proposed. The Task Force on the Budget Process of the House Committee on Rules took the lead in the House, while several members of the Senate Budget Committee sponsored similar legislation in the Senate. In both chambers, however, the issue of credit control was ultimately subordinated to spending and deficit uses.[27] The Balanced Budget and Emergency Deficit Control Act of 1985 (popularly known as Gramm-Rudman-Hollings) finally expanded the congressional budget process to cover federal loan programs. Gramm-Rudman-Hollings made several important changes in the budgetary treatment of credit programs. First, it defined direct loan obligations and loan guarantee commitments as "credit authority," which then was made subject to the same restrictions as budget authority and other spending authority for purposes of meeting annual spending and deficit totals.[28] Thus, the automatic cuts or sequestration under Gramm-Rudman-Hollings were to apply to credit authority. Second, FFB financing activities – both the purchases of loan assets and the financing of guaranteed loans – were attributed to the originating agency and the off-budget measurement for FFB outlays was therefore abolished.

Under Gramm-Rudman-Hollings Congress is required to set aggregate limits for direct loan obligations and loan guarantee commitments in its annual budget resolutions. Credit authority totals are also included in the budget reconciliation process. Finally, allocations to the Appropriations Committees and their subcommittees now include new direct loan obligations and new loan guarantee commitments. Over the past six years, therefore, the budgetary treatment of credit programs has progressed a good deal. What Congress continues to resist, despite repeated urgings by OMB and by many budget policy experts, is measuring the subsidies in credit programs and incorporating these costs into the spending budget. As Herman Leonard states: "Whatever method is adopted for heightening credit accountability, credit programs desperately need an appropriate profile of cost information in the budget...but the prerequisite – recognizing credit program costs in the budget – has eluded two decades of government credit program reformers."[29]

COSTING FEDERAL CREDIT

Primarily as a result of executive branch pressure, credit programs and credit policy have emerged from obscurity to occupy at least a modest status on the policy agenda. Federal credit activity now receives much greater attention in both the executive branch and Congress. Credit budgets have been initiated. Legislators have gained some idea of the hidden costs and economic effects of credit intervention.

Despite these positive changes, the budgetary treatment of credit programs remains deficient. Federal credit programs affect the allocation and cost of credit, but there is a good deal of uncertainty about the magnitude and direction of these effects. Unfortunately, and despite a good deal of speculation, there is no clear-cut evidence about the impact of federal credit intervention on capital markets in general or even on submarkets, such as housing.

A more comprehensive congressional budget process – with separate spending, tax, and credit aggregates – represents an improvement in federal budgeting. It increases the visibility of credit programs, and it might eventually encourage greater scrutiny of program management. A much more complicated problem is how to set – and then to protect – credit budget totals. The primary concern with credit budget totals is, after all, their economic impact, both for capital markets in general and particular credit submarkets. In preparing annual budget resolutions, for example, the House and Senate Budget Committees presumably are seeking to set an "appropriate" level of federal credit intervention. It is not at all clear, however, how this level should be measured, much less set. The problem is illustrated by comparing credit to direct spending.

While the macroeconomic effects of various types of spending may differ, depending upon what the money is spent for or who receives it, the differences are sufficiently modest to be usually ignored. Therefore, the *composition* of the spending budget has a political and programmatic relevance that greatly outweighs its economic impact. For credit programs, variable economic effects are difficult to ignore. As Elizabeth H. Rhyne explains, the composition of the credit budget is of major importance:

Some supporters of the credit budget as a control device hope that the macroeconomics of federal credit will soon become well enough understood that the "right" aggregate level can be chosen ... However, because subsidies differ, the fiscal implications of a credit budget made up largely of near-market FHA-insured mortgages would differ sharply from one containing the same volume of mortgages made under the Farmers Home Administration's low-interest Rural Housing Insurance Fund. The credit budget framework is useful, but it cannot yet offer much assistance.[30]

A formal credit budget, together with more accurate budgetary treatment of credit programs, improves the congressional and executive decision-making processes, but it does not provide a clear-cut basis for control. It may be possible, however, to provide that control by focusing on credit subsidies.

Two facets of credit program costs can serve as control points. The first is the interest subsidy provided by a direct loan or a loan guarantee. The second involves the defaults and delinquency costs in the administration of credit programs. By integrating these costs into the unified budget, it becomes possible to force tradeoffs between spending and credit assistance, to shatter the illusion that the latter are cost-free, and to provide decision makers with incentives to scrutinize and control credit activity.

It is generally agreed that credit and direct spending are not sufficiently comparable, either in programmatic or economic terms, to allow simple dollar-for-dollar budgeting tradeoffs. The *costs* of credit are not necessarily the same as the *amounts* of credit. The costs of direct spending, for all intents and purposes, are the same as the budget amounts. In order to integrate budgetary decisions on spending and credit in a meaningful fashion, it is necessary to provide a direct spending equivalent for a given credit program level. This can be done by estimating the present value of the interest subsidy: "The equivalent cash grant value of a federal loan or loan guarantee."[31]

This interest subsidy is not just the difference between the interest rate charged by the government and the government's own borrowing costs. Rather, it is the difference between the loan terms a borrower receives under a federal credit program and the loan terms that same borrower would face in private credit markets without federal assistance. If there were private market surrogates for every federal credit program, interest subsidies could be readily and reliably measured on a program-by-program basis. Many federal programs have no private market equivalents, however, and in some instances federally assisted borrowers are such high risks that private credit might not be available under any circumstances. The estimating problem associated with the latter would be especially pronounced for single-borrower and high-risk guarantee programs.

This focus on subsidies is hardly a new idea. The 1955 Hoover Commission recommended that lending agencies be charged for interest subsidies by the Treasury.[32] The 1961 Report of the Committee on Money and Credit also stressed that deliberate subsidies be identified for all credit programs.[33] President Kennedy's Committee on Federal Credit Programs recommended that

all proposals to create new credit programs or to broaden existing credit programs should be accompanied by an appraisal of the relationship between the interest rate charged by competitive and efficient private lenders and the rate necessary to cover the Government's costs…. The normal reviews of all existing Federal credit programs should include discussion of these relationships.[34]

The 1967 President's Commission on Budget Concepts suggested that separate budget presentations for loans and direct spending be included in the budget in order to facilitate analysis of their respective impact "on incomes and employment," but emphasized that the "subsidy elements in all such loans should be included and specifically disclosed in the expenditure rather than the loan account."[35] The Reagan administration for years strenuously argued that "the subsidy element in Federal credit programs needs to be measured more accurately and targeted more effectively."[36]

Once interest subsidies, including default risk, are integrated into the unified budget, a rigorous basis for credit control would be established.

Instead of disembodied credit totals, whose chief contribution to credit control consists of sheer size and *possible* economic effects, credit budget totals would have tangible and immediate budgetary costs. This would not guarantee control, but it would at least provide incentives for control.

DISCUSSION

An assessment of Congress's participation in credit policy-making must necessarily take into account the budgeting process and system it uses. The handling of credit programs, from this perspective, does not appear to be especially well suited for the types of decision-making usually associated with macroeconomic policies. While all areas of public policy would doubtless benefit from improved coherence, economic management policies would appear to have obvious and particular needs in this regard.[37]

Consistency and coherence, however, are difficult to achieve, given the characteristic decision-making organization and procedures in Congress. The entire congressional budgetary process is, by most accounts, the most decentralized and fragmentary among the Western democracies. Party leadership and control are comparatively weak, opportunities for interest group intervention and influences are abundant, and distributive tendencies are pronounced. According to Sundquist, the result has been severely to limit the "capability of the legislative branch to develop integrated and coherent policy."[38]

For economic management policies, such as credit policy, these shortcomings tend to raise serious questions about institutional competence. LeLoup emphasizes that "Congress has failed to create an institution or process capable of making economic policy or responding to the president's proposals coherently and consistently."[39] And the central problem he identifies is that the "legislative process tends to facilitate the achievement of individual goals at the expense of collective policy making."[40]

The congressional record on federal credit programs parallels this general indictment. It has taken a very long time to correct basic budget accounting weaknesses, primarily because these helped to shelter programs that served important constituencies. More important, the continuing failure to include credit subsidies in budget totals has undermined the consistency, accuracy, and comprehensiveness of the unified budget. While spending and deficit figures are no longer seriously understated, functional resource allocations are misleading, and credit costs are hidden.

Credit policy, like budget policy generally, finds Congress to be atypically active in comparison to other national legislatures. Unlike the tax and spending components of the budget, however, credit policy has lacked visibility or salience for much of the public and even for many members of Congress. In effect, credit programs have proved to be a fertile area for congressional activity, precisely because they have not been widely understood or publicized. They are an exception to the proposition that "The policy activity of parliaments is greater on issues which are new rather than old, salient rather than quiet, and which activate diverse and numerous publics rather than a small and homogeneous public."[41]

This perhaps reinforces the point that we need to examine more carefully interactive effects among variables affecting legislative policy activity. The starting point, for example, appears to be constitutional and structural. The constitutional division between the president and Congress creates opportunities for independent congressional action. Since centralized parties have never truly bridged this division, the scope of potential legislative activism is widened still further.

We have, therefore, a constitutional invitation to act along with an institutional capacity to do so. What are missing are the incentives that make the activity worthwhile, and it is here that the role of interest groups in the electoral and policy processes needs to be incorporated. The involvement of highly specialized interest groups in the proliferation and expansion of federal credit programs has been crucial.[42] And the operative rules for this involvement have followed classical distributive politics, since credit follows the general pattern for subsidy arrangements:

The recipients usually do not compete with each other for the subsidies, but rather they seek a high level of support for themselves without being particularly aware of the other recipients and their subsidies. The petitioners typically seek direct access to the bureaus in the executive branch and the subcommittees in the House and Senate that are primarily responsible for setting their level of subsidy. Once the level of subsidy is set, the implementation of that subsidy is also delegated back down to the bureau level of the executive branch – often with close involvement of personnel from the relevant subcommittees.[43]

As Ripley and Franklin go on to explain, these distributive policy subgovernments can and do change in response to pressures from the White House or congressional control committees, but they are "remarkably persistent and tenacious."[44] Further, they are likely to resist very strongly efforts to change the distributive character of their policy areas. The congressional resistance to, first, the inclusion of credit programs in the unified budget and, more recently, to the budgetary accounting of credit subsidy costs is easily understood in this context.

Including subsidy costs in the unified budget would make credit programs compete not only against each other but also against direct spending programs.

The very conditions that promote legislative policy activity, then, may mitigate against effective policy-making. The absence of clear macro-economic guidelines with regard to spending and tax policy have become rather evident with the unprecedented deficits of recent years. The problem is even more pronounced with credit, since there are no clearcut standards against which to measure credit levels. In sum, the "problems in directing or controlling Federal credit are enormous and systemic."[45]

CONCLUSION

This case study of credit policy strongly indicates the importance of internal and external decentralization in promoting legislative policy-making on matters of budget and finance. While the powers of many parliaments on budgetary policy have been sharply curtailed,[46] the US Congress has jealously guarded its prerogatives. In doing so, it has relied heavily on procedures and organization that focus on discrete programs rather than broad policy objectives. Moreover, its focus on these programs has been largely divorced from appropriate evaluative standards relating to costs and economic objectives. As a recent study of the economics of credit programs concluded, "None of the [evaluative] factors are stressed in the federal budget or in the congressional evaluation of individual programs."[47]

By resisting coordinated and comprehensive treatment of credit programs, Congress is able to maintain considerable discretion in its committees and in operating agencies within the executive branch. If federal credit programs used the accounting practices of private or even government-sponsored financial enterprises, Congress would have a "direct measure...enabling it to evaluate the costs relative to the benefits before making a commitment."[48] At the same time, congressional committees and the operating agencies in the executive branch would lose much of their discretion.

Moreover, the benefits to Congress of such a change would be minimal. Congress, like many other legislatures, is ill-suited to compete with the executive when policy requires consistency, coherence, and integration. Moving credit programs into a decision-making framework that facilitates these conditions would inevitably mean ceding control to the executive. Congress would be able, in Mezey's formulation, to do "what it can do well – to publicly discuss policy problems and alternative solutions, to aggressively oversee the development and implementation of public policy...and to represent to the executive the needs and demands of individual constituents as well as the constituency as a whole. "[49] This might correspond to congressional capabilities. It does not appear to reflect what members of Congress see as their individual and institutional interests.

Notes

1 David M. Olson and Michael L. Mezey, "Parliaments and public policy", this vol., ch. 1.
2 Ibid., p. 7.
3 Barry P. Bosworth, Andrew S. Carron, and Elisabeth H. Rhyne, *The Economics of Federal Credit Programs* (Washington, D.C.: The Brookings Institution, 1987), p. 13.
4 Ibid., p. 1.
5 Michael L. Mezey, "The legislature, the executive and public policy: the futile quest for congressional power," *Congress and the Presidency*, 13 (Spring 1986), 2.
6 Olson and Mezey, "Parliaments and public policy," p. 17.
7 That the amount of time and energy has expanded greatly since passage of the 1974 Budget Act is clear, but the results are something else entirely. Louis Fisher, for example, argues that "reform" has simply made matters worse: "Appropriations bills are enacted later than ever, and sometimes not at all, the government operates for longer periods of time on continuing resolutions, and deficits are larger, far larger, than before the passage of the Budget Act. Basic functions of Congress – the authorizing and appropriating of funds – have lost priority to perennial battles over budget resolutions and reconciliation bills," Louis Fisher, "The Budget Act of 1974: a further loss of spending control," in *Congressional Budgeting*, W. T. Wander *et al.*, eds. (Baltimore: Johns Hopkins University Press, 1984), p. 185.
8 See Dennis S. Ippolito, *Hidden Spending: The Politics of Federal Credit Programs* (Chapel Hill: University of North Carolina Press, 1984).
9 For a discussion of how this protects specific programs, see Herman B. Leonard, *Checks Unbalanced: The Quiet Side of Public Spending* (New York: Basic Books, 1986), pp. 84–93.
10 Control over credit programs has, up until recently, been the nearly exclusive province of authorizing committees. Even with the introduction of credit budgets during the 1980s, the authorizing committees have preserved much of their control over programs. As Bosworth *et al.* have noted, credit budget ceilings apply to only about half of total lending and "Congress tends to be generous in setting the loan ceilings well above any realistic projection of lending activity," *The Economics of Federal Credit Programs*, p. 156.

11 On the impact of decentralization, see Kenneth A. Shepsle and Barry R. Weingast, "Legislative politics and budget outcomes," in *Federal Budget Policy in the 1980s*, G. B. Mills and J. L. Palmer, eds. (Washington, D.C.: Urban Institute Press, 1984), pp. 343–67.

12 Olson and Mezey, "Parliaments and public policy," p. 12.

13 Ibid., p. 9.

14 Ibid.

15 Shepsle and Weingast, "Legislative politics and budget outcomes," pp. 344–5.

16 President's Commission on Budget Concepts, *Staff Papers and Other Materials Reviewed by the President's Commission* (Washington, D.C.: Government Printing Office, 1967), p. 292.

17 President's Commission on Budget Concepts, *Report* (Washington, D.C.: Government Printing Office, 1967), p. 49.

18 Ibid., p. 47.

19 See section 3(a)(2) and 401(c)(2).

20 Senate Committee on Rules and Administration, *Report No. 93–688, Congressional Budget Act of 1974* (Washington, D.C.: Government Printing Office, 1974), p. 13.

21 Allen Schick, *Congress and Money* (Washington, D.C.: Urban Institute, 1980), p. 79.

22 Herman B. Leonard and Elizabeth H. Rhyne, "Federal credit and the 'Shadow Budget,'" *Public Interest*, 65 (Fall 1981), 57.

23 *Special Analysis F, Federal Credit Programs, Budget of the United States Government, Fiscal Year 1984* (Washington, D.C.: Government Printing Office, 1983), p. 50.

24 Elisabeth H. Rhyne, "Federal credit activities," in *Setting National Priorities: The 1984 Budget*, J. A. Pechman, ed. (Washington, D.C.: Brookings Institution), p. 236.

25 *Fiscal Year 1982 Budget Revisions* (Washington, D.C.: Government Printing Office, March 1981), p. 17.

26 *Special Analysis F. Federal Credit Programs, Budget of the United States Government, Fiscal Year 1986*, (Washington, D.C.: Government Printing Office, 1985), pp. F-52–F-54).

27 Which is not to say that the credit control proposals were not highly controversial on their own. As the *Congressional Quarterly* reported in assessing House reactions to the Rules Committee Task Force's recommendation, "Many members are not anxious to bring additional scrutiny – and more frequent votes – to a number of programs that are now off-budget... " *Congressional Quarterly Weekly Report*, 42 (Aug. 8, 1984): 2020.

28 For an explanation of how this procedure operated for fiscal 1986, see General Accounting Office, *Budget Reductions for FY 1986, Balanced Budget and Emergency Deficit Control Act of 1985* (Washington, D.C.: General Accounting Office, January 1986).

29 Leonard, *Checks Unbalanced*, p. 105.

30 Rhyne, "Federal credit activities," p. 236.

31 Ibid., p. 235.

32 See President's Commission on Budget Concepts, *Staff Papers and Other Materials Reviewed by the President's Commission*, p. 301.

33 Ibid.

34 Ibid.
35 President's Commission on Budget Concepts, *Report*, p. 47.
36 *Special Analysis F. Federal Credit Programs, Budget of the United States Government, Fiscal Year 1987* (Washington, D.C.: Government Printing Office, 1986), p. F-53.
37 See Mezey, "The legislature, the executive and public policy," pp. 2-7, for a discussion of optimal public policy and legislative capabilities.
38 James L. Sundquist, "Congress, the president, and the crisis of competence in government," in *Congress Reconsidered*, L. C. Dodd and B. I. Oppenheimer, eds. (Washington, D.C.: Congressional Quarterly, 1981), p. 361.
39 Lance T. LeLoup, "Congress and the dilemma of economic policy," in *Making Economic Policy and Congress*, A. Schick, ed. (Washington, D.C.: American Enterprise Institute, 1983), p. 32.
40 Ibid.
41 Olson and Mezey, "Parliaments and public policy," p. 17.
42 See Ippolito, *Hidden Spending*.
43 Randall B. Ripley and Grace A. Franklin, *Congress, the Bureaucracy, and Public Policy* (3rd edn. Homewood, Ill.: Dorsey Press, 1984), pp. 98–99.
44 Ibid., p. 135.
45 *Special Analysis F, Fiscal Year 1986*, p. F-4.
46 Olson and Mezey, "Parliaments and public policy," p. 3.
47 Bosworth *et al.*, *The Economics of Federal Credit Programs*, p. 174.
48 Ibid., p. 21.
49 Mezey, "The legislature, the executive and public policy," p. 15.

4

Industrial policy agenda and options in Congress and the executive in the United States

DAVID M. OLSON, ROGER H. DAVIDSON, and W. THOMAS KEPHART

The term "industrial policy" in the American setting is not so much a discrete policy proposal as an umbrella term for a debate about a whole range of economic policies. The long-standing imbalance between imports and exports, and the evident decline of heavy industry and textiles have led to a searching debate in the United States about both what other countries are doing better, and what government policy should be.

The twin characteristics of the industrial policy issue in America – its union of the practical with the ideological, and its tentative and beginning stages in the policy cycle – provide a distinctive example of how Congress and president interact in formulating public policy. We seek to understand how Congress contributes to policy formation, how it functions, and how its activity is shaped by outside circumstances. We will consider the growing congressional interest in industrial policy over the span of three Congresses, and then examine the three specific cases of congressional and executive branch action which received the most attention (Congressional Budget Office (CBO), 1983; Scott and Lodge, 1985; 484–93).

INDUSTRIAL POLICY AT THE BEGINNING: FORMING THE AGENDA

A large number of bills on industrial policy were introduced in the three Congresses in the 1979–84 period. We include under "industrial policy," proposals for coordinated government action to address concerns for industrial competitiveness, productivity, and development. Many of the proposals also incorporated related issues such as research and technology, exports and trade, and adjustment assistance for structurally disadvantaged workers.

The idea of coordinated government action toward American industry surfaced about 1980, when several professional and popular articles advocated steps to counter what was feared to be American industry's long-term decline in its capacity to compete internationally (Reich, 1980; Thurow, 1980). This diagnosis of economic ill health was given visibility and credibility by rising unemployment, declining trade, and rampant inflation. In addition, the Chrysler "bailout" legislation of 1979 provided a clear and dramatic example of both a problem industry and a government response. The imminent collapse of one of the major manufacturers in one of America's major industries was a "focusing event" which elevated the broader issue from a potential to an active issue on the governmental agenda (Kingdon, 1984).

Over the six-year period of 1979–84, at least 150 bills were introduced to address problems raised in the industrial policy debate (Table 4.1). In the first period, almost half dealt with export promotion. Most measures were particularized; none embraced the comprehensive approach envisioned by at least some academic proponents of industrial policy. The only bill to pass in the 1979–80 Congress was the Technology Innovation Act of 1980 (Sen. Adlai Stevenson, III., Democrat, Illinois, and Rep. John Wydler, Republican, New York).

Attention in the second period remained on export promotion. The only enacted bill was the Export Trading Company Act (Sen. John Heinz, Republican, Pennsylvania, and Rep. Don Bonker, Democrat, Washington). The declining economy perhaps accounts for the increased number of bills concerned with worker assistance and retraining.

Although the number of industrial policy bills declined in 1983–84, the bills became more comprehensive in scope. This period featured active congressional concern with broad industrial policy as a means of responding to pervasive problems of the whole economy. The three cases we shall concentrate on in this paper emerged during the 1983–84 Congress.

The Senate consistently was less active than the House on industrial policy legislation. In the 98th Congress, Senate bills dropped off sharply. Two of the nine Senate bills were comprehensive, introduced by Sen. Carl Levin (Democrat, Michigan) and Sen. Edward Kennedy (Democrat, Massachusetts).

The stage was set, however, by the 1980 presidential election, which brought Ronald Reagan to the White House, and Republican control to the Senate for the first time in over twenty-five years. Republican policy

Table 4.1 *Industrial policy bills, by category, 96th to 98th Congresses*

	Congress						
	1979–80 96th		1981–82 97th		1983–84 98th		
Category	House	Senate	House	Senate	House	Senate	Total
1 Export policy and promotion	14	11	12	7	1		45
2 Industrial innovation and technology	7	2	1		3	1	14
3 Industrial competitiveness	1	1	2	1	5	1	11
4 Worker retraining and trade adjustment assistance	6	1	12	5		1	25
5 Industrial investment, promotion, and development	5	6	9	5	8	2	35
6 Plant closings and dislocation policy	1	1					2
7 Joint ventures			1	4	1		6
8 Capital market regulation					2		2
9 Broad industrial policy					4	2	6
10 Trade reorganization	1	1			3	2	7
Total: Chamber	35	23	37	22	27	9	
Total: Congress	58		59		36		153

Source: SCORPIO bill status computerized data base (US Library of Congress).

was to be made in the executive branch and protected in the Senate. Congressional Democrats were thrown back on their own considerably reduced resources.

One Democratic Party response to its demoralized condition was the Committee on Party Effectiveness created by the House Democratic caucus in February 1981. Its purpose was to revive Democrats' sagging electoral fortunes by exploring new policy approaches. Its formation coincided with the publication of industrial policy ideas by external policy entrepreneurs, whose ideas found a receptive audience in the Committee's Task Force on Long-Term Economic Policy. Chaired by Rep. Tim Wirth (Democrat, Colorado), the committee contained some members who thought industrial policy a meritorious concept, while others saw it as a means of uniting their more usual concerns over employment with strategies for economic growth (Baker, 1985).

The House Democratic Task Force on Long-Term Economic Policy report advanced the topic of industrial policy on the legislative agenda, stimulating further debate and activity (House Democratic Caucus, 1982). The Task Force report reflected consensus among a consciously representative crossection of Democrats, both ideologically and regionally. The members agreed on the industrial competitiveness problem and its causes, as well as on a proposed Economic Cooperation Council which would combine governmental, labor, and business representatives. The House Democratic Task Force report provided a departure point for many Members of Congress and outside observers in refining their approaches and strategies on the industrial policy issue. The substantial, perhaps unusual, degree of party activity among both Democrats and Republicans illustrates the anticipated utility of the industrial policy issue in the coming presidential election of 1984.

In these early stages of agenda formation, the most active promoters of industrial policy were three House Democrats with institutional platforms for their advocacy. One, Rep. Wirth (Democrat, Colorado), chaired the House Democratic Task Force on Long-Term Economic Policy. Rep. John LaFalce (Democrat, New York), chaired the critical House committee unit to assert jurisdiction over related legislation. Rep. Stan Lundine (Democrat, New York) held memberships on both the Democratic Task Force and on the LaFalce subcommittee.

OPTION FORMATION IN THE COMMITTEES

Each of the three 1983–84 political responses to the industrial competitiveness issue considered here was prompted by a congressional committee or presidential commission. While election trends, perceived economic crises, and party task forces contributed to setting the agenda, the specific policy options were developed by formal panels. Congressional committees proposed legislative initiatives while the Reagan administration responded by establishing a commission – a familiar executive device often utilized for policy questions apparently lacking widespread consensus.

Congress processes legislation through an extensive committee and subcommittee system, which performs a special function in managing the congressional agenda. Committees select those topics on which they will deliberate and attempt to formulate the options which go to the floor. A committee's ability to influence the chamber's decisions on the floor places a premium on developing consensus within the committees. While the committees could place industrial policy on their own agendas, their inability to generate consensus over policy options beyond the membership of the committee (sometimes among committee members as well) effectively prevented their own bills from reaching the floor.

We shall discuss first the emergence of broad-gauged industrial policy bills in the House. Second, we will turn to the Senate, where the issue arose in conjunction with a bill to create a Department of Trade. The third case is the response of the Reagan administration.

In the House: industrial policy

The Committee on Banking, Housing and Urban Affairs' Economic Stabilization Subcommittee, which had industrial policy jurisdiction, was the arena for considering industrial policy in the House throughout 1983–84. Two bills, HR 4360 on industrial competitiveness, and HR 4361, to create an Advanced Technology Foundation, were reported by the committee but failed to reach the floor. A long series of subcommittee hearings, and the ensuing legislation, represented the culmination of active congressional consideration of industrial policy.

A vigorous advocate of a national initiative on industrial policy, Rep. LaFalce used his post as the subcommittee's chairman to shape the debate by convening an extended series of hearings in 1983 and fashioning the legislative vehicles the committee then considered. The immediate stimulus to these bills was the economic recession of 1982–83. In addition, several Democratic Members of the subcommittee represented declining industrial "smokestack" districts. On the Republican side of the subcommittee, however, several Members came from districts with growing "high tech" industries. Thus, the opposing positions taken on the issue were differentiated by political party undergirded by contrasting types of constituencies.

The task for the subcommittee chairman and staff was to define a policy problem, formulate a legislative response, and obtain sufficient support to enact that legislation. Public hearings by the LaFalce subcommittee were the basic device to accomplish the task of placing industrial policy on the active congressional agenda.

Two sets of hearings were held. The first, and the longest in time and in printed pages, was exploratory (Banking Committee, Subcommittee on Economic Stabilization, *Industrial Policy*: Hearings, 1983–84). Problem definition and policy option exploration were their purpose and accomplishment.

They provided a forum for outside witnesses to present their analyses of economic problems and their suggestions for appropriate government

action. A wide-ranging array of outside witnesses, including economists
and other academic "experts," labor leaders, industrial and financial
representatives, and state and local government officials uncovered
conflicting economic analyses, scholarly approaches, and policy objectives. Panel members approached the hearings from a number of
perspectives, expressing widely differing underlying premises (WP Nov.
16, 1983: A4; CQWR Aug. 20, 1983; 1679–87). These exploratory
hearings were often referred to subsequently as helping to define both the
problem and the response.

Administration witnesses also testified in opposition to the major
concepts emerging in the larger policy debate: they defended the market-
oriented approach of the administration, and belittled the suggestions of
a tripartite industrial council and of an industrial development bank. The
administration witnesses instead urged support of the Senate bill to create
a Department of International Trade and Industry (Hearings, Part 5;
364–570).

The initial hearings also helped identify the underlying configuration of
political forces on the resulting bills, for the summary statement of
findings from the hearings was issued by the Democratic majority, with no
Republican participation (*Forging*, 1983). The subcommittee's Democratic report dismissed the administration's position and characterized the
newly appointed Presidential Commission on Industrial Competitiveness
as neither representative of America's economy nor independent of the
administration. The partisan gauntlet had already been thrown down (WP
Nov. 8, 1983; A3).

The initial hearings occupied almost six months. Then, events moved
rapidly. The hearings ended in late October 1983. The Democratic
members of the subcommittee issued their recommendations on
November 8, and the main industrial policy bill, HR 4360, was introduced
by LaFalce on November 10. He proposed a Council on Industrial
Competitiveness and a Bank for Industrial Competition to provide
venture capital.

The second set of hearings, on HR 4360 and the other bill which
resulted from the exploratory hearings, began promptly on November 16.
By this time, the term "industrial policy" had been dropped in favor of
the administration's own phrase, "industrial competitiveness." LaFalce
referred to his initiative as "industrial strategy."

The administration, represented by witnesses from the Departments of
Commerce and of Treasury, opposed the whole bill, either with or without
the name change. Commerce also opposed the second bill, which
proposed an Advanced Technology Foundation (HR 4361). Adminis-

tration witnesses could point to their own positive actions as a means to blunt the push for these specific subcommittee bills. They pointed to Sen. William Roth's (Republican, Delaware) trade department bill, having been reported favorably by his Senate committee, as an "administration proposal" – though no one asked in the hearings if the administration also accepted the industrial policy amendments to that bill. In addition, the administration witnesses pointed to the recent creation of the president's Commission on Industrial Competitiveness, though it was only in the beginning stages of its work at the time of these hearings (Econ. Stab. Subcommittee, Industrial Competitiveness Act Hearings, pp. 205–56).

The chairman's response was predictable: "Yesterday we had an opportunity to hear the administration's view... and I can say quite frankly that I was appalled..." He characterized the administration as "pursuing illusions" (Hearings, p. 267). The main source of support for his own position in the hearings came from organized labor.

The proposed bank was the main source of contention. While Republican members of both the subcommittee and the full Banking Committee opposed industrial policy as an idea, as did the administration, they targeted the bank as the object of their opposition. Their minority report declared their intention to offer a substitute on the floor to remove the whole title of the bill containing the Bank (Committee on Banking, *Industrial Competitiveness Act Report*, 1984; 164).

The bank proved to be the main obstacle to Democratic Party unity as well (NYT Jan. 12, 1984; D6; WP Oct. 17, 1983: A2). Though the bill was reported from committee with unified Democratic majority support, the bank promised to generate Democratic opposition on the floor (WP Feb. 9, 1984: B1, B4). Thus, the bill was held at the Rules Committee while Democratic leaders attempted to negotiate a compromise. That effort failed, and the bill was never brought to the floor (Baker, 1985).

Brookings economist Charles Schulze, adviser to two Democratic presidents, Johnson and Carter, played a pivotal role in undermining House Democratic consensus on industrial policy (Schulze, 1983). He argued that the American political system would not allow potential losers to fail; political pressure would override general policy concerns to mandate subsidizing or protecting threatened industries. Schulze buttressed this view with an argument widely invoked by conservatives: that government attempts at economic planning – centralizing decisions in the hands of those concerned with the general welfare rather than with profit maximization – were unworkable. Inefficient enterprises would be perpetuated rather than being permitted to shrink or die.

What had begun as a major Democratic initiative against the administration, and also as a show of party unity, failed through party disunity. The Schulze dissection of the proposals both signalled the split and undermined the credibility, even among Democrats, of the industrial policy idea.

In the Senate: Department of Trade

The only directly relevant bill to be reported by a Senate committee in the 98th Congress was Sen. Roth's Trade Reorganization Act (S. 121). The proposal to create a new Department of Trade, unifying the scattered agencies concerned with trade policy into a single cabinet level department, was a long-term interest of Sen. Roth, chairman of the Committee on Governmental Affairs. Since his committee held jurisdiction over agency reorganization matters, he was able to conduct committee hearings on his bill. It was to this bill that industrial policy amendments were grafted after the House had given visibility to the issue.

The hearings were used mainly to prod the administration into taking a position supporting the trade reorganization bill, for there was no clear administration position at the beginning. One of the major difficulties in forming an administration position was the problem the bill was designed to remedy – split agency responsibilities between the Department of Commerce with its International Trade Administration, and the US Representative for Trade. Though the heads of both were appointees of the president, though both were loyal members of the cabinet, and though both professed a cooperative working relationship with each other, they did not immediately endorse the bill which would have merged their two agencies (WSJ, Aug. 18, 1983: 48; WP, Dec. 12, 1984: D1).

Administration support did come, slowly, with considerable prodding by Sen. Roth. Indeed, the hearings were delayed for two weeks to give the administration time to develop a position. Endorsement by the president came on June 1. Sen. Roth observed, at the opening of the next hearings on June 24, that "We had some pretty tough negotiations in trying to reach a consensus..." (Hearings, p. 290). These negotiations had brought the administration view into sufficient agreement with the Roth bill, so that it became the administration bill.

Commerce Secretary Baldridge announced that President Reagan put the proposal on a "fast track" and "hoped for passage this year" (WP, May 4, 1983: D9). But, the publicly expressed endorsement of the president was not sufficient to win adoption of the bill.

One problem was that the Department of State, whose secretary had considerable personal experience in international economics, was increasingly active in that field. Indeed, by 1985, the State Department had become the leading agency in US–Japanese trade negotiations.

Agriculture was another major unresolved problem (WP, March 18, 1983: C8). Farmer organizations looked to the Department of Agriculture as their voice in international trade negotiations. Many midwestern farm state Republican senators could be expected to vote against the bill should it reach the floor. Though the bill had gained administration support, it faced a split among the Senate Republicans because of opposition from the agricultural groups.

In markup, the bill acquired the further liability of becoming a vehicle for industrial policy views. Several Democratic Senators (Thomas Eagleton, Mo., and Carl Levin, Mich.) offered amendments to create tripartite councils to monitor the performance of the economy and to recommend needed policy changes. While the strongest of their proposals were defeated in committee, several milder versions were added. The bill thereby attracted opposition rather than additional support, for numerous senators of both parties would not accept such a notion, and the administration was strongly opposed to any suggestion of an industrial policy (WP, Sept. 22, 1983: C12). The strongest of the amendments offered in committee on industrial policy, to create a Council on Industrial Strategy, was the one roll call decided on a straight party line vote (Committee Governmental Affairs, Report, 1984: 45–46).

Though this bill, like the others we are considering, was approved in committee, it was never brought to the floor. Clearly it would have split the majority Republican Party. Neither the agricultural state Senators nor the advocates of open trade would accept the bill. Furthermore, the administration's position was in doubt. The public endorsement by the president was not sufficient to convince the advocates that genuine administration support could be obtained in the crunch of floor action. Not only did the president face the problem of divided agency loyalties within the Executive Branch, but the successful use of the bill by Democrats as a vehicle for industrial policy amendments greatly diminished administration enthusiasm for the bill as a whole. In addition, there was the strong possibility that, in the House, the bill would have been used there, too, as a vehicle for industrial policy amendments both in committee and on the floor (WP Nov. 16, 1983: A4).

Presidential Commission on industrial competitiveness

Just as Congress explored problems and attempted to define options through specialized committees, so the executive branch created a presidential commission to examine industrial competitiveness. Its membership was largely drawn from the chief executive officers of growth, exporting, and high-tech companies. In addition, several university economists and representatives of organized labor were included.

The Commission's report, issued in February 1985, recommended, among forty-four different items, creation of two new cabinet departments – Trade, and Science and Technology – and paid particular attention to the need for research and development and for the facilitation of exports (Commission Report, Jan. 1985; WSJ Feb. 14, 1985: 6; WP, Feb. 17, 1985: E6; NYT, Feb. 14, 1985: D1; NJ, Dec. 1, 1984: 2298–301).

The report contained no suggestions of "industrial policy." Many related broad questions apparently did not arise in the formal deliberations of either the full commission or its subcommittees. For example, neither a tripartite industrial council nor sector-specific policies were considered. Neither were staff studies requested on such topics. The work and discussion of the commission remained within the confines of the policy orientation of the administration. Unlike congressional committees, presidential commissions do not have a structured basis for internal disagreements.

The administration's preferences were clearly signalled by President Reagan's legislative recommendations released after he met with the commission as they began their work. Changes in the antitrust laws were recommended to permit companies to enter into joint ventures for research into and development of new technology (WP Sept. 13, 1983: A1; NJ Oct. 1, 1983: 1992–96). Presidential announcements of the formation and membership of the commission likewise carried the twin emphasis upon "high technology" and continuation of the administration's fiscal policies (Weekly Compilation Presidential Documents, June 28, 1983: 936, and Aug. 4, 1983: 1091).

By appointment of the commission, the administration gained both time and ideas. Its creation in effect froze any further congressional action until after the 1984 presidential election. Republican advocates of a unified Department of Trade could not act against their own administration, and Democratic proponents of industrial policy legislation were effectively blocked from further action on their own initiative. The report was issued in February 1985 after the 1984 elections, though the initial report data had been defined as one month prior to those elections.

To emphasize the adverse position of the administration on the industrial policy issue, Rep. LaFalce's subcommittee held hearings in early March 1985 with the chairman of the president's commission, in which the former commended the latter, expressing the hope that the administration would act positively on the recommendations. In the

Senate, the Finance Committee also held a hearing to review the commission findings. Simultaneously, Sen. Roth was holding his trade bill in abeyance, pending announcement of the president's decisions about the commission's recommendations, one of which agreed with Sen. Roth's own Department of Trade proposal (National Journal, March 9, 1985).

The report of the commission was received by the Secretary of Commerce, not by the president. The recommendations were referred to the Cabinet Council on Commerce and Trade, which in turn, would make recommendations to the president. Little information was available about how the Cabinet Council was thinking about the report's recommendations, or about how the president was being informed and what he was thinking. Though an administration draft bill was transmitted to Congress, it was not until mid-March that it was revealed unofficially that the president had decided not to recommend a department of trade (WSJ, Mar. 18, 1985: 64). Shortly thereafter, the whole formal structure of White House policy advice was revised; the Cabinet Council which had received the report was dissolved (NYT Apr. 14, 1985: A15).

FACTORS RELATED TO CONGRESSIONAL POLICY PARTICIPATION

There was, as one participant put it, lots of activity but no action. Individual Members, subcommittees and committees, committee chairmen and staff, and party task forces and leaders, were all active on industrial policy and trade department bills. But, there was no collective and authoritative decision. While the originating committees could act, neither party nor chamber made subsequent decision. While outside policy entrepreneurs and inside Congressmen could place industrial policy on the active congressional agenda, and could also formulate specific legislative options, they could not move the issue toward an authoritative policy decision. The result was, at least in the short run, policy stalemate, both between president and Congress, and within Congress itself.

Three broad sets of factors have been identified in the opening chapter which are related to the extent to which, and the means by which, legislatures are active on issues of public policy: environment, institutionalization, and policy. Congressional activity on industrial policy provides an example by which these factors may be examined.

Environment: Executive Branch

1 Constitutional structure. This factor is explicitly cross-system in effect and is hard to evaluate within a single nation. Certainly, Members and the congressional parties and committees were free to develop and to act upon

their own policy preferences. For Republicans in the Senate, part of their
activity was aimed at the administration of their own party. The trade bill
sponsors saw no hope of obtaining senatorial approval in the absence of
strong presidential endorsement. Most actions within one branch seemed
at least partly designed to influence the other, at all stages of the policy
cycle.

2 Executive branch centralization. The relatively open and decentralized American executive branch confronted both president and Congress
(Campbell, 1983). The president and his advisors required a considerable
period of time to resolve internal differences among agencies prior to
announcing support of the trade bill. Neither the executive nor senatorial
supporters of the trade bill obtained full support from either the
Agriculture or State Departments. The administration did have more
internal unanimity in opposition to industrial policy bills, perhaps because
the latter raised more of an ideological and generalized issue, than in
support of the more specific trade reorganization bill.

3 Executive level. The wide scope of both sets of bills removed them
from the jurisdiction of any one agency, thus creating potential conflicts
among agencies and causing the issues to rise within the structure of the
executive branch to the White House for resolution. The wide scope of the
bills thus had similar organizational consequences in both branches of
government (Ripley and Franklin, 1984). The diversity of views among
the administrative agencies increased both the opportunities for congressional activity and the necessity for White House involvement.

Presidential support of the trade bill was not as steady or clear as was
administration opposition to industrial policy. Congressmen were most
alert to the nuances of the "real" administration position in the crunch of
floor action. To congressional supporters of the trade bill, presidential
rhetoric did not match prospective administration inactivity. Since then,
presidential support of a department of trade has been withdrawn. At
least one factor in that decision was the prospect of congressional defeat.

The president and congressional committees were the targets of each
other's actions; this committee–presidential relationship is perhaps
unusual in the American policy setting, in which committees and agencies
are the usual interactive partners (Ripley and Franklin, 1984).

The multiple agency scope of industrial policy and of trade reorganization had the same effect within the executive branch as within
Congress: conflict at lower levels drove the issue upward into the
congressional party leadership and into the White House. The "open"
American executive branch (Hypothesis 2) did stimulate congressional
activity in developing and defining issues, but as the issue came to White

House attention (Hypothesis 3), congressional autonomy was reduced. Our examples paradoxically confirm both hypotheses.

Environment: elections

The impact of party versus candidate centered campaigns is a cross-system difference, hard to evaluate within any one country. The potential importance of industrial policy (but not the trade bill itself), however, in the coming elections of 1984 was a very strong consideration in the thinking of both proponents and opponents. The presumed electoral utility of the issue activated task forces within both congressional parties and perhaps stimulated the administration to create the Presidential Commission on Industrial Competitiveness. The electoral relevance of the issue had both a polarizing and centralizing impact upon how the issue was handled.

The industrial policy issue ultimately was handled in a European parliamentary manner, in that it was treated as a national party electoral issue. The congressional party task forces and the strong views of the administration in opposition to industrial policy produced stalemate in the American policy process until after the 1984 presidential election. Reagan's reelection effectively prevented further congressional action on the issue for the next several years. On this issue, the American electoral system became, at least relatively, centralized, thus confirming the lack of final congressional action expected by Hypothesis 4.

Environment: interest groups

1 Interest group type. As with congressional committees and administrative agencies, the diversity of affected elements produced both activity and stalemate. Many interest groups were active in presenting testimony to congressional committees, in developing their own study groups and reports, and in lobbying on both the Hill and within the executive branch.

These many outside participants illustrate the importance of "issue networks" and "policy communities" as opposed to formal and presumably powerful interest groups (Heclo, 1978). The uncertainty of the problem and the fluidity of ideas were matched by the constant interchanges among the participants, and by the porousness of the governmental structure itself.

2 Group–agency relationship. In some instances, an interest group may disagree with the actions of the administrative agency with which it has its primary relationship, thus opening the way for congressional involvement. In our cases, however, each tended to agree with the other in opposition to the administration and to other groups. The diversity of groups and the diversity of agencies produced conflicts and stalemate.

3 Inter-group relationships. The extensive conflicts among the affected groups provided ample scope for congressional activity. Management and labor from declining regions and distressed industries have a common point of view against those from high-tech areas. There has been more apparent division, however, among businessmen than labor unions on this type of issue. Again, the result was stalemate.

4 Group involvement. The new issue of industrial policy has not yet stimulated the formation of new interest groups. It does, however, have the potential to stimulate the formation of new coalitions among existing groups. Industrial policy raises a question of the relationship among existing policies and groups more than it raises a new issue in either substance or group composition. The result in Congress to date has been more the activation of existing constituency and ideological coalitions than the formation of new combinations among members, committees, or political parties.

Institutionalization

The internal organizational capacity of a legislature to act affects both the extent and means of legislative involvement in public policy. This set of factors mostly concerns political parties and committees as the main means by which legislatures are organized to work.

1 Party system. Control of both the presidency and Congress by a single party or coalition could depress legislative policy activity. The absence of single party control, by contrast, would encourage such activity. To have the two chambers of Congress controlled by different parties, and thus, to also have split party control between the presidency and one chamber, is perhaps the most unstable condition of party composition of which the American government is capable (at least within a two party system). Yet, the conditions for congressional activism against the president are maximized when both houses are controlled by the opposition party, as during the Nixon administration, rather than to have split party control between the two houses as during the Reagan years.

2 Internal party organization. Decentralization and fragmentation within both of the two congressional parties encouraged congressional activism, but prevented either party from taking a clear decision. Neither Republicans in the Senate nor Democrats in the House were sufficiently unified to be able to adopt a bill on the floor. Perhaps atypically, task forces of both House parties and among Senate Democrats did issue industrial policy reports. Republicans found it easier to agree to oppose, than Democrats did to support, industrial policy proposals. But if decentralization encourages individual or small group activism, it also prevented the larger units of party and chamber from reaching a decision.

3 Party external links. In the United States, the question of external linkages from congressional parties to outside sources of direction exists only for the party of the president. The Reagan administration has been thought to have had an effective relationship with, as opposed to "control" over, its congressional party in its first term (Ornstein, 1982). Though the administration had solid congressional Republican support in its opposition to industrial policy, it was not able to obtain positive support for the Trade bill from Senate Republicans.

The circumstances of American political parties were thus ideally suited to both the stimulation of the issue of industrial policy and to its stalemate. Party disunity created openings for individual congressman to attempt to find and define a new issue. Once an issue was defined, party unity assumed different characteristics. In support of their president, Republicans could unify to oppose Democratic initiatives more readily than either party could unify in positive support of any policy. Both the lack of single party control (Hypothesis 10) and the fragmented party organization (Hypothesis 11) of the American Congress in the first term of the Reagan administration were ideally suited to stimulate congressional activity at the early stages of the policy cycle. But, these same characteristics also made definitive decision less likely.

4 Committee system. Committees in the US Congress are considered to be more active and powerful than are committees in other national parliaments (Lees and Shaw, 1979). Committee chairmen proposed bills and organized hearings in support of their bills. Both option formulation and agenda setting are functions for which congressional committees are especially well suited (Jones and Strahan, 1985).

But, no one committee had exclusive jurisdiction over either industrial policy or trade reorganization bills, thus giving opponents multiple forums within which to oppose the bills. Congressional respondents speculated that had the bills received more support, and had better prospects of actually coming to the floor, other committees would have more actively asserted jurisdiction. The consequence would have been either amendment or defeat of the proposed legislation. Nevertheless, the main activity on both sets of bills centered in one committee in each chamber.

The consequence of multiple committees and subcommittees, with overlapping jurisdiction, has been to both encourage congressional activism but discourage a positive decision on either legislative initiative.

In the 1983–84 Congress, nearly one-quarter of all legislation was considered by two or more committees (Oleszek, Davidson, and Kephart, 1986). Given the scope and complexity of industrial policy bills, multiple committee jurisdictions were unavoidable. If either industrial policy or trade policy administrative organization had been within the jurisdiction of any one committee, perhaps either issue could have been resolved more easily than it was. The hypothesis about committee structure in parallel with administrative structure (Hypothesis 13) needs modification: an important additional element is the congruence of an issue with the jurisdiction of any one committee.

Policy

1 Manifest content. Industrial policy is an issue which encourages active legislative involvement. It offers the promise of providing socioeconomic benefits to wide segments of the population as a distributional issue, and also of rescuing distressed industries as a redistributional issue (Ripley and Franklin, 1984). It also suggests a wide range of regulations to accompany a wide range of potential benefits. Its content places this issue within the category of socioeconomic policy, which encourages congressional activity, rather than the much narrower one of finance (which would discourage congressional activity).

2 Circumstances. Industrial policy affects a wide and diverse range of population and economy. Furthermore, it affects differently the various economic subcategories within the population. That is, many persons, economic segments, and regions are affected, but are affected for different reasons and in different ways. Nevertheless, the issue itself probably was known to only the elites of these diverse segments. The width of the publics is more a statement of the potential impact rather than current attentiveness. The issue was more on the governmental agenda than the public one (Cobb and Elder, 1972: 160–61). Diversity and disagreement among the elites accompanied congressional activity. The issue was highly salient to the elites in part because of its potential use in the coming 1984 presidential campaign. Though the issue was low in public visibility, it was high in conflict among the political elites (Price, 1978: 569–570).

3 Stage. This policy question in the United States was at the beginning stages of agenda setting and options formulation (Kingdon, 1984). Agenda setting and issue agitation are frequently congressional activities, while formal option preparation is more often an executive activity. Given the opposition of the Reagan administration, however, the proposal of new policy was left by default to Congress and especially to the committees (Jones and Strahan, 1985).

Taking all three components of policy together, both the manifest content and the attributes of industrial policy would suggest an active congressional involvement in the issue, at least in its beginning stages.

Industrial policy, however, has two additional attributes: it is both comprehensive and ideological. Though the bills themselves proved to be fairly modest in scope, industrial policy was ultimately interpreted by friend and foe alike as a non-incremental policy embodying comprehensive changes in governmental economic policy. It attempts to coordinate and integrate many different sectors of activity. The trade department bill would perform the same function for the many facets of foreign trade. Yet, Congress is not organized to enact such comprehensive legislation, of which the Carter administration's energy plan is an illustration (Oppenheimer, 1980).

Industrial policy, at least in the United States, also became highly ideological. Though addressed to hard economic realities, it is debated in terms of first principles. Both the emotive quality of the issue and its potential electoral utility also stimulated congressional activity, especially among Democrats, while the same factors stiffened Republican opposition in both Congress and the administration. The American politics of industrial policy does not so much negate as expand and complicate the hypotheses in chapter 1 concerning attributes of issues. Both the comprehensive and ideological attributes of this issue, submerged the manifest content of the policy question and activated preexisting lines of cleavage within existing publics more than stimulated new groups and publics. It may be that the combined comprehensive-ideological nature of industrial policy was particularly important at the beginning stages of the policy cycle.

CONCLUSION

The result of these many factors was stalemate between president and Congress, and internally within Congress and within each congressional party as well. Stalemate confirms existing policy and practices. Given the preference of the Reagan administration for the avoidance of overt governmental action as a positive public good, the administration was the winner on industrial policy, at least in the beginning. Prospective congressional majorities, never tested in floor fights, were also the winners in their presumed opposition to industrial policy legislation.

These three economic policy questions show the capacity of Congress, through its many committees, to help shape both the governmental agenda and the policy options. Committee autonomy from either external control or internal party management, and their very number and diversity, give them ample opportunities to seize issues and to attempt to formulate policy options. But both the presence of sustained opposition on the floor and from the administration, and the absence of crisis to overcome that opposition, prevented the issue from proceeding past the committees.

References

BOOKS AND PERIODICALS

Adams, F. Gerard and Lawrence R. Klein, eds. (1983) *Industrial Policies for Growth and Competitiveness* (Lexington, Mass.: D. C. Heath).

American Enterprise Institute (1984) *Proposals to Establish a Department of Trade* (Washington, D.C.: AEI, Legislative Analysis No. 43, May 1984).

Business–Higher Education Forum (1983) *American's Competitive Challenge: The Need for a National Response.* A Report to the President, Washington, D.C.

Campbell, Colin (1983) *Governments Under Stress* (Toronto: University of Toronto Press).

Cobb, Roger W. and Charles D. Elder (1972) *Participation in American Politics: The Dynamics of Agenda-Building* (Boston: Allyn & Bacon).

Committee for Economic Development (1984) *Strategy for U.S. Industrial Competitiveness*: A Statement by the Research and Policy Committee. New York (April).

Driscoll, Robert E. and Jack N. Behrman, eds. (1984) *National Industrial Policies* (Cambridge, Mass.: Oelgeshlager, Gunn and Hain).

Friedman, Benjamin M., *et al.* (1985) "Do we need an industrial policy? a forum," *Harper's*, (February), 35–48.

Friedman, Miles (1982) "The political question: can we have a national industrial policy or a national regional policy?" in Michael E. Bell and Paul S. Lande, eds., *Regional Dimensions of Industrial Policy*, (Lexington, Mass.: Lexington), pp. 21–46.

Heclo, Hugh (1978), "Issue networks and the executive establishment," in Anthony King, ed., *The New American Political System*, (Washington, D.C.: AEI), pp. 87–124.

Jones, Charles O. and R. Strahan (1985) "The effect of energy politics on congressional and executive organization in the 1970s," *Legislative Studies Quarterly*, 10 (May), 151–80.

Johnson, Chalmers (1978), *Japan's Public Policy Companies* (Washington, D.C.: AEI).

Kantrow, Alan M., ed (1983) "The political realities of industrial policy: a roundtable," *Harvard Business Review*,) 61 (September–October), 76–86.

Kingdon, John W. 1984 *Agenda, Alternatives, and Public Policies* (Boston: Little, Brown).

Lees, John D. and Malcolm Shaw, eds. (1979) *Committees in Legislatures: A Comparative Analysis* (Durham, N. C.: Duke).

Maunder, Peter, ed. (1979) *Government Intervention in the Developed Economy* (New York: Praeger).

Merrill, Stephen A. 1984 "The politics of micropolicy: innovation and industrial policy in the United States," *Policy Studies Review*, 3 (May), 445–52.

Olson, David M. (1980) *The Legislative Process: A Comparative Approach* (New York: Harper and Row).

Oppenheimer, Bruce I. (1980) "Policy effects of U.S. House reform: decentralization and the capacity to resolve energy issues," *Legislative Studies Quarterly*, 5 (February), 5–30.

  (1983) "How legislatures shape policy and budgets," *Legislative Studies Quarterly*, 8 (November), 551–98.

Ornstein, Norman J., ed. (1982) *President and Congress: Assessing Reagan's First Year* (Washington, D.C.: AEI).

Phillips, Kevin P. (1984) *Staying on Top* (New York: Random House).

Price, David E. (1978) "Policy making in congressional committees: the impact of 'environmental factors'," *American Political Science Review*, 72: 548–74.

Reich, Robert B. (1983) *The Next American Frontier* (New York: Penguin Books).
  1982 "Making industrial policy," *Foreign Affairs* (Spring), 852–81.
  1980, "Pie-slicers vs. pie-enlargers," *The Washington Monthly*, 12 (September), 13–19.

Ripley, Randall B. (1983) *Congress: Process and Policy,* 3rd edn, (New York: Norton).
  and Grace A. Franklin (1984) *Congress, the Bureaucracy, and Public Policy*, 3rd edn (Homewood, Ill.: Dorsey).

Schulze, Charles L. (1983) "Industrial policy: a dissent" *The Brookings Review*, 2: 3–12.

Scott, Bruce R. and George C. Lodge, eds. (1985) *U.S. Competitiveness in the World Economy* (Boston: Harvard Business School Press).

Shepsle, Kenneth A. and Barry R. Weingast. 1984 "Legislative politics and budget outcomes," in Gregory B. Mills and John L. Palmer, eds., *Federal Budget Policy in the 1980s* (Washington, D.C.: The Urban Institute), pp. 343–67.

Spitzer, Robert J. (1983) *The Presidency and Public Policy: The Four Arenas of Presidential Power* (Alabama: University of Alabama Press).

Thurow, Lester C. (1980) "There are solutions to our economic problems," *New York Times Magazine*, August 10, 1980, pp. 30–46.

Warnecke, Steven J. and Ezra N. Suleiman, eds. (1975) *Industrial Policies in Western Europe* (New York: Praeger).

NEWS PUBLICATIONS (WITH ABBREVIATIONS USED IN NOTES)
Business Week, 1984–85
Congressional Quarterly Weekly Report, 1983–84 (CQWR)
National Journal, 1983–85 (NJ)
New York Times, 1983–May 1, 1985 (NYT)
Wall Street Journal, 1983–July 1, 1985 (WSJ)
Washington Post, 1983–May 1, 1985 (WP)

GOVERNMENT DOCUMENTS: US CONGRESS

House:

Committee on Banking, Finance, and Urban Affairs. *Industrial Competitiveness Act (HR 4360)*. April 24, 1984. Report 98–697 Part I.

Advanced Technology Foundation Act (HR 4361). 1984. Report 98-693 Part I.

Subcommittee on Economic Stabilization. *Industrial Policy*. Hearings. June 9, 1983–February 15, 1984, Parts 1–6. Serial 98-39, -44, -45, -47, -53, -66.

Forging an Industrial Competitiveness Strategy; A Report with Legislative Recommendations from Democratic Members. November 8, 1983. Committee Print 98–8.

Industrial Competitiveness Act; Hearings on HR 4360. November 16, 1983– February 2, 1984. Serial No. 98–70.

Secondary Market for Industrial Mortgages. Hearings March 13 and 20, 1984. Serial No. 98-79.

The Advanced Technology Foundation Act; Hearings on HR 4361. March 14–28. Serial No. 98-77.

Committee on Energy and Commerce. Subcommittee on Commerce, Transportation and Tourism. *Industrial Competitiveness Act*. Hearings. May 17, 1984. Serial no. 98-155.

Industrial Competitiveness Act (HR 4360). Report. June 6, 1984. Report 98-697, Part II.

Senate

Committee on Governmental Affairs. *Trade Reorganization Act of 1983; Hearings on S. 121*. March 17–September 15, 1983. S. Hrg. 98-474.

Trade Reorganization Act of *1983; Report on S. 121*. April 3, 1984. Report 98-374.

Committee on Finance. *Review of Findings of the President's Commission on Industrial Competitiveness; Hearing*. March 29, 1985. S. Hrg. 99-75.

Subcommittee on International Trade. *Trade Reorganization Plans*; Hearings I and II. S. Hrg. 98-858. February 21–27, 1984.

Joint Economic Committee (listed by date)

Joint Economic Committee. *Industrial Policy, Economic Growth and the Competitiveness of U.S. Industry*; Hearings Parts 1–3. June 24–October 31, 1983. S. Hrg. 98-299 pts 1–3.

Industrial Policy: The Retraining Needs of the Nation's Long-Term Structurally Unemployed Workers. Hearings, September 16–October 26, 1983. S. Hrg. 98-639.

Antitrust Policy and Joint Research and Development Ventures. Hearing. November 3, 1983. S. Hrg. 98-829.

The Service Economy and Industrial Change. Hearing. April 4–11, 1984.

Policies for Industrial Growth in a Competitive World; A Volume of Essays. Joint Committee Print. Prepared for Subcommittee on Economic Goals and Intergovernmental Policy. April 27, 1984. S. Prt. 98-187.

Industrial Policy Movement in the United States; Is it the Answer? A Staff Study. Joint Committee Print. June 8, 1984. S. Prt. 98-196.

102 DAVID M. OLSON, ROGER H. DAVIDSON, AND W. THOMAS
KEPHART

Congressional Budget Office (listed by date)

The Industrial Policy Debate, December 1983
Federal Support of U.S. Business, January 1984
Federal Support for R & D and Innovation, April 1984
The Federal Role in State Industrial Development Programs, July 1984
The Effects of Import Quotas on the Steel Industry, July 1984

Congressional political parties

House Democratic Caucus. Special Task Force on Long-Term Economic Policy.
"Rebuilding the Road to Opportunity." September 1982.
House Republican Research Committee. "National Industrial Policy: New
Rhetoric, Old Ideas," February 6, 1983 (mimeo).
House Republican Research Committee. The Steering Committee of the Task
Force on High Technology Initiatives. "Targeting the Process of Innovation:
An Agenda," 1st edn, May 1984.
Senate Democratic Caucus. "Jobs for the Future: A Democratic Agenda."
November 16, 1983.

Other

Congressional Research Service. "Industrial Policy" Background Material Info
Pack (various items, dates).
Oleszek, Walter J., Roger H. Davidson and Thomas Kephart 1986. "The
incidence and impact of multiple referrals in the House of Representatives,"
Washington.
GOVERNMENT DOCUMENTS: EXECUTIVE BRANCH
Commission on Industrial Competitiveness. *Global Competition: The New Reality.*
vol 1. The Report of the President's Commission, January 1985.
Council of Economic Advisors. *Economic Report of the President, 1984.*
Transmitted to the Congress February 1984.
Secretary of Defense. *Annual Report to the Congress FY 1985:* On the FY 1985
Budget, FY 1986 Authorization Request and FY 1985–89 Defense Programs.
February 1, 1984.
Weekly compilation of presidential documents 1983–84.
UNPUBLISHED PAPERS
Baker, Ross K. 1985 "What's in it for me?: Benefits to House members for
association with industrial policy." 1985 Annual Meeting of American
Political Science Association, New Orleans, La.
1986 "The bittersweet courtship of congressional Democrats and industrial
policy." 1986 Annual Meeting of the Midwest Political Science Association,
Chicago, Ill.

PART III
MICROECONOMIC POLICY

5

The British House of Commons and industrial policy

DAVID M. WOOD

In Britain, as in many other countries, the process of policy-making is executive-dominated. The literature is voluminous and essentially unanimous in relegating the British parliament to a secondary role in economic policy-making (e.g. Richardson and Jordan, 1979; Coombes and Walkland, 1980; Rose, 1982). However, there is a minority view which, while accepting the central premise, insists upon the potential of the legislative arena to generate considerable influence over this executive-dominated process (Norton, 1981; Schwarz, 1980; Rasmussen, 1984). Here the focus is on the backbench members of parliament (MPs), who, when acting in sufficient numbers, can thwart or deflect government policies, especially through their ability to withhold support when the House of Commons divides to vote. Regarding the separate policy-making stages, identified in this book as gestation, policy preparation, policy deliberation and decision, and policy implementation, back-bench MPs may have influence if their voices add up to a considerable volume in favor of action in one direction or another. However, there is consensus in the literature concerning the negligible role in policy-making of the *individual* back-bench MP. This essay will support the minority view, while according somewhat greater importance to the role of the individual MP in industrial policy *implementation*.

The extent to which MPs are able or motivated to participate at the various stages of policy-making will vary according to the nature of the issues being addressed. Hypothesis 14 in the Introduction proposed that legislative policy participation is likely to be most extensive in the case of policies involving "social benefits and regulation" and those involving values of basic civic and religious rights. In the latter category party

103

leaders in Britain often give back-bench MPs a "free vote," unconstrained by the party whips, thus making possible a wider range of options for activism than is true of issues where the vote is whipped (Hibbing, 1985). On the other hand, it is hypothesized that policies found in the "social benefits and regulation" category are often cases where there is strong interest group pressure and/or strong constituency pressure that may bring about divergence from party lines by individual MPs or groups of MPs (chapter 1, Hypotheses 5, 6, 8, 14). Another hypothesis in the Introduction (15) suggests that legislative policy activity is likely to be greater when issues are new, when they are salient, and when they "activate diverse and numerous publics." Some of the issues that involve "social benefits and regulation" have newly arisen or else have taken on new dimensions during the recent years of industrial decline, business failure, and unemployment, problems that Britain has experienced in more acute form than have most advanced industrial countries. But to the extent that other countries have experienced these problems, some of the hypotheses examined here may likewise be relevant to them. Whether or not new groups have arisen along with these issues (Hypothesis 9), there have been newly activated publics emerging at local or regional levels, seeking to protect their areas against further decline, pursuing government assistance, and enlisting local MPs in support of their causes (King, 1983; Wood, 1987).

Much of the assistance sought and provided for localities and regions to counter the territorially specific impact of Britain's industrial decline can be put under the heading of industrial policy, if that term is taken to mean a broad spectrum of policy options and tools designed to have an impact upon the structure and location of industry. The options range from the effort to halt the decline of troubled industrial sectors, employing as policy tools subsidies and protection against competing imports, to the conscious attempt to speed along the process of adaptation to new technology and world market conditions, channeling government assistance into rationalization of existing industry and development of high technology and new products (Wolf, 1979). In Britain, unlike some countries such as Japan and France, industrial policy has tended to be subordinated to macroeconomic policy (Grant and Wilks, 1983; Zysman, 1983). This is not to say that there has been no industrial policy; rather there have been industrial *policies*, often *ad hoc*, but seldom adding up to a coherent industrial policy strategy that could stand on its own, independent of whatever macroeconomic commitments prevailed. Keynesian-oriented governments, when in expansionist phases, were relatively short-lived, usually overtaken by balance of payments crises, by rapidly rising inflation, or by both at the same time (Stewart, 1977; Rose, 1984). With Keynesianism at least temporarily discredited, Mrs. Thatcher's monetarism abhors government intervention in the economy and is therefore committed to scaling down much of what passes for industrial policy in Britain. Yet studies of her government's policies and their impact have shown that her follow-through in this area has been less than overwhelming (Beer, 1982; Riddell, 1983).

The question of what industrial structure will best serve Britain's needs as the country moves towards the twenty-first century is not the same question as that of what role government should play in seeing that the proper industrial structure emerges. The first is a question of ends, the second one of means. But in Britain the question of means tends to be tied up in the general ideological debate between and within parties over macroeconomic policy. It especially involves the balance to be struck between the public and private sectors. Each side accuses the other of advocating strategies that would have disastrous economic consequences, but the consequences are couched in terms of broad macroeconomic indicators such as growth rates, unemployment levels, and inflation figures. On the other hand, the question of structural transformation of British industry is a "social/regulatory" question in the sense that different envisaged outcomes for the early twenty-first century imply different winners and losers in the process of change. Party ideologies tend to view winners and losers in class terms; but in fact gains and losses will be registered much more unambiguously (and have been for several years) in *territorial* terms (Townsend, 1983). Members of parliament are elected by territorially specific constituencies that tend to be differentiable on class grounds (McAllister and Rose, 1984). But the economic decline of traditional heavy industry in the British periphery has meant a growing tendency recently for party support trends to diverge on regional lines (Curtice and Steed, 1982). The appearance of the Social Democratic Party and the success of the Liberal–Social Democratic Alliance in capturing considerable public support transformed the electoral picture in the 1980s and rendered safe middle-class constituencies no longer safe for the Conservatives and once reliable working-class constituencies no longer automatically in the Labour column (McAllister and Rose, 1984). Candidates for parliament must take local concerns into account today to an extent that was not true twenty years ago. The industrial policy strategies they evoke can win or lose votes depending on how accurately they reflect local needs (Cain, Ferejohn and Fiorina, 1984). Accordingly, members of parliament may have views on industrial policy that do not necessarily coincide with official party positions on macro- or microeconomic policies, and they may seek ways in which to demonstrate their fidelity to these views to their constituents.

The House of Commons of the late 1980s is not the House of Commons of the post-World War II years. Its back-bench members are more attentive to the needs and opinions of blocs of voters in their constituencies, whether they are organized or not. They no longer can rely on or resign themselves to national swings between the two parties to keep them in or propel them from office, if for no other reason than the fact that there is now a three-party system throughout Great Britain which makes many more seats marginal than was the case not very long ago. But the reasons for the change are deeper than a single dimensional electoral analysis would suggest. They go to the basis of the relationship between "center and periphery" in Britain, which has itself been undergoing profound change in the past two decades although it is beyond the scope of the present chapter. According to Jim Bulpitt (1983), for much of the twentieth-century center–periphery relations in the United Kingdom featured what he calls a "dual polity" in which politics in the center and politics in the periphery operated in isolation from one another. The role of the member of parliament, whether Labour or Conservative, was almost that of a buffer between the two spheres, or even that of *a representative of the center to the periphery*, rather than the opposite. His job was to filter local grievances, virtually to cleanse them, in such a way as to make them manageable for a decision-making machinery at the center (party center as well as governmental center) that was more preoccupied with national, or in economic terms, macro problems and viewed the problems of the periphery as cases of broader national problems. As representative of the center to the periphery, the MP was expected to interpret the problems of local constituents in national terms, to assure or convince them that what they were experiencing was typically experienced by people like them (solid subjects of the Crown, citizens entitled to social benefits, or deprived workers at the mercy of the capitalist system) *all over the country*.

In the past two decades the periphery has been in revolt against the center, although the intensity of the revolt has been in descending order from Northern Ireland to Scotland to Wales to the North of England and most recently to the West Midlands and London. Members of parliament are having to choose whether to join the revolt, accommodate themselves to it or actively to resist it. In many cases, recent entrants to parliament have themselves been part of the revolt. One indicator of the change occurring in the local orientation of incoming MPs is the fact that the incidence of those entering parliament *with local authority experience* has been growing over the years. Table 5.1 shows that, when currently sitting MPs entering parliament before 1970 are compared with those entering in 1983, the percentage with local authority experience rises from 9.4 percent to 35 percent in the Conservative Party and from 21.5 percent to 58.8 percent among Labour MPs. With the exception of a slight dip in percentage registered by Labour MPs entering in the early 1970s, the upward movement of these percentages is steady from cohort to cohort in both parties. Not coincidentally, the sharpest rise in that incidence of local authority experience has coincided with the decline in economic fortunes that has made the problems of British industry a national preoccupation.

Industrial policy is treated in this chapter as a focal point for bringing into sharper relief tendencies that are manifesting themselves less dramatically in other policy areas. It has served as the focal point for comparative works (Shonfield, 1965; Zysman, 1983) and edited volumes of single-country studies (Cox, 1982; Dyson and Wilks, 1983), but attention in these has seldom been directed to the effect that changes in industrial and employment patterns may have for the roles of legislators and legislative bodies. As Bulpitt insists, in many ways the older British pattern for center–periphery relations was unique (Bulpitt, 1983: 83). If so, we would not expect center–periphery relations and the role of legislator in other countries to have undergone the same changes. But we would expect profound economic changes to bring about some important political changes along the dimensions examined here.

The remainder of the chapter will examine industrial policy and Britain as a policy domain with which to test the conventional view that the House of Commons is a legislative body whose policy-making activity is peripheral to the mainstream of policy-making for the country (Rose, 1986). If the House of Commons is not central to the industrial policy-making process, it may be argued, then it is unlikely to be central to policy-making in those domains that the elite political culture regards as central to the physical and material security of the nation, i.e., "high politics" (Rose, 1982; Bulpitt, 1983). In testing the hypothesis that parliament is not central to industrial policy-making I shall employ (1) data from the public record, including the record of voting in divisions in the House of Commons and the record of interventions by MPs in debates and parliamentary questions, and (2) data drawn from interviews with 70 Conservative back-bench MPs and 62 Labour MPs[1] during the parliamentary session 1983–84, the first year following the General Election of June 1983, which returned the Conservative government of Margaret Thatcher with an enlarged majority. Evidence of a substantial amount of activity on industrial policy matters will be regarded as

DAVID M. WOOD

Table 5.1 *MPs entering parliament with local authority experience*

	Local authority experience	Total MPs	%
Conservatives first elected:			
Before 1970	9	96	9.4
1970–73	7	58	12.1
1974–78	13	70	18.6
1979–82	22	73	30.1
1983	35	100	35.0
Labour MPs first elected:			
Before 1970	14	65	21.5
1970–73	7	36	19.4
1974–78	13	38	34.2
1979–82	19	36	52.8
1983	20	34	58.8

Source: The Times Guide to the House of Commons, 1983.

subjecting the conventional wisdom to question. In the following sections, hypotheses regarding parliament's role in the stages of industrial policy-making are tested.

POLICY IMPLEMENTATION

Hypothesis 16 in chapter 1 suggested that the *implementation* stage of policy-making is the stage where the greatest incidence of parliamentary activity occurs, while the stage of *proposal preparation* takes place with a minimum of parliamentary involvement. In between fall the stages of *genesis* and *policy deliberation and decision*. The literature concerning parliament and policy-making in Britain leaves little doubt that the minimal parliamentary role is played in proposal *preparation*, wherein the role of civil servants advising their ministerial superiors is clearly paramount, and Westminster must await rather passively the product of Whitehall efforts. Norton, who is more attentive than most to evidence of legislative influence, says flatly:

In short, the House as a collective entity cannot expect to wrest domination of the initiative and formulative stages from government and those co-opted into the decision-making process. The role of the House, collectively and individually, is essentially a reactive one, and its reaction is one among several that the Government will normally be concerned to consider. (Norton, 1981: 85)

The interview data support the proposition that the implementation stage attracts the greatest amount of legislative activity.[2] MPs from constituencies with high levels of unemployment must deal with the individual problems that families of the unemployed must face. These, as well as many related problems of the less advantaged constituents are broached in letters or brought to weekend surgeries. The MP hears the problems, suggests remedies and/or seeks to assist the constituent with representations made to central or local government agencies. The literature has established this function quite clearly and has noted that it has grown in proportion in the past decade (Cain, *et al.*, 1984; Marsh, 1985).

The interviews also revealed a different sort of activity performed by many MPs that transcends the handling of individualized constituents' problems in scope, if not in frequency, of occurrence. This involves a sort of "economic interest lobbying" by MPs on behalf of local economic units, more often than not manufacturing units (Wood, 1987). Despite a party belief system that regards lobbying on behalf of economic interests to be one of the problems that correct application of economic principles must overcome, slightly over half (36) of the 70 Conservatives interviewed testified to having sought ministerial support for local industries as a fairly normal part of their legislative role definition. Not surprisingly, the incidence of such lobbying varies with the difficulty of one's constituency situation, both in economic and in political terms. Conservative MPs are more likely to lobby if they represent areas with levels of unemployment that are high by the standards of Conservative-held constituencies, or that are relatively marginal in electoral terms (Wood, 1987). The incidence of Labour lobbying on behalf of economic interests is higher (61 percent), although it is limited today by the fact that Labour MPs from some inner city constituencies no longer have much industry left on behalf of which to advance claims to ministers.

Most MPs indicated in the interviews that the lobbying they do on behalf of local economic interests constitutes the minority proportion of the work they perform on behalf of their constituencies, the majority of such time being spent on problems of individual constituents. Of their total time spent as MPs, constituency concerns appear to be a growing preoccupation, although most MPs regard their work of a national or functional, rather than territorial (Rose, 1982), nature to be more important to them (Searing, 1985).[3] The visible side of their activity, i.e., that which can be documented by reference to the evidence available in Hansard, suggests that this is still true. To gauge the amount of publicly displayed MP activity, the first half of the 1983–84 parliamentary session,

Table 5.2 *Oral and written questions (in %)*

	Local economic	National economic	Other	Total	N
		Conservative MPs			
16.6	35.7	47.6	99.9	1,785	
Labour	14.1	40.6	45.4	100.1	2,647
N =	669	1,712	2,051	4,432	

Source: House of Commons Debates, 1983

Table 5.3 *Debates, Commons (%)*

	Local economic	National economic	Other	Total	N
Conservative MPs	14.9	48.8	36.6	100	570
Labour	14.3	58.3	27.4	100	1,199
N =	256	977	536	1,769	

Source: House of Commons Debates, 1983

from June to December 1983, has been examined. Interventions in parliamentary debate and in oral and written questions by 70 Conservative and 61 Labour respondents[4] were classified according to whether they were devoted to economic issues of direct relevance to their constituencies. The interviews established certain constituency economic characteristics and preoccupations of the MPs themselves, which facilitated judgments as to which debates and questions were relevant to local economic interests for each MP. For example, an MP with coal mines in his constituency, when participating in a debate on the coal industry, is clearly speaking to issues of local relevance. On the other hand, an MP who indicated in the interview that he serves as a spokesman for the Scotch whisky distillers industry, but who represents a constituency that is nowhere near an area where Scotch whisky is distilled, when putting down a question regarding that industry, is coded as addressing a national economic question, not a constituency-specific one.

Tables 5.2 and 5.3 indicate that, in the half-session in question, Conservatives devoted a slightly higher percentage of their questions and of their debate time to matters of local economic interest than did Labour Members. However, the absolute level of Labour activity of both kinds was greater than that of the Conservatives. The 61 Labour MPs put down an average of 43.4 questions, against an average of 25.5 for the 70 Conservatives. The difference was greater in the case of debate time. An average of 19.7 columns of Hansard contained Labour interventions in debate, versus 8.1 columns in the case of the Conservative respondents. As for questions of local economic concern, there was an average of 6.1 put down by Labour MPs and an average of 4.2 by Conservatives, while debate interventions of local economic relevance by Labour MPs averaged 2.8 columns, against 1.2 for the Conservatives. Still, the incidence of visible local economic initiative is not impressive for either party, when put in terms of total visible initiative. This suggests that those MPs who lobby on behalf of local businesses and the local economy generally put greater emphasis on direct contacts with ministers than on participation of a more visible nature. One writer has recently specified that MPs, including Opposition MPs, will typically try the direct route first, resorting to public complaint or attention calling only if the direct avenue proves, in the opinion of the MP, unjustifiably fruitless (Marsh, 1985: 83).

The interviews showed that the involvement of individual MPs in influencing the local implementation of industrial policy is an important part of the role of many MPs, especially those with considerable amounts of industry in their constituencies or at least in their local "travel-to-work" areas. It is also a *growing* involvement. Letters were received from 22 Conservative MPs to a follow-up inquiry in the spring of 1986. Of 18 responses that addressed the question of whether constituency economic interest lobbying was on the increase, 14 answered that it was, although reasons were not always given and those that were varied. Some felt that a general growth in the self-confidence of the MP accounted for the trend more than exogenous factors affecting the constituency. Others saw a link with adverse economic trends, and one pointed to the rise of the Alliance as having marginalized many formerly safe Conservative constituencies, thus forcing the incumbents to pay more attention to constituency needs. One particularly comprehensive answer by a London MP is quoted nearly in full:

I certainly believe that the phenomenon of "local economic interest lobbying" is widespread, and that with one or two obvious exceptions it is of reasonably recent origins. I think that it also reflects part of a trend in the changing role of MPs in general and that because it can probably embarrass a Minister more than say representations by civil servants or the general public, particularly where the MP is a member of the same Party, then it is likely to grow more common.

I'm not sure whether I made the point in our interview, but it is undeniable that even in the relatively short time (seven years) that I have been an MP there has been a perceptible growth in correspondence in general, accompanied by an increase in the perception of the general public that the role of the MP is primarily "pavements and lamp-posts" in other words the spokesman for the local community rather than the "check on the Executive." It seems inevitable to me therefore that this has led and will continue to lead to greater pressure on MPs to lobby on behalf of those constituents. I believe that although my constituents may be mildly interested at this or that parliamentary initiative that I have taken, unless it coincides with an area which *they* regard as highly important I will rarely receive any subsequent responses. I contrast that with, to take a current example, the tendency for whole roads of constituents to write to me about a change in a bus route and expect me to stop it!

In addition to believing that the change is inevitable, I am on balance in sympathy with the trend, since I believe it further cements the identification of the MP with those who have the power to elect or reject him. I believe that to be a very important feature of democracy, which was by and large underplayed or ignored in the immediate postwar years, let alone much earlier, and that within reason could be said to be a good 'binding' agent within the community. It is none the less undeniable that much time and energy is expended and the answer is probably to extend MPs' back-up facilities to some extent (extra secretarial or research assistance handles much of this increase) rather than revert to the "Edmund Burke role" which for a democrat in any event is fatally flawed.

POLICY GESTATION

Given these trends, it would appear that preoccupation with constituency problems can also have the effect of increasing the importance of back-bench and even opposition MPs in the gestation stage of industrial policy-making. Through both their publicly visible and invisible actions, MPs whose constituencies are adversely affected by current government policy can make it known to ministers that the policies are unpopular at least in certain areas of the country. While opposition claims of this kind may fall on deaf ears, if substantial numbers of majority back-benchers weigh in on the side of a policy change, it is likely to have an effect. A case in point in the realm of industrial policy is the reassessment of regional assistance policy that has been taking place in Britain ever since the mid-1970s. Interviews with both Labour and Conservative MPs uncovered frequent complaints about the local impact of regional policies that favored location of firms in certain areas rather than in others. As economic conditions worsened, regional policy, while cushioning the blow somewhat for the assisted areas, came to be seen as actively contributing to the industrial decline of non-assisted areas, such as Greater London and the West Midlands (Birmingham region), against which regional policy deliberately discriminated through restrictions on office building and location (Massey and Meegan, 1982: 189). Members of Parliament from these areas, whether Labour or Conservative and whether under Labour or Conservative governments, persistently complained about the adverse effects of the policies on their regions throughout the late 1970s and early 1980s. Starting with the 1974–79 Labour government and continuing under the present Conservative government, the emphasis of government policy has been to reduce the territorial scope of regional assistance, confining it to smaller areas that have been worst hit by industrial decline (Department of Trade and Industry, 1983). When the Thatcher government took office in 1979 it abolished the policy of restricting office building in the once prosperous areas of the southern half of England. Another change, which began under the previous Labour government, was a greater emphasis on assistance to troubled industrial sectors rather than to troubled regions, a change that had been strongly urged upon governments by MPs from the West Midlands and other areas where the automobile industry and its components manufacturers are located (Grant, 1982: 59–60, 86). In the late 1970s and early 1980s, while not enjoying special regional assistance status, the West Midlands experienced the most rapid growth in unemployment of any region in Britain except the Northwest, whose growth in unemployment it nearly equaled (Townsend, 1983: 109).

The negative view of West Midlands MPs toward regional policy is expressed in two very similar responses to questions about their attitudes toward regional policy, one from a Conservative member and the other from a Labour member, both representing Greater Birmingham constituencies:

Conservative MP: I don't think there is any evidence to show that it has been efficient in securing employment, and I would like to see it diverted toward the provision of infrastructure and the creation of opportunity. I find, indeed, in my own experience before I came into politics, the company I was in, we moved our factory ten miles and we were going to invest and expand anyhow, but we got the money from the government, which is crazy. I don't believe that the government should be putting money into business directly in that way, and there's no evidence in the studies to show that it has been effective. It has led to distortion and diversion, because actually it wasn't the money; the regional policy was backed by the so-called industrial development certificates, so that it was impossible to get planning permission for expansion of the premises. That was the damage. So that in the West Midlands, the new industries and expanding industries were driven out of the region and we were left with a heavily biased and declining industrial structure. That was the problem. No amount of regional policy is actually going to help that very much.

Labour MP: You see, what happened when my government was in office, we had industrial development certificates issued: firms had to go to areas of high levels of unemployment. My area, my region, had never had high levels of unemployment. My region had never had it, so therefore firms moved out. It was like bribery. In retrospect it wasn't a very good policy, but there it was. It was well meant, because how could a government say well we're not going to do anything about South Wales and Scotland when you've got high levels there and here's the West Midlands [sic]. So it was well meant but this is what happened. Firms moved out and they've got a lot of money so to do. Therefore there was that sort of robbery of industrial establishments and activities as a result of that.

In the Labour Party, which officially supports a re-extension of regional assistance, as well as a regionalization of industrial planning, 40 respondents expressed support for these aims, all but 5 of whom represented Scotland, Wales, or North of England constituencies, i.e., the regions that had been the heaviest recipients of regional assistance. On the other hand, among the 18 Conservatives expressing strongly negative opinions about regional policy, only 2 are from these "peripheral" areas, as against 16 from the hitherto prosperous Midlands and South. In the Conservative Party, voting patterns in recent decades have intensified the within-party strength of MPs from the Midlands and southern regions. It is clear that their voices have influenced the genesis of new regional policy departures by the Thatcher government. In the case of the Labour Party, the effect has been to divide the party between proponents of regional assistance (including some who seek devolved financial power to regional legislative bodies) and proponents of industrial strategies that substitute an industrial sector for a regional basis of allocating resources. Recent Labour Party pronouncements have downplayed the regional dimension, varying the message depending upon the audience targeted.[5] Both parties provide examples of how the legislator's involvement in the implementation of policy generates dissatisfaction with the policy itself, bringing the influence of the legislator to bear on the genesis of new policy. Insofar as industrial policy is concerned, the British MP plays an important role in feeding back information regarding the effects of ongoing policy, possibly displaying more sensitivity to some dimensions of these effects than would normally be true of the civil servants responsible for their implementation.[6]

POLICY DELIBERATION AND DECISION

Constituency oriented MPs have little scope for affecting the outcome of legislation once the legislative process has begun. Disciplined majorities ensure that the outcome of the process will be what the government intended. Amendments that have the disapproval of the government can be defeated by dividing the House. Such divisions, and divisions on the bill in its entirety at second and third reading, seldom find members crossing into the opposite lobby, not, at least, in the case of industrial policy bills or general debates on industrial policy. During the 1983–84 session the principal issues in which the Conservative Party exhibited disagreement in its ranks were those of: (1) the death penalty (an unwhipped issue); (2) the Trade Union Bill, on which right-wing Members sought a stronger policy on trade union restriction; (3) the issue of the toughness of Mrs. Thatcher's bargaining position on the European Community budget, in which a handful of hard-line anti-European MPs dissented; and (4) the issue of central government restrictions on local authority financial power which produced dissent from the left side of the party. Although economic issues were involved in three of the four cases, none concerned industrial policy.

The importance of divisions in the House of Commons could increase substantially if no party emerged from a general election with a majority in the House of Commons. The strength of the Alliance in 1983–84 made such a result a distinct possibility. The years of minority or near minority Labour government in the 1970s were the years in which the greatest incidence of intra-party dissent occurred in House of Commons divisions since the nineteenth century (Schwarz, 1980; Rose, 1986). In such circumstances divisions on industrial policy issues as well as other issues could become problematic. However, in addition to the fact that party unity tends to prevail on both macro- and microeconomic issues, the very diversity of local economic circumstances within and across regions of Britain makes it unlikely that a significant cluster of industrial policy dissenters might emerge that would differentiate voting patterns on industrial policy from those on other economic policy issues.

Within-party economic policy divisions

It is nevertheless true that conflict over economic policy models can be found within as well as between parliamentary parties in the House of Commons. Questions were asked of the interview respondents regarding the overall role that government should play in the economy and the strategy government should employ in dealing with the problems of inflation and unemployment, both questions interpreted as macro-economic policy questions. In macroeconomic terms, the Conservatives ranged from neoliberals on the right to Keynesians on the left, while Labour MPs ranged from Keynesians on the right to socialists on the left.[7] In the Conservative case neoliberals on the right saw curbing inflation as having higher priority than reducing unemployment, even though British inflation had been reduced substantially by 1983–84 while unemployment remained at a high level. Neoliberals also wanted to limit government intervention in the economy. Keynesians, on the other hand, saw unemployment as the central problem to be solved and prescribed various modes of government intervention as ways to reduce it. In between were Conservatives who eschewed government intervention on general principle, but who agreed with the Keynesians that some measures were necessary to cope with unemployment, although they would not go as far as the Keynesians in turning their backs on efforts to limit government spending and to control the money supply. A scale was constructed from the Conservative responses that placed 32 MPs on the neoliberal right, 14 on the Keynesian left, and 18 in the center. Six respondents were excluded from the scale due to inconsistent responses.[8]

On the Labour side there were no respondents who gave inflation a higher priority than unemployment, although there were a few who still had a nagging concern for inflation. Basically, however, all took a Keynesian pump-priming approach to getting the economy back in motion and reducing unemployment. Many went further, advocating what might be called "post-Keynesian" or socialist measures, including exchange and import controls, nationalization of lagging industries, and government planning with elements of compulsion up front or in reserve. Traditional Keynesians on the right of the party were those who placed faith in classic public investment projects, building or rebuilding roads, schools, hospitals, and sewer systems as means of generating employment and encouraging new private sector investment and expansion. In the center of the Labour spectrum were post-Keynesians who saw a need to guide public investment in industry with government planning of industrial sectors, preferably with the cooperation of industry, but coupling financial carrots with the stick of tighter regulation or even the threat of nationalization. Those on the left wanted to go further, nationalizing specified industries, and/or imposing import and exchange controls, and seeking ways of combining job creation with a real redistribution of income and wealth. It was possible to align 53 of the 62 Labour respondents along a single macroeconomic scale involving these issues. When this was done, 26 members were classified in the Keynesian right position, 16 in the post-Keynesian center, and 11 on the socialist left.

The interview responses also revealed that there is mutual constraint (Converse, 1964) across the macro/microeconomic divide within both parliamentary parties. Within each party, those who take a left-of-center stance on macroeconomic policy are more concerned about the preservation of employment in threatened industries than are those on the right. It may be assumed that the economic policies favored by the left side of the Conservative Party and by the right side of the Labour Party, i.e., a Keynesian approach to macroeconomic policy and an effort through government intervention to ease the process of industrial adaptation in a humane fashion, will accord with the preferences of the Alliance parties. Since the latter are the potential arbiters in a "hung parliament" scenario, then whichever party, Labour or Conservative, has a moderate wing that is better placed than the extreme wing to determine party policy may be better placed to steer a safe course as a minority or near minority government. The interviews suggest that moderation on economic policy issues was stronger within the parliamentary Labour Party than within the Conservative Party in parliament. But two caveats are in order: (1) the interviews did not go beyond issue domains in which the economic dimension was predominant, and (2) the position of the Alliance parties on even the economic issues are only *assumed* to lie in the center of the spectrum.

Non-economic issues

There are ways of testing whether or not party alignments on economic issues are in accord with those on other issues of significance for British politics. One can determine through examination of the public record whether Conservative MPs on the left, or "wet," side of economic issues are party wets when it comes to issues like capital punishment, trade union regulation, or central government efforts to bring the local authorities under control. There were publicly recorded votes in which the party divided over these issues in 1983–84. By identifying a wet or a "dry" on one of these issues, could one predict his/her position on the others, and could one predict from votes on these issues to the stances taken on economic issues in the interviews? Could one proceed in the opposite direction, predicting the votes in the House of Commons from views expressed in the interviews?

It was possible to construct a Guttman Scale out of six of the divisions taken in 1983–84, including the issues of capital punishment, trade union regulation, local authority control, and the EEC budget. The appendix provides details of the scaling procedure, as well as a table showing the distribution of the entire membership of the parliamentary Conservative Party on the scale. As was found in the interviews, the party is skewed to the right on the issues of the scale, in this case because the issue of capital punishment is the cutting point between left and right, and more Conservatives support capital punishment than oppose it. Although skewed to the right, the scale takes on the some of the aspects of a normal curve. Most members of the government are found in intermediate scale positions. Members of the cabinet fall evenly, 8 to the right of center (including Mrs. Thatcher) and 8 to the left of center. Junior ministers represent the overall party configuration more accurately, as 31 are to the right of center and 26 to the left.

The scale can be fairly said to represent in very rough form the spectrum of positions within the Conservative Party on a variety of policy issues. When the interview respondents are examined separately, it is possible to see whether there is a fit between their scores on this scale and their positions on the left–right macroeconomic scale discussed above. The fit is a good one, the Pearson r correlation being 0.54. This suggests that both scales, the one drawn from roll call data and the other from interview data, are reliable indicators of the left–right spectrum among Conservatives. Constraint within the Conservative sample between the macroeconomic responses and those on industrial policy issues was demonstrated in a factor analysis of response patterns in which both types of issues were found to load highly on the principal factor (Wood, 1985). Disagreement with Thatcherite policies on most issues, economic and non-economic, was found among a minority of Conservative MPs in 1983–84, most of whom could be relatively easily identified from their statements of policy criticism and occasional abstentions or dissenting votes in the House. There will have to have been a sea change of opinion among MPs in the broad center of the party, which was skewed to the right in 1983–84, toward the left of the party center on these issues, for the party to be well positioned after a subsequent loss of majority in an election to play the game of coalition or minority government politics.

In the case of the Labour Party, there were not sufficient divisions in the House of Commons on which the opposition party divided within itself in 1983–84 and in which the further requirement was satisfied that most of the Members actually participated in the division, to permit construction of a scale for Labour paralleling that constructed for the Conservatives. However, a surrogate is available that in some ways more than suffices. Prior to the October 1983 Labour Party conference an "electoral college" of Labour MPs, trade unionists, and constituency activists voted for a new leader and deputy Leader of the party. The MPs' votes were made public (*The Guardian*, October 3, 1983), so that it was possible to construct a six-point scale of the MPs based on assumptions about the locations of the candidates for the two party offices on the left–right spectrum.[9] This scale was then correlated with the macroeconomic scale derived from the interview responses, producing a Pearson r of 0.65. The "leadership scale" can be regarded as reflecting MPs' positions over a variety of issues. It would certainly reflect views on foreign and defense policies, which were at least as prominent as economic policy in differentiating left and right in the party during the year 1983 (Dunleavy and Husbands, 1985: 89–91). According to the leadership vote, the parliamentary party was skewed slightly to the right, with 38 voting on the left, 90 in the center, and 49 on the right.

From this analysis, it appears that the moderate side of the parliamentary Labour Party was in a stronger position within the parliamentary party than was its moderate counterpart within the Conservative Party in 1983–84. If anything, it appears that the Neil Kinnock and Roy Hattersley leadership that was elected in October 1983 has since moved that party's national image in a moderate direction (*The Economist*, May 16, 1986: 17–20), undoubtedly with considerable input from their parliamentary colleagues. However, one should not discount the likely influence of the extra-parliamentary party on the later Labour Party policy. Nor should it be forgotten that, if Labour is returned at a later election with enough seats to form a government, majority or minority, it will mean an influx of many new members, the ideological distribution of whom could be to the left of the parliamentary Labour Party found in 1983–84.

Of greater significance for possible post-election coalition politics is the fact that both the Conservative and Labour parliamentary parties appeared in 1983–84 to have distinct and consistent left–right structures that make it possible to assess the significance of shifts on one direction or the other for future behavior of the party in or out of office. The parliamentary Conservative Party had by 1983–84 become a battleground between left and right that was more coherent and parsimoniously analyzable than had been the case a decade earlier (Wood and Jacoby, 1984). The battle within the parliamentary Labour Party has been more complex and multidimensional, but the above analysis makes it clear that economic policy positions (including industrial policy) of the party are at stake in the battle between left and right. These conflicts in both parties would loom larger if no party emerged from an election with a solid majority. Whichever party gained power, and whichever wing of that party appeared to be in the ascendancy, MPs on the other wing could, as was the case of the Labour Party left in the Wilson–Callaghan years, have a considerable influence on policy decisions made at all stages because of their ability to withhold support at the ultimate stage of policy decision, when the House of Commons divides to vote.

The question of coalition

There remains the problem of the location of the former Alliance parties
(then, the Liberals and the united Social Democrats) between the
Conservative and Labour parties on the spectrum, which would be of
considerable importance in determining which of the major parties
formed a government in the event of a close election outcome.
Unpublished research by Mark Hagger and this author reveals that the
Alliance supported the Conservative government in only 11 percent of the
divisions which we examined from the 1983–84 legislative session. The
data set included all those divisions in which one or both of the major
parties voted in sufficient percentages to indicate that the party whip was
in force. On economic policy issues Alliance support dropped to only 4
percent in divisions where macroeconomic issues were at stake and 8
percent in industrial policy divisions. By contrast, the Alliance supported
the government in 41 percent of the divisions involving trade union
regulation and 32 percent of the divisions involving external relations
(foreign and defense policy and European Community questions). The
Alliance voted with the Labour Party against the government in 80
percent of all of the divisions examined, including 86 percent of the
macroeconomic divisions and 85 percent of the industrial policy divisions.
Alignment with Labour occurred in only 35 percent of the divisions
involving trade union regulation and in 55 percent of those involving
external policy. Of course, a vote with the major opposition party against
government policy does not represent as solid a commitment to any
particular policy position as does a vote in favor of government policy.
Thus it is likely that, while the Alliance stood closer to the Labour Party
on economic policy issues aside from trade union regulation (especially
considering the moderate tilt within the parliamentary Labour Party on
economic issues), it stood closer to the Conservatives on external policy
questions. In fact, on the issues involving the EEC, it is likely that the
Alliance was even further to the pro-European side than was the
Conservative mainstream. Alliance votes against government policy on
European issues would not be proceeding from the same premises as
Labour votes, which largely reflected opposition to government policy
from the anti-European direction.

  Support for any minority government could be a very complex
proposition, involving support from different quarters on different issues,
depending on which party holds borrowed-time power. Or there could be
something similar to the "Lib–Lab pact" of the late 1970s. This would
represent a complex tradeoff of policy positions on domestic and external

policies that would inevitably put the moderate wing of the stronger party in a commanding position in within-party terms, but leave the pact vulnerable to specific acts of dissent from the outside wing of that party.

To summarize what has been said about the role of the House of Commons at the various stages of policy-making, the hypothesized order of stages according to the degree of parliamentary influence is borne out by the findings. Policy *implementation* is clearly the stage at which the back-bench MP is likely to be the most active and to have the greatest individual effect, keeping in mind that the impact of the implementation stage is largely confined to individual cases, or else to the type of case, especially in the realm of industrial policy, in which important localized interests are at stake. Sometimes, however, these localized effects can have cumulative significance, such that the *generative* stage of policy-making comes into play. Existing policy is reassessed by central policy-makers in Whitehall, but if the signals from Westminster are consistent and clear, it is a safe prediction that they will be taken into account as new policy departures are contemplated, significantly increasing or decreasing the chances that policy will be changed and that the changes will be in certain directions. This generalization probably accords greater weight to parliament in policy genesis than the literature on British policy-making would suggest, and it must be acknowledged that such parliamentary influence is probably the exception rather than the norm in most policy areas. Industrial policy may be a domain in which parliament exercises its greatest influence, because industrial policies have an inescapable discriminatory effect along territorial lines. As for the role of Parliament in policy *deliberation and decision*, it is usually, as the literature suggests, more *pro forma* and symbolic than productive of different outcomes; but this ceases to be true whenever there is the absence of a comfortable majority in the hands of the government of the day. At that point, not only do the votes of the smaller parties become crucial, but also those of minority blocs of back-benchers of the governing party, as the 1974–79 parliament demonstrated. Finally, it is acknowledged that the policy *preparation* stage is dominated by civil servants and essentially outside the realm of parliamentary influence, which is at any rate exercisable at earlier and later stages.

Appendix

The Guttman scale reported in the paper was constructed out of six divisions of the House of Commons taken between July 13, 1983 and April 2, 1984, and includes the four issues that most sharply divided the Conservative parliamentary party when it came to voting in the division lobbies. All of these were votes in which at least 75 percent of the membership of the House of Commons voted on one side or the other, as well as at least 75 percent of the Conservatives. The largest number of dissents from the Conservative majority was 134, constituting 37 percent of the Conservative MPs voting. This division (no. 16) concerned the issue of restoring the death penalty. The majority of Conservatives were in favor of restoration, but the minority added their votes to those of other parties to defeat the measure. This was a private member's initiative, and the division was not whipped. Dissents in the Conservative ranks on the other five divisions, all constrained by the government whip, were much less numerous, ranging from 7 dissents on a motion advocating a tougher bargain position by the Thatcher government in negotiations over the European budget (no. 84) to 42 on an amendment to the Trade Union bill to strengthen its provisions restricting the use of union funds for political purposes (no. 218). Both of these were right-wing motions; the support for them by Conservatives constituted dissent from the main body of the party. The rest of the dissents came from the left, or "wet" side of the party, all on the issue of local authority rate-capping, in which the "wets" took exception to the proposed legislation. Dissents on these three divisions (no. 205, no. 207, and no. 211) ranged from 8 to 11 MPs.

The scale places the two divisions bearing right-wing dissent on one end and the three rate-capping divisions with left-wing dissent on the other. In between is the capital punishment division. Table 5.4 displays the ordering of the divisions and the ideal response pattern corresponding to each scale score. Scoreable individual voting patterns deviated from the ideal only in

Table 5.4 *Ideal scale patterns*

Scale score	84	218	16	211	207	205	N
6.0	+	+	+	+	+	+	4
5.5	0	+	+	+	+	+	12
5.0	−	+	+	+	+	+	23
4.5	−	0	+	+	+	+	21
4.0	−	−	+	+	+	+	159
3.5	−	−	0	+	+	+	19
3.0	−	−	−	+	+	+	103
2.5	−	−	−	0	+	+	3
2.0	−	−	−	−	+	+	1
1.5	−	−	−	−	0	+	7
1.0	−	−	−	−	−	+	0
0.5	−	−	−	−	−	0	2
0.0	−	−	−	−	−	−	6

the substitution of absences for "positive" or "negative" votes. Positive votes are those regarded as right-of-center on the issue, negative votes as left-of-center.

There were 25 MPs who, because of excessive absences (more than half of the divisions), could not be given scores, and another 13 with non-scale patterns, i.e., containing at least one "error of reproducibility," who were likewise not scored. The total scale had a coefficient of reproducibility of 0.99 and a coefficient of scalability of 0.93. Because absences are taken into account in the scoring when they fit on the margin between positive and negative votes (scale scores 5.5, 4.5, etc.), further tests were made which took non-fit absences as half-errors and added them to total scale errors and total marginal errors (McIver and Carmines, 1981: 44–51). This produced a coefficient of reproducibility of 0.93 and a coefficient of scalability of 0.60, both narrowly within the confines of conventional acceptability (*ibid.*), although including absences in the tests makes it much harder for the scale to satisfy these standards.

Inspection of the right-hand column of Table 5.4 reveals that the parliamentary Conservative Party is skewed to the right on the issues in the scale. Division 16 regarding restoration of the death penalty divides the party in such a way that MPs scoring above 3.5 may be regarded as right-of-center. The 19 MPs scoring 3.5 absented themselves from division 16, and therefore may be regarded as occupying a mid-point on the spectrum. There are 219 MPs to the right of center, against 122 to the left.

Notes

1 Both samples were designed to be representative of the respective parliamentary parties. In the Conservative case, the population from which the
sample was drawn was confined to back-benchers. In the Labour case, only 5
present and former leaders and deputy leaders were excluded from the
population: James Callaghan, Michael Foot, Dennis Healey, Neil Kinnock,
and Roy Hattersley. Exclusions were based on the expectation of inaccessibility. In fact, there was greater accessibility to the Conservative MPs,
where the sample adhered closely to the criteria chosen for representativeness:
seat marginality, region (grouped according to unemployment levels), length
of tenure in the House of Commons, and past or present offices held. In the
Labour case, a fifth criterion, vote for leader and deputy leader in October
1983, was employed (see note 8). The greater difficulty in obtaining interviews
with Labour MPs resulted in an underrepresentation of Welsh MPs vs. an
overrepresentation of Scottish MPs, and an underrepresentation of the center-
left of the party vs. an overrepresentation of the center-right. The author
wishes to thank Wang Sik Kim and Yogesh Grover for their assistance with
data analysis.

2 Some of the activity discussed in this section may more properly be said to
involve activities by MPs in response to the individualized or localized
consequences or policy implementation, or policy non-implementation, or
even of *non-policy*. In other terms, MPs are finding a role in areas of "low
politics," regarding which central policy-makers have traditionally shown low
energy levels (Bulpitt, 1983; ch. 5).

3 This is actually a matter disputed in the literature. Marsh writes of "the
enormous satisfaction" that constituency work gives MPs (1985: 75). The
interviews drawn on here are inconclusive. Many Labour and some
Conservative MPs were heavily involved in the fortunes of the areas they
represented, often building up reputations as specialists in certain national
problems *because* they were of particular interest to their own constituents.
But some respondents in both parties appeared to view constituency work as
interfering with the national roles they preferred for themselves.

4 A sixty-second Labour MP was omitted from this analysis, whose entry into
the House of Commons occurred via a by-election held after December, 1983.

5 These commitments were included in the 1983 Labour Party election

124

manifesto. The institutional aspects had been given sharper definition by a 1982 report of a parliamentary spokesmans' working group headed by John Prescott, MP. It called for the creation of Regional Assemblies and coordination of national and regional plans through establishment of a Regional Planning Council at national level (Parliamentary Spokesmans' Working Group, 1982). However, in a fifteen-page 1985 industrial policy statement released by the Labour Party, only a brief paragraph was devoted to the regional dimension, and it was referred to as a way to "assist the growth of local economies" (Labour Party, 1985a: 11). On the other hand, a pamphlet devoted to the problems of the Yorkshire–Humberside region is studded with headlined references to the "regional bank," and a "Regional Enterprise Board" (Labour Party, 1985c). Meanwhile, one may search almost in vain through large and small print for any use of the word "region" in the companion pamphlet for the West Midlands. There the emphasis is on specific industries, and there is little discussion of an institutional framework (Labour Party, 1985b).

6 I have not addressed the question of what role in policy gestation is played by the relatively new select committees of the House of Commons. To the extent that the interviews shed light on the matter, it appeared to be the judgment of MPs in 1983–84 that the Select Committee on Trade and Industry was not among the most effective of the new select committees. However, others were clearly participants in the policy gestation process. Christopher Price, MP, former chairman of the Select Committee on Education, Science and Arts, put it this way: "Curiously these apparently impotent Select Committees have achieved some influence... but only when they make themselves more expert than ministers and civil servants. The former isn't too difficult; the latter will take a little time." Quoted in Downs (1985), which is a good survey of the role of select committees as of the mid-1980s.

7 Somewhat different modes of questioning were involved in these two intra-party classifications. In the Conservative interviews respondents were posed two sets of polarities to choose between: (a) reduction of government intervention in the economy vs. government intervention at accustomed levels; (b) priority given to reducing inflation vs. priority given to reducing unemployment. In the Labour interviews respondents were posed three open-ended questions: "What should government do to reduce the high level of unemployment in Britain? What role should government planning play? How would you answer the objection that these policies would be inflationary?" Classification of MPs in both parties often had to sort out contradictory statements and discern the central thrust of the answers. In both parties classification was based on a scale constructed from two three-point items that were highly inter-correlated: macroeconomic strategy and role of government, or the distinction between policy objectives and policy instruments.

8 Issues involving aid to declining regions and industrial sectors had high loadings on the first factor. One issue relating to industrial policy, that of import controls, had a zero-order loading on the first factor and a high loading on the second. Also loaded highly on the second factor were issues involving the EEC and the subjective judgment of the MP regarding the constituency's economic type, manufacturing or non-manufacturing. Briefly, the second factor reveals a protectionist strain among MPs who represent

constituencies where particular industries in decline, such as textiles, automobiles, and fishing, are locally dominant (Wood, 1985).

9 Scoring was a follows: votes for Eric Heffer for leader and Michael Meacher for deputy leader (the left-most choices) were scored as 1.0; Neil Kinnock–Meacher, 2.0; Kinnock–Roy Hattersley, 3.0; Hattersley–Hattersley, 4.0; Peter Shore–Hattersley, 5.0; and Shore–Gwyneth Dunwoody, 6.0. Votes for Denzil Davis for Deputy Leader posed a problem because he attracted votes of fellow Welshmen located further to the left on the spectrum than where he probably is located himself (his vote was for Peter Shore for Leader, the right-wing choice). Kinnock–Davies votes were scored 2.5; Hattersley–Davies, 4.5; and Shore–Davies, 5.5. There was one Hattersley–Dunwoody combination, which was scored 5.0. Abstentions for deputy leader (four cases) were scored as if they had been votes for Davies. One MP who voted for Hattersley for deputy leader, but abstained in the leader vote, was placed in the middle of the scale at 3.5.

References

Beer, Samuel H. (1982) *Britain Against Itself: The Political Contradictions of Collectivism* (New York and London: W. W. Norton & Company).

Bulpitt, Jim (1983) *Territory and Power in the United Kingdom: An Interpretation* (Manchester: University of Manchester Press).

Cain, Bruce E., John A. Ferejohn, and Morris P. Fiorina (1984) "The constituency service basis of the personal vote for U.S. representatives and British members of parliament," *American Political Science Review*, 78 (March), 110–25.

Converse, Philip E. (1964) "The nature of belief systems in mass publics," in *Ideology and Discontent*, David E. Apter, ed. (New York: Free Press), pp. 206–61.

Coombes, David, and S. A. Walkland, eds. (1980), *Parliament and Economic Affairs* (London: Heinemann).

Cox, Andrew, ed. (1982) *Politics, Policy and the European Recession* (New York: St. Martin's Press).

Curtice, John, and Michael Steed (1982) "Electoral choice and the production of government: the changing operation of the electoral system in the United Kingdom since 1955," *British Journal of Political Science*, 12 (July), 249–98.

Department of Trade and Industry (1983) *Regional Industrial Development*, Cmnd. 9111 (HMSO).

Downs, Stephen, J. (1985) "Structural changes: selection committees: experiment and establishment," in *Parliament in the 1980s*, Philip Norton, ed. (Oxford: Basil Blackwell), pp. 69–93.

Dunleavy, Patrick, and Christopher T. Husbands (1985) *British Democracy at the Crossroads: Voting and Party Competition in the 1980s* (London: George Allen & Unwin).

Dyson, Kenneth, and Stephen Wilks, eds. (1983) *Industrial Crisis: A Comparative Study of the State of Industry* (Oxford: Martin Robertson).

Economist, The (1984–86)

Grant, Wyn (1982) *The Political Economy of Industrial Policy* (London: Butterworth).

Grant, Wyn and Stephen Wilks (1983) "British industrial policy: structural change, policy inertia," *Journal of Public Policy*, 3 (February), 13–28.

Guardian, The (1983)

128   DAVID M. WOOD

Hibbing, John R. (1985) "Parliament without parties: voting patterns of British MPs on free votes," paper presented at the 1985 American Political Science Association Conference, New Orleans.

King, Roger, ed. (1983) *Capital and Politics* (London: Routledge and Kegan Paul).

Labour Party (1985a) *Jobs and Industry: Labour Working Together for Britain* (London: The Labour Party).

    (1985b) *Regional Plan: The West Midlands Can Make It* (London: The Labour Party).

    (1985c). *Regional Plan: Yorkshire and Humberside Can Make It* (London: The Labour Party).

Marsh, James W. (1985) "Representational changes: the constituency MP," in *Parliament in the 1980s*, Philip Norton, ed., (Oxford: Basil Blackwell), pp. 69–93.

Massey, Doreen, and Richard Meegan (1982) *The Anatomy of Job Loss: The How, Why and Where of Employment Decline* (London & New York: Methuen).

McAllister, Ian, and Richard Rose (1984) *The Nationwide Competition for Votes: the 1983 British Election* (London and Dover, N.H.: Frances Pinter).

McIver, John P. and Edward G. Carmines (1981) *Unidimensional Scaling* (Beverly Hills and London: Sage Publications).

Norton, Philip (1981) *The Commons in Perspective* (New York: Longmans).

Parliamentary Spokesmans Working Group (1982), *Alternative Regional Strategy: A Framework for Discussion* (London: Parliamentary Labour Party).

Rasmussen, Jorgen S. (1984) "Is parliament revolting", in *Dilemmas of Choice in British Politics*, Donley T. Studlar and Jerold L. Waltman, eds. (Jackson, Miss.: University Press of Mississippi).

Richardson, J. J. and A. G. Jordan (1979) *Governing Under Pressure: The Policy Process in a Post-parliamentary Democracy* (Oxford: Martin Robertson & Company Ltd).

Riddell, Peter (1983) *The Thatcher Government* (Oxford: Martin Robertson).

Rose, Richard (1982) *The Territorial Dimension in Government: Understanding the United Kingdom* (Chatham, New Jersey: Chatham House Publishing, Inc.).

    (1984) *Do Parties Make a Difference?*, 2nd edn (London and Basingstoke: Macmillan Press).

    (1986) "British MPs: more bark than bite?" in *Parliaments and Parliamentarians in Democratic Politics*, Ezra N. Suleiman, ed. (New York and London: Holmes & Meier).

Schwarz, John E. (1980), "Exploring a new role in policy making: the British House of Commons in the 1970s" *American Political Science Review*, 74 (March), 23–37.

Searing, Donald D. (1985) "The role of the good constituency member and the practice of representation in Great Britain," *Journal of Politics*, 47 (May), 348–81.

Shonfield, Andrew (1965) *Modern Capitalism: The Changing Balance of Public and Private Power* (New York and London: Oxford University Press).

Stewart, Michael (1977) *The Jekyll and Hyde Years: Politics and Economic Policy Since 1964* (London: Dent).

Times Guide to the House of Commons, The (1983) (London: Times Books).

Townsend, Alan R. (1983) *The Impact of Recession: On Industry, Employment and the Regions, 1976–1981* (London and Canberra: Croom Helm).

Wolf, Martin (1979) *Adjustment Policies and Problems in Developed Countries: A Study of the Problems Created By, and Policies Toward, the Imports of Manufactures from Developing Countries* (Washington: World Bank Staff Working Paper No. 349).

Wood, David M. (1985) "Macroeconomic vs. microeconomic policy orientations among back-bench Conservative MPs: economic policy and party polarization," paper presented at the Midwest Political Science Association Conference, Chicago.

(1987) "The Conservative Member of Parliament as lobbyist for constituency economic interests," *Political Studies*, 35 (September), 393–409.

and William G. Jacoby (1984) "Intra-party cleavage in the British House of Commons: evidence from the 1974–79 parliament, *American Journal of Political Science*, 28 (February), 203–23.

Zysman, John (1983) *Governments, Markets and Growth: Financial Systems and the Politics of Industrial Change* (Ithaca and London: Cornell University Press).

6

Congress and the development of a computer industry policy in Brazil

ABDO I. BAAKLINI and ANTONIO CARLOS POJO DO REGO

Of the many challenges facing legislature in contemporary societies, that of effectively participating in initiating and shaping industrial development policy is perhaps the most critical. Traditionally, legislatures were suited to perform a number of important functions, such as representation, legitimization, socialization of political leadership, and communication between government and constituencies and *vice versa*.[1] However, the challenge of advanced industrialization and the harnessing of science and technology to formulate industrial policies caught many legislatures unprepared even in the most developed society with a strong legislative system such as the United States of America. To effectively participate in shaping industrial policies legislatures needed to equip themselves with staff and information capabilities, previously unavailable to them. They also found that the decentralized structure that facilitated their traditional functions was ill-suited to the function of long-range planning and integration of science and technology into public policy. Yet legislatures do play an important role in shaping industrial policy, even when their function has been drastically curtailed as is the case with the Brazilian Congress, under the military dominated regime (1964–85).

This chapter explores the role the Congress played in shaping a very important aspect of Brazil's industrial policy, that of the manufactur and use of computers, semi and superconductors, integrated circuit, and the necessary software that goes with it, known in Brazil as the policy of "informatics." It is not our intention to evaluate the economic wisdom of congressional intervention as compared to executive proposals and plans.[2] We seek to explore the modalities and directions of congressional intervention. By modalities, we mean the instruments that the Congress utilized to shape the informatics policy. The direction refers to the aspects of the policy and the concerns that preoccupied congressional actions in this policy area. Once the modalities and the directions of this intervention have been discussed, we shall advance some propositions to explain the role of the Congress in the informatics policy, and to relate these hypotheses to those developed by Olson and Mezey in chapter 1, such as the changes within the executive during military government. It is important to emphasize, at the beginning, that the informatics policy was developed and elaborated by a small group of technocrats aptly called by Adler the "pragmatic antidependency guerrillas" within the executive who "used their scientific, technological and managerial knowledge, as well as their access to political power, to mobilize not only the know-how and know-what but also the know-where-to regarding computers."[3] Given the supremacy of the executive in setting public policy during the authoritarian regime in Brazil, congressional participation was gradual and contingent on the degree of conflict within the executive, and the opening and relaxation of the political climate within the country, as suggested in the first set of hypotheses in chapter 1.

THE CONGRESS UNDER AUTHORITARIAN RULE 1964–1985

The Federal Congress of Brazil consists of two chambers. The Senate, elected for eight years, made up of three Senators from each state, one-third of them elected every four years, and the Chamber of Deputies, elected every four years. Although the distribution of seats within the Chamber of Deputies is supposed to reflect the principle of one man one vote, in reality large states of the Southeast such as São Paulo, Rio de Janeiro are underrepresented, while smaller states in the North and the Northeast are overrepresented.[4] Electoral laws define each state as a single electoral district. Although, between 1964 and 1985, certain characteristics of the Brazilian Congress and the balance of political forces represented in it changed from one administration to another, its role in public policy was circumscribed by certain constitutional, political, structural, and ideological features, which remained on the whole constant.

Constitutionally, the role of the Congress in public policy was severely restricted.[5] The military abolished all existing political parties in 1965, and by fiat, created two new parties, one to represent the government and the other the loyal opposition.[6] Through the manipulation of the electoral laws and the election, and by using repression and persuasion, it made sure that the party representing the government (ARENA) dominated both houses of the Congress. Thus, whatever minimal role the constitution[7] reserved for the Congress was taken away through manipulation of the parties, electoral laws, and processes.

Structurally, the military regime, in the name of equality of opportunity, bureaucratized the Congress and weakened its leadership. The institutional leadership of each house, known as the Mesa, was elected to a non-renewable two-year term. The committee leadership was elected to a one-year non-renewable term in the chamber and two years non-renewable term in the senate.[8] By limiting the term of office of leaders, and by separating the institutional leadership from party leadership, the executive insured that the Congress would not develop the expertise, the continuity, or the power base to challenge executive initiatives. While the Congress was permitted to hire its own staff, the bureaucratic structure of its organization rendered them irrelevant to public policy.

Finally, the ideology of the military, of state intervention to achieve industrialization, and rapid economic development through comprehensive planning and the harnessing of science and technology[9], left no doubt that legislatures with their parochial outlook, archaic structures, and meager comprehension, are neither equipped nor entitled to participate in this process. However, the role of Congress in shaping the informatics policy between 1971 and 1985 reveals some surprises. Its role varied from marginal in nature, such as a random criticism of government policy in 1971 to eventually acting as arbitrator among conflicting groups within the bureaucracy, thus participating in the shaping of the informatics policy in 1985.

INFORMATICS POLICY: EXECUTIVE INITIATIVE AND
CONGRESSIONAL REACTION

In the military's development ideology a computer policy occupies a prominent position. The regime was committed to a development policy that would encourage the rapid transfer of technology and capital from the advanced Western countries to Brazil. The regime was also committed to an economic policy that would encourage local capital to develop industries, not only for import substitution, but also in order to compete internationally. The main issue was what type of technology should be imported from overseas, or manufactured in Brazil by subsidaries of foreign multinationals, and what should be reserved for Brazilian manufacturers. Adler identified two groups with distinct ideologies within the Brazilian intelligentia that sought to define the economic model of Brazil's relationship with the international economic order. The "structural dependency" group, with classical Marxist logic, argued for an end to dependency on the multinational corporations (MNCs) as the only road to achieve Brazilian autonomy in the economic and technological arena. But this call for autonomy was judged to be beyond Brazil's reach because the solution required global structural changes. The solution therefore required concerted action among all developing countries to change the international economic system. Brazil's elites were either unable or uninterested in following such a path, because their existence in power depends on the support of those forces that they need to change.

The second group, while accepting the theoretical logic of the dependency theorists, believed that it was possible to end this structural dependency by following a pragmatic approach, emphasizing a mixture of state intervention, national capital, and the MNCs. It is this group of "pragmatic anti-dependency" under the leadership of men like Jose Pelucio, Ricardo A. C. Saur, and others, that eventually succeeded in defining and implementing the informatics policy of Brazil.[10]

Another reason why informatics policy occupied a special position in the ideology of the military regime as well as that of its critics, was the close connection between computers, data bases, intelligence gathering, and controlling and intimidating political dissidents. This connection led to questions about the effect of technology on privacy, on the regime's ability to suppress opposition, and on the labor market. The questions raised dealt with organizational structure in the formation of informatics policy, who should take part in it, to whom should they report, and how wide its jurisdiction would be.

As early as 1971, Brazil recognized the need to develop a policy in the area of informatics. Between 1971 and 1985, an intense debate ranged first within the executive and later within the Congress as to the appropriate policy the country should follow. During that period the role of Congress in setting the informatics policy ranged from the marginal to the pivotal. For the purpose of understanding the issues raised and the role that Congress played, three periods can be distinguished: 1971–78, 1979–81, and 1981–86.

The formative period (1971–1978)

The first official act to address the informatics policy occurred in 1971,[11] when the government created a special working group composed of naval officers and some bureaucrats from the Ministry of Planning, working under the auspices of the navy.[12] This working group had the task of planning the development and manufacture of an electronic computer prototype for naval operations. The immediate goal was to equip a number of navy frigates being purchased from British and Brazilian suppliers with such computers as were needed.

From this military beginning the need for an industrial policy for the manufature and operation of data processing equipment (hardware), programs (software), and human resources began to emerge. Both the National Development Plan of 1972–74[13], and the Basic Science and Technology Development Plan of 1973–74 mentioned the need for the development of a mini-computer industry and the establishment of a computer technology.

To address those needs, a presidential decree[14] established, in 1972, the Electronic Processing Activities Coordinating Commission (CAPRE), an executive agency under the Secretary of Planning (SEPLAN).

CAPRE established a market reserve policy for mini and micro-computers which meant that they were to be built in Brazil by Brazilian companies. They could neither be imported nor manufactured in Brazil by foreign corporations. The rationale for such a policy was that, although multinational corporations operated in Brazil building mainframes, Brazilian companies should have a monopoly on the mini-computer market, since the technology was available and the necessary capital investment was relatively small. However, enunciating a policy, and implementing it, are two completely different things, since the Brazilian companies who would produce these computers were yet to be established.

CAPRE'S authority to examine and set up various aspects of the informatics policy was augmented both in 1975 and 1976. In 1975, with the deepening foreign exchange crisis, Brazil's Foreign Commerce Council (CONCEX)[15], in an effort to cut down on computer imports, empowered CAPRE to examine all aspects of data processing imports. In 1976, another presidential decree created a special plenary council to oversee CAPRE'S work and at the same time gave CAPRE wide-ranging powers to propose the goals for a national information policy and to present it to the newly established plenary council, representing various civilian and military departments. While CAPRE was to have the executive power to set up the policy and implement it, the council would set policy guidelines and hear administrative appeals in cases of disagreement among the various administrative units affected by the policy.[16]

In that same year, CAPRE selected four private companies and a newly established public corporation, Computadores e Sistemas Brasileiros (COBRA), to build the first new mini-computer, still using foreign technology in their production.

There was increased international pressure against Brazil's market

Table 6.1 *Legislative action on computer policy (1971–78)*

1. Dep. Silvio Barros (RIC 12/71) – requests information from the executive on projects on use of computers for research and development in Brazil.
2. Dep. Francisco Amaral (PL 1071/72) – establishes a six-hour work day for data processing employees.
3. Dep. Amadeo Geara (PL 528/75) – forbids night work for women (among the exceptions: data processing activities).
4. Dep. Nina Ribeiro (PL 371/75) – increases SERPRO competence to provide services to private companies.
5. Dep. Geraldo Bulhoes (PL 973/75) – limits number of work hours for data processing employees.
6. Dep. Francisco Amaral (PL 1434/75) – forbids invasion of individual privacy by the use of computerized information.
7. Dep. Francisco Amaral (PL 2728/76) – six-hour work day for data processing workers.
8. Dep. Jose Camargo (PL 2924/76) – six-hour work day for computer operators.
9. Dep. Siqueira Campos (PL 3279/76) – considers a felony the development or use of adulterated computer programming.
10. Sen. Nelson Carneiro (PLS 96/77) – establishes protection of computerized information, and access to data stored.
11. Dep. Faria Lima (PL 4365/77) – establishes a national registration for data bases to protect individual privacy.
12. Dep. Jose Camargo (PL 4368/77) – regulates the kind of information that can be provided by data processing centers about files on individuals, for the protection of individual privacy.
13. Dep. Isreal Dias-Novaes (PL 5758/78) – regulates the professions in the area of electronic data processing.
14. Dep. Israel Dias-Novaes (PL 5773/78) – regulates the work hours of data processing professionals.
15. Dep. Israel Dias-Novaes (PL 1205/79) – regulates the professions in the area of electronic data processing.
16. Dep. Jose Camargo (PL 1463/79) – establishes reduced work hours for data processing personnel.

reserve policy, especially by American multinational corporations. IBM, which lobbied against the market reserve policy affecting production of its mini-computer line, presented in 1977 five new equipment projects to be produced in Brazil, in apparent violation of the market reserve policy. Against fierce opposition,[17] within the plenary council of CAPRE, the largest two of the five projects were approved.

This decision split CAPRE's council and brought into the open the conflict over informatics policy. The press, the national companies, the users, and the Congress criticized the decision to allow IBM to produce certain kinds of computers in Brazil as a sellout to the interest of the multinationals and as a serious violation of the market reserve policy.

Stripped of its most important powers and placed under severe constitutional and political limitations, the Congress was in no position to initiate or to meaningfully affect public policy. Yet, a review of the official record shows that individual members of the Congress during 1971 to 1978 presented thirteen bills and one request for information, all intended to draw the government's attention to what the Congress considered important areas relevant to informatics policy. Nine of the bills presented had to do with the implication of information technology on those who work in it. Thus, some of the bills suggested the establishment of a six-hour workday for data processing employees. Other bills raised the issue of privacy and its protection. Table 6.1 gives the various bills presented in Congress between 1971 and 1978.

During this period the role of the Congress in setting up the informatics policy was limited to requests for information and to sensitizing the executive to areas of privacy, labor implications, and some areas of possible use. Congressional activity did not involve policy-making nor the review and control of whatever policy was formulated by the government.

Informatics was an executive preserve, debated and promulgated by CAPRE under the domination of the military and the bureaucrats. In fact, informatics policy emerged in, and continued to a large extent to be controlled by, the bureaucratic and intelligence organizations of the military regime. As long as there was agreement within the executive regarding this policy, even when the policy was ambiguous and in flux, the Congress had neither the power nor the means to contribute. It could only wage individual "guerilla acts," whose purpose were to embarrass the government or to draw public attention to some facets of the policy.

The "limited engagement" period (1979–1981)

During the second phase, the institutions involved in making the policy were changed. The newly installed administration of President Joao Figueiredo gave informatics policy top priority and called for a comprehensive study in response to the mounting criticism against CAPRE discussed above. Having openly committed himself to the policies aimed at the opening up of the political system known as "Abertura," Figueiredo called for a comprehensive study of informatics policy. On April 19, he appointed a commission composed of members of the National Information Service (SNI), the National Security Council, the Ministries of Planning, Foreign Affairs, and the Armed Forces

General Staff (EMFA), to examine the structure and the present status of the data processing industries, and to propose a new structure to control all informatics policy. The commission was given 120 days to present its recommendations. Ambassador Paulo Cotrim, whose only achievement in the field of informatics came from having been chief of a division in the Ministry of Foreign Affairs in charge of administrative application of computers within the ministry, was appointed as head of the commission. Cotrim's appointment was widely criticized by the press and the data processing professional community, since he was not known to be knowledgeable in the informatics policy area. It was feared that his appointment was window dressing to give civilian legitimacy to a commission clearly dominated by the military.

The commission report presented in September 1979 was critical of CAPRE's work and policies.[18] It called for the dismantling of the CAPRE council, and the creation of a Special Secretariat for Informatics (SEI), to operate under the Secretary of the National Security Council, headed by General Danilo Venturini. The commission recommended an increase in the market reserve to include medium-size computers in addition to the mini, a strengthening of "national enterprises," and a freeze on government creation of new public corporations in the computer sector.

The Cotrim commission's recommendations were sharply attacked. In a meeting in Bahia, the data processing professional association (APPD) charged that

the debate on informatics policy should not be restricted to a closed group. A closed commission, made up of of elements unacquainted with the problems of computer industry, is incompatible with the professed political liberation of the regime. The question should be debated not only within the data processing community, but by other groups as well, especially the legislative branch, which with the technical support of the professional community, is the only legitimate forum for the formulation of this policy.[19]

Notwithstanding the negative reaction against the commission's recommendations, a presidential decree accepted the recommendations and established SEI in October 1979.[20] The reaction against the establishment of SEI was swift. On October 25, at a university meeting in Porto Alegre, the data processing community adopted a resolution to condemn the "authoritarian process of creating SEI, a process that does not take into consideration the views of technical and scientific personnel, in total contradiction with the process of political liberalization."[21]

CAPRE's demise, according to Adler, signaled the erosion of the political base of the "pragmatist anti-dependency guerrillas" and its "egalitarian nationalism" type of economic policies. Since its establishment, CAPRE policies have met with intense resistance from many different quarters. SEPLAN under Minister Antonio Delfim Netto in 1979 was not very hospitable to the reserved market policies. While he could not totally eliminate the policies established under his predecessors, he tried to weaken the interpretation of those policies. CAPRE, in spite of its valiant attempt to mobilize all the government sectors behind its technological autonomy quest, failed to do so. Several ministries and state enterprises maintained their autonomy and on several occasions adopted policies and purchasing practices favoring foreign producers. Small national enterprises opposed certain aspects of the policy, such as the standards specified by the National Institute of Industrial Property (INPI), for the absorption of technology by the national enterprises. Disagreement among the scientific community as the policy progressed became apparent. Those in academia engaged in pure scientific research felt that the policy discriminated against them in favor of applied science and economic development. Finally, the various government entities engaged in one aspect or other of the informatics and science policies failed to maintain adequate coordination among themselves leading to conflict over area, bottlenecks, overlapping, and contradictions.[22]

SEI, under Octavio Gennari as secretary, was a true reflection of the predominantly military influence that brought it into existence. Though Gennari was a civilian electronics engineer, the policies of SEI fell under the total sway of the military who occupied senior positions throughout the organization, and to whom SEI reported. The establishment of SEI under the National Security Council was intended to consolidate all informatics policy under one agency and to end bureaucratic squabbles about the direction of that policy. Consolidation was achieved, but not the ending of confusion and bureaucratic conflict between those in favor of a market reserve and those who under international pressure favored a relaxation or even the total elimination of the market reserve policy.

In May 1980, SEI reaffirmed the market reserve policy and rejected a proposal by IBM to build in Brazil two medium-sized computers (Models 38 and 4331).[23] SEI argued that such a request violated the established market reserve policy. In August, however, SEI reversed its decision, and allowed IBM and Burroughs to build medium-sized computers, and Hewlett-Packard to manufacture micro-computers for scientific applications. Except for a slight increase in memory, the IBM request was identical to the one rejected in May of the same year.

SEI's informatics policy was in shambles and conflict broke out again between the proponents of a market reserve and those proposing a free market, each trying this time to mobilize public opinion and congressional support. On the one side, there were the users and the electronic trade associations, who supported the new policy. On the other side, stood the computer manufacturers' trade association which opposed the relaxation of the market reserve policy. A lobby group called Alliance for the Defense of National Technology was formed to support market reserve. It consisted of associations of professionals and manufacturers. The controversy was joined by new groups of university professors, government employee organizations, and the Brazilian Society for the Advancement of Science.

Between 1980 and 1982, the power and jurisdiction of SEI continued to expand, in spite of mounting criticism both from within Brazil and from the international computer manufacturers. In March of 1981, for example, the government issued a decree increasing the mandate of SEI to "plan, supervise and control research and development and industrial policy of semi-conductors and micro-electronic components."[24] SEI was branching out into other industrial areas where electronic chips were being increasingly used, such as communication equipment. This increase in the power and jurisdiction of SEI went hand in hand with increased policy ambiguity and internal conflict as to the course to follow. The greater the internal conflict, the more SEI found itself in need of external support and legitimization, especially from the Congress.

When, in 1982, Gennari departed as secretary general of SEI for "personal reasons," an army colonel, Joubert Brizida, was made secretary and Edson Dytz, another colonel, was made executive secretary, thus completing the "militarization" of the organization under the overall supervision of Danilo Venturini, the head of the National Security Council.

This "militarization' of SEI did not help much in eliminating the conflict over which policy would ultimately be adopted. In October of 1982, for example, Venturini stated that "future entrance of foreign enterprises in the reserved market would depend on further government studies." This announcement worried the pro-reserve lobby, since it raised the possibility of another policy shift and added another uncertainty to the market.

During this second phase, the role the Congress played increased in boldness and sophistication. The creation of SEI, and placing it under military control, outraged politicians from both the right and the left. Free traders, such as Senator Roberto Campos, objected to the market reserve policy adopted by SEI, and argued for its liberalization in favor of an open trade policy. The nationalists were outraged by the domination of

Table 6.2 *Legislative action on computer policy (1979–1981)*

1. Dep. Israel Dias-Novaes (PL 1205/79) – regulates professions in the area of electronic data processing.
2. Dep. Jose Camargo (PL 1463/79) – establishes reduced work hours for data processing personnel.
3. Dep. Marcello Cerqueira (PL 2709/80) – forbids foreign-owned companies to provide data processing services.
4. Dep. Cristina Tavares (PL 2796/80) – ensures citizens access to information stored in computerized data bases.
5. Dep. Henrique Eduardo Alves (PL 3034/80) – six-hour work day for computer operators.
6. Dep. Helio Duque (PL 3455/80) – reserves for Brazilian-owned companies the market for data processing services.
7. Dep. Cristina Tavares (RIC 80/80) requests information on export of data processing services to Africa and Latin America.
8. Dep. Marcello Cerqueira (RIC 97/80) – (RIC 97/80) – requests information on data processing services provided to Federal Savings Corporation (Caixa Economica Federal).
9. Dep. Cristina Tavares (PL 4810/81) – institutes registry for computerized data bases and information access.
10. Dep. Oswaldo Lima (PL 4833/81) – establishes 20 per cent pay increase and special retirement age for computer operators.
11. Dep. Carlos Wilson (PL 5012/81) – institutes National Informatics Day.
12. Dep. Cristina Tavares (PL 5117/81) – establishes guidelines for an informatics policy, forbids computer manufacturing by multinational corporations.
13. Dep. Rafael Faraco (PL 5314/81) – regulates use of computers in elections, for voting and counting of ballots.
14. Dep. Mauricio Fruet (PL 5332/81) – creates Informatics Commission to oversee SEI, composed of representatives of data processing professionals association, Brazilian Bar Association and Brazilian Press Association.
15. Dep. Victor Faccioni (PL 5356/81) – regulates the data processing professions.
16. Dep. McDowell Leite de Castro (PL 5502/81) – limits work day for computer operators to four hours.
17. Dep. Pacheco Chaves (PL 5679/81) – limits workday for computer operators to six hours.
18. Dep. Israel Dias-Novaes (PL 5758/81) – regulates the professions of system analyst and programmer.
19. Dep. Cristina Tavares (PRC 238/81) – creates Committee on Informatics in the Chamber of Deputies.

the informatics policy by the military and security organs of the state. They feared that such a monopoly over information policy, and the use of data processing technology, would undoubtedly strengthen the repressive institutions of the regime and lead to abuses and violations of individual rights, in addition to opening the door to corruption and profiteering. They also feared that those advocating free trade policies within the military would soon give in to international pressure and abandon the market reserve policy.

During this phase, the Congress initiated nineteen bills and requests for information related to informatics policy as shown in table 6.2.

Some of these bills dealt with familiar issues such as privacy and regulating work conditions in the new technology. Others, however, broke new ground. The requests for information by Deputy Cristina Tavares (RIC 80/80), asked for information regarding Brazil's export of data processing services to Africa and Latin America. Deputy Marcello Cerqueira (RIC 97/80), requested information on the data processing companies engaged by the Federal Savings and Loan Association. The two most important bills, however, were introduced during the 1981 session in the Chamber of Deputies. Bill 5117/81 introduced by Deputy Tavares, established guidelines for a national informatics policy, and forbade computer manufacturing by multinational corporations. The second bill was introduced by Deputy Mauricio Fruet.[25] It called for the creation of an Informatics Commission to oversee the work of SEI, to be composed of representatives of the data processing professional association, the Brazilian Bar Association, and the Brazilian Press Association.

For the first time Congress tried, though unsuccessfully, to create public policy and devise mechanisms to control the actions and policies of the executive. What began in the first phase as uncoordinated individual "guerrilla skirmishes" with the government developed in the second phase into limited engagement, where Congress, though cognizant that it could not have its way against government policy, none the less, ventured to suggest policy, control the executive, and mobilize the concerned public. With appropriate changes in the political climate, the Congress was ready and eager to engage the government in fully fledged battled aimed at determining informatics policy and controlling executive action. Such a change was to occur during the third period between 1983 and 1985.

The third period (1983–1985)

During this period the role of the Congress began to change dramatically. Two main reasons account for this change. First, there are the political reforms introduced by the policy of "Abertura" initiated by Figueiredo in 1979, and second, the intensification of conflict within the executive branch over the future direction of informatics policy and the institutions that should be put in charge of shaping and implementing such a policy.

"Abertura" set in motion a series of political reforms such as political amnesty, abolition of Institutional Act No. 5, changes in the electoral laws allowing the formation of a multi-party system, the opening up of the electoral process, direct election of state governors, and an increase in the freedom of the press. During the 1982 election, the opposition, in spite of government efforts at manipulating electoral laws, emerged with new strength. The deteriorating economic conditions, and the boldness of the opposition, necessitated the hastening of political liberalization. Figueiredo was committed to seeing that his successor be chosen by an electoral college rather than imposed by the military. Thus, by the early eighties, the nature of the bureaucratic-authoritarian regime in Brazil began to change. The implications of this gradual return to democracy were very significant for the evolution of the informatics policy:

Abertura has had an effect on science and policy. As the political system was freed, as dissident voices began to be heard and opponents of the military government returned to Brazil, the nationalist rhetoric and the egalitarian–nationalist and Marxist attacks against foreign investment increased, pressuring elites and government agencies to take a more nationalistic stand.[26]

Furthermore, with the second oil shock in the late seventies, the economic policy of the government was facing its severest challenge in the form of mounting inflation, a recession, and an extremely high foreign debt. The political relaxation and the worsening economic climate both contributed to accentuate the bureaucratic conflict over informatics policy.

Thus, in 1983, while Brizida was reasserting SEI's policy of market reserve to a group of US businessmen, Mario Garneiro, president of the Brazilinvest Finance Corporation, and a close ally of foreign interest in Brazilian industry, gave a lecture at the Ministry of Communication in which he stated that the government was studying the unification of communication and computer industrial policy, implying the acceptance of joint ventures to build computers. In seeking support for his market reserve policy, Brizida began lobbying opposition members in the

Congress who were known to favor the nationalistic policy of market reserve.

In 1984 Brizida left SEI to take the position of Military Attaché to the Brazilian Embassy in London, leaving Colonel Dytz in charge of SEI. At the same time SEI announced the results of a bid by Brazilian enterprises that qualified to build a new type of computer called the super-mini. Eight companies were chosen, all owned entirely by Brazilians, but five of them needed to acquire the necessary technology abroad. This was considered a deviation from the market reserve policy, since SEI has maintained, from the beginning, that the upper portion of the market would be filled by Brazilian mini-computer manufacturers, upgrading the technology in their research facilities, rather than importing the technology. The super-mini-computer was one size larger than the mini-computers which were being built in Brazil, and therefore should have been manufactured by upgraded technology developed internally.

These sudden shifts in reinterpretation of existing policy gave additional fuel to the critics of the bureaucracy as an instrument of setting public policy in an area where its upper echelon was divided on the proper policy to follow. While SEI, representing the intelligence community and supported, oddly enough, by the opposition parties, was committed to a market reserve policy, the government's top economic team, headed by Planning Minister Delfim Netto, was skeptical of the whole policy arguing that it would undermine the on-going negotiations on the Brazilian foreign debt. Two other important ministers in Figueiredo's cabinet, Communication Minister Mattos and Industry and Commerce Minister Camilo Penna, were also opposed to the market reserve policy on the grounds that it ruled out joint ventures, which are permitted in the communication industry.[27]

Congress suddenly became the subject of intense lobbying by the various feuding factions within the government. The stage was set for a strong congressional role in the determination of informatics policy and the structure of its management, implementation, and control.

During this period the Congress became the place for sorting out the conflict among senior administrative officials. The Chamber of Deputies, where the opposition party was better represented, emerged as the champion of a market reserve policy, but to be controlled by civilian institutions. The opposition party wanted SEI to be controlled by civilians, and to declare itself unequivocally in favor of a strict market reserve policy, while the government party objected to SEI policy, and sought to have it controlled by ministries that were in favor of free trade, such as Planning, Communication, or Industry and Commerce. The

Table 6.3 *Legislative action on computer policy (1983–1984)*

1. Sen. Mario Maia (PLS 2/83) – transforms the National Information Service (SNI) into a civilian-administered "National Informatics and Telematics Institute."
2. Dep. Francisco Amaral (PL 210/83) – six-hour work day for computer terminal operators.
3. Dep. Marcello Cerqueira (PL 406/83) – forbids government hiring companies to provide data processing services.
4. Dep. Dante de Oliveira (PL 871/83) – establishes computerized election records to prevent fraud.
5. Dep. Leopoldo Bassone (PL 1031/83) – regulates the use of computers in credit research.
6. Dep. Wilmar Pallis (PL 1261/83) – requires the use of computerized voting machines.
7. Dep. Cristina Tavares (PL 1384/83) – regulates the manufacturing, sale, and import of data processing equipment.
8. Dep. Nelson do Carmo (PL 1628/83) – regulates the use of computer-readable bar codes in commerce.
9. Dep. Flavio Bierrenbach (PL 2442/83) – requires the use of Portuguese language characters in computer keyboards.
10. Sen. Roberto Campos (PLS 48/84) – regulates National Informatics Policy.
11. Sen. Carlos Chiarelli (PLS 93/84) – defines regulations for the National Informatics Policy.
12. Dep. Lelio Souza (PL 3274/84) – regulates the use of computers in credit control.
13. Dep. Amadeo Geara (PL 3560/84) – forbids contract with private data processing companies for election services.
14. Dep. Ruy Codo (PL 3589/84) – forbids the use of computers in primary and secondary schools.
15. Dep. Cristina Tavares (PL 3634/84) – regulates the use of industrial robots and industrial automation devises.
16. Dep. Salles Leite (PL 3659/84) – creates National Informatics Council, under the Ministry of Industry and Commerce, with representatives from Executive, Chamber of Deputies, Senate, National Industrial Confederation, Computer Manufacturing Association, and Brazilian Press Association.
17. Dep. Armando Pinheiro (PL 3969/84) – forbids foreign-owned data processing companies to provide electoral services.
18. Dep. Luiz Antonio Fayet (PL 4038/84) – establishes National Informatics Policy.
19. Dep. Pacheco Chaves (PL 4173/84) – limits work day for computer operators to six hours.
20. Dep. Joao Carlos Vasconcellos (PL 4659/84) – creates Informatics Technology Foundation in Recife, Pernambuco.
21. Dep. Cristina Tavares (PL 4646/84) – assures the right of privacy, regulates the operation of data bases.

22. Dep. Paulo Lustosa (PL 4724/84) – considers the city of Fortaleza as "informatics export district."
23. Dep. Jose Jorge (PL 4766/84) – regulates the access of private citizens to information filed in data bases.
24. Dep. Cristina Tavares (PL 4810/84) – requires government to divulge list of existing data bases.
25. Dep. Freitas Nobre (PL 4856/84) – regulates citizen access to information stored in data bases.
26. Sen. Roberto Campos (RQS 83/84) – requests information on Brazilian exports of data processing equipment.

heavy-handed methods used by the government, first in setting up the Cotrim Commission, and later in establishing SEI and placing it under the control of the intelligence community, seemed to have galvanized the opposition, both within and outside the Congress. SEI's policies and actions, unlike those of CAPRE, were watched by a number of strong computer related organizations which came to existence mainly in the seventies, such as the Association of Data Processing Service Enterprises in 1976, the Brazilian Association for Computer and Peripheral Equipment (ABICOMP), the Association of the Data Processing Professionals (APPD), the National Laboratory of Computer Network, and the Brazilian Computation Society (SBC) all in 1978.[28] All of these groups supported a pragmatic market reserve policy and resisted any move on the part of SEI or the other government institutions that were promoting a more open policy towards the MNCs. Indeed, in 1980, a coordinating committee representing all of these bodies, was organized to lobby the Congress, the executive, and the judiciary and to use all the legal means available to prevent the reversal of the informatics policy.

Between 1983 and 1984 Congress assumed a strong policy role. Twenty-six bills dealing with informatics policy were introduced. Hearings and seminars were conducted and speeches were delivered, all dealing with informatics policy.

Bills introduced

Of the twenty-six bills introduced in the Congress, two in the Chamber of Deputies and two in the Senate are the most noteworthy. The two bills introduced in the Chamber, were by Deputy Marcello Cordeiro and Deputy Cristina Tavares, both from the opposition party, Party of the Democratic Brazilian Movement (PMDB), while the two bills introduced in the Senate were by Senators Roberto Campos and Carlos Chiarelli, both from the pro-government party, the Social Democratic Party (PDS).

The Cordeiro bill[29] was intended to regulate data processing services furnished to government agencies, stipulating that the contracts for such services should only be given to Brazilian companies. The bill introduced by Tavares[30] was a broad-range bill, calling for the regulation of the entire computer industrial policy by laws enacted in Congress rather than through administrative acts, directives, or simply by fiat. As the author mentioned in the bill's justification, the bill aimed at

giving a legal foundation to the national policy for the production of data processing equipment, a policy that, up to now, has been regulated by administrative fiat of the Special Secretariat for Informatics of the Presidency of the Republic, an organization whose technical expertise is undeniable, but that is not the proper form for discussions and implementations of an industrial policy of the highest importance for the Country.

Tavares' bill called for the imposition of import restrictions by an act of Congress, rather than an administrative act. It also called for a complete embargo on foreign capital in companies manufacturing computers.

In the Senate, the bill introduced by Senator Campos[31] called for the deregulation of the computer industry, and, contrary to SEI's policy, advocated a return to a free trade policy. Senator Chiarelli's bill,[32] on the other hand, tried to strike a balance between the Tavares and the Campos bill, by calling for a mild government reserve as advocated by SEI, with increased Congressional oversight over informatics policy.

Other bills dealt with measures to prevent abuses and arbitrariness by SEI, and with the application of the new technology to the electoral process, its effects on privacy, and on consumer credit, among others.

Seminars and speeches

Another method used by the Congress to shape the informatics policy was through a series of seminars and speeches that it sponsored for the purpose of educating the Congress and the concerned public regarding the various dimensions of informatics policy. In 1981, for example, the Chamber's Committee on Science and Technology held a five-day seminar on National Informatics Policy under the leadership of Deputy Tavares. During the seminar, the committee was able to hear a presentation by Gennari, the SEI's secretary general, former CAPRE executive secretary Saur, computer industry trade leaders, presidents of government computer companies as well as several university professors. As a result of this seminar, the final report of the committee concluded that the country needed a coherent and consistent policy and that Congress and not SEI was the appropriate forum to formulate such a policy.

During 1983 and 1984, as the national debate over informatics policy intensified, a great many speeches about the policy were made on the floor of the Congress. Senate majority leader Aloysio Chaves and Senators Roberto Campos, Fernando Henrique Cardoso, Marco Marcel, Fabio Lucena, Henrique Santillo, Jutahy Magalhaes, Nelson Carneiro, and others, representing all sorts of diverse policy orientations, gave frequent speeches on the floor of the Senate regarding the informatics policy.[33]

In June of 1983, the Senate held a seminar on informatics dealing with government policy, the question of the "informatization" of society, the national computer industry, and informatics and national sovereignty. Among the participants were SEI Secretary Brizida, Communication Ministry Secretary General Romulo Furtado as well as representatives of trade associations (manufacturers, users, and service bureaus), academics and politicians of various political orientations.[34]

Hearings

In 1984, for the first time, the Senate's Economic Committee, chaired by an influential and outspoken critic of the market reserve policy, Roberto Campos, held a well publicized hearing, in which he was able to give extensive coverage for his bill calling for the deregulation of the computer industry and a return to free trade. The committee undertook a wide-ranging debate on the whole industrial policy of the government in the high technology area in which high government officials (Venturini, Mattos, and Penna), industrialists, politicians, and even the two presidential candidates (Tancredo Neves and Paulo Maluf) were called to testify.[35]

All of these activities served the purpose of educating the Congress and the public on the controversies surrounding the informatics policy. The openness of the discussion and the opportunities that these activities provided for the various protagonists were in sharp contrast to the way SEI undertook its deliberations or aired its policy differences. For the first time in twenty years, Brazil was able to develop its public policy in free and open congressional deliberations.

The Congress enacts the Informatics Bill

The gestation period came to a climax when, on July 30 1984, the executive sent to Congress a bill[36], detailing its informatics policy. The government requested that it should be reported out of Congress in forty-five days, lest it should be promulgated as an executive decree, in accordance with the prevailing constitutional provisions. Instead of resolving the ongoing controversy, the executive bill seemed to have fueled it afresh. In an editorial, *Jornal do Brasil* called it an "Orwellian nightmare" through which the "intelligence community" was "fostering the dream of transforming the authoritarian state into a totalitarian state, that is to say, the very opposite of all we intended to achieve with the political liberalization process and our endeavor to create institutions that would guarantee democracy." The paper called upon the Congress "to give priority to the question of informatics policy." The Congress, it added, "cannot absent itself and permit the approval of such a totalitarian measure, since it contradicts the liberalization process."[37]

The government bill called for the continuation of the market reserve policy. It also kept SEI under the supervision of the National Security Council. A new council drawn exclusively from senior government officials was to oversee the Secretariat. According to the provisions of the bill, SEI was given a free hand to decide the informatics policy and supervise its implementation, only this time (if the bill passed the Congress as presented), with the full blessing and legitimacy of the Congress.

Although the government tried to argue that all concerned parties were consulted before the bill was presented, according to one of the participants in these so-called consultations, the presidential palace merely called them in to inform them of what had already been decided, rather than to consult with them. None of the suggestions made were taken into consideration. True to its practices in the last twenty years, the military seemed unable to incorporate ideas that conflicted with its own thinking. The military was unwilling to recognize the rapidly changing political landscape in Brazil.

In August 1984 a Congressional joint committee was created to study the bill. The pro-government party, PDS, was represented in the committee by eleven senators and deputies; nine senators and deputies represented the major opposition party, PMDB, while one deputy represented another opposition party, PDT. Although PDS had a one vote majority in the joint committee,[38] the voting pattern in the committee was not along party lines, since many of PDS members were against the government's market reserve policy. During the committee's deliberations of the bill, more than 261 amendments were presented and 72 of these amendments were finally approved by the committee. The hearing conducted by the committee involved eighteen people, including Minister Murilo Badaro (Industry and Commerce), Minister Haroldo Mattos (Communication), Danilo Venturini (National Security Council) and Colonel Edson Dytz, secretary of SEI.

The committee also heard the testimony of the two presidential candidates, trade association representatives, and industrialists. Brazil's divergent elements were on hand for the first time, to legitimize, for both domestic and international opinion, whatever policy the Congress might choose to enact.

While the government bill was still in committee, Senator Tavora presented a substitute bill that eventually was adopted by the Congress in place of the government bill.[39] While maintaining many of the points of the government bill, Tavora's bill increased the scope of the market reserve, established enforceable goals for the companies benefiting from market reserve, created export districts in the North and Northeast with special tax incentives, set up an annual informatics plan to be submitted by the Executive to Congress (thus sharply limiting SEI autonomy), and established a National Commission on Informatics and Automation (CONIN), to operate under the presidency rather than the National Security Council.

CONIN's composition was expanded to include, in addition to representatives from the executive, persons who would represent professional, scientific, trade, manufacturing, and citizens' organizations. The main function of CONIN was to oversee the work of SEI, which was removed from under the National Security Council, and placed under the direct authority of the president. Later, after the new civilian regime was installed in March 1985, SEI was placed under a newly established Ministry of Science and Technology.[40]

Two amendments to Tavora's bill presented by a deputy from the Workers' Party (PT), although rejected by the committee were approved by the plenary session of the Congress. The two amendments dealt with the protection of individual privacy, and called for the assistance of those workers who lose their jobs as a result of automation. Both of these amendments were later item-vetoed by the president.

MODALITIES AND DIRECTIONS OF CONGRESSIONAL ACTIONS

It is not our intention in this chapter to argue that congressional intervention led to a better or worse public policy outcome. It is important however, to point out that congressional intervention follows certain modalities and highlights policy dimensions different from the modalities and policy concerns of the Executive.

Modalities of congressional intervention

Students of the US Congress often emphasize the confrontational dimension of the executive–legislative roles in public policy. While this approach is relevant to a strong legislature such as the US Congress, it fails to capture the subtleties of the methods used by a weak legislature operating under adverse executive pressures. In the case of Brazil for example, the Congress utilized a number of strategies to force the executive to discuss and reconsider its informatics policy.

1 Requests for information. During the early seventies, the Brazilian Congress lacked the power to participate in an open debate regarding informatics policy, or any other policy. Yet, as Table 6.1 indicates, a number of requests for information were presented to the executive. These requests were intended to draw the attention of the executive to certain policy concerns not taken into consideration under the existing policy. In many cases these requests were directed at the executive to force clarifications in areas of ambiguity.

2 Lectures and press interviews. Another method used by members of Congress is to resort to lectures and press interviews to influence and mobilize the concerned public behind certain policy orientations in the hope of influencing the executive. In Brazil, these methods included speeches on the floor, lectures to professional associations and manu-facturers, and interviews with the press. All were intended to educate and mobilize public opinion.

3 Seminars. During the period of military domination, the Congress of Brazil resorted to sponsoring seminars as an ingenious way of educating itself and the public about important public policy concerns, of forcing the executive to publicly explain its policy, and of allowing the dissidents within the executive to publicly state their policy differences. In almost all cases, the proceedings of the seminars were published by the printing press of the Congress and distributed to opinion leaders in the country. While these seminars were not conducted as hearings or investigations, they attempted to arrive at some policy recommendations and set the stage for new legislative initiatives. Both the Chamber of Deputies and the Senate held such seminars in which leading policy makers from the executive, the manufacturers, the users, and academics participated and elaborated on existing policies and outlined the new initiatives needed.

4 Hearings. Committee hearings in the Brazilian political settings were resorted to after the Congress had regained some of its power, and after the conflict within the executive over the policy to adopt became public. Both Houses held public hearings that were widely publicized. These hearings raised many of the issues covered in the seminars, but from an advocacy perspective with the specific intent to devise policy.

5 Introduction of bills. Even when the Congress had no chance of winning, a number of bills were introduced, particularly in the Chamber of Deputies. Some of these bills dealt with specific issues within the general policy area, others attempted to cover the fundamentals of the policy.

Table 6.4 *Direction of legislative concern (1971–1984)*

Categories	Frequency	%
Labor regulations	19	32.1
Privacy	10	16.9
Overall policy	5	8.4
Computer use in elections	5	8.4
Control of executive policy	4	6.7
Data processing services	3	5.0
Computer exports	2	3.3
Regional economy	2	3.3
Use by government	2	3.3
Use by credit industry	2	3.3
Computer use in education	1	1.6
Computer use in commerce	1	1.6
Use of Portuguese language	1	1.6
Computer crime	1	1.6
Observance ("computer day")	1	1.6
Total	59	

Although few of those bills were ever approved, they none the less provided the executive with the opportunity to become aware of some of the concerns of Congress and the public. In the final analysis, many of the concerns expressed in those bills were adopted as public policy and were embodied in the 1988 constitution.[41]

Directions of congressional concerns

The direction of the policy concerns of Congress are equally as important as the methods it used to express those concerns. An examination of the bills introduced, including the bill finally approved, reveals that congressional concerns in public policy often stress aspects left unaddressed by the executive. Table 6.4 demonstrates the policy concerns included.

1 Labor. Of the fifty-nine bills presented between 1971 and 1983, eighteen bills (30.5 per cent), dealt with the impact of the new technology on labor. Some of these bills tried to regulate the number of work hours for computer programmers, the scheduling of work so that women would not have to work at night and leave their families, and preparation and certification of computer specialists. Other bills dealt with measures that needed to be taken to protect those workers displaced as a result of the introduction of the new technology. In all of these cases, the direction of

legislative action was to regulate an emerging profession and ameliorate any adverse effects on those who would be involved in it or affected by it. The bills, though sponsored by a minority, raised the issue of the welfare of the labor force. In the Brazilian context, where labor welfare has been systematically neglected by the military's economic and industrial policies, the congressional initiatives in this regard were politically very significant, since they implied strong criticism of the prevailing policies.

2 Utilization of the new technology. Another important concern of congressional initiatives, were the uses of, and consequently, the segments of the population that would benefit from, the new technology. Legislatures, by their very political nature, are interested in the allocation of resources among their supporters. The Congress in Brazil, during the period under discussion presented over thirteen bills (21.4 per cent), dealing with areas in which the new technology could be utilized, such as the reporting and tabulation of elections' results, in certain government agencies, credit control, education, and commercial activities. The Congress wanted to insure that the benefits of the new technology were properly shared by various segments of the population and throughout the regions of the country.

3 Protection of privacy. A major concern of congressional action was the protection of individual privacy from the new technology. It should be remembered that the informatics policy in Brazil emerged in, and continued to be controlled by, the intelligence organizations of the military regime. Legislators were always aware of the actual and potential abuses of this technology by the intelligence and security communities. The fear that the new technology would be used by the military to harass and persecute political dissent in the country was paramount. Hence, many of the bills presented dealt with the need to define the type of information that could legally be collected about individuals, the need to divulge, the type of data base already available to the executive, and the type of information collected on individuals, the right of individuals to know what has been collected about them, and who would have access to legally collected information. This is not unlike those concerns embodied in the Freedom of Information Act in the United States. The Congress of Brazil introduced ten bills (16.9 per cent), dealing with the protection of privacy.

4 Policy. Another concern of bills introduced by the legislators, was the direction of public policy. Legislators, by and large, advocated a nationalistic policy, in favor of a market reserve and placing limitations on the activities of the multinational corporations in the field of informatics. Advocates of this policy in the executive were quick to

capitalize on this legislative support, both as an instrument to out-maneuver their domestic opponents in the executive who were advocating an open policy, or at least a relaxation of the market policy. More importantly, this legislative support was used to withstand tremendous pressure from the multinationals and their governments. In fact, the gradual involvement of the Congress in informatics policy came about, in large part, in response to divisions within the executive as to the proper policy to follow, and in order to enable those in the executive advocating nationalistic policies to withstand international pressures.

5 Control and accountability. A primary thrust of bills introduced by legislators in the informatics area, is the concern with control and accountability of executive policies and implementation of those policies. Several bills dealt with issues such as where informatics policies should be made, who should participate and how those who promulgate, elaborate, and implement those policies can be held accountable for their actions. The Congress introduced four bills on these issues (6.7 per cent). The final bill approved by the Congress included many of those concerns.

6 Educational and communication concerns. One of the main concerns of the Congress throughout this period, whether through bills, questions, seminars, requests for information, or even hearings and investigations, was that of educating itself and the public and building support for whatever policies were finally adopted. In analyzing the role of legislatures in public policy, this important function is often neglected.

CONCLUSIONS

As a collegial body representing diverse interests, Congress provided many channels of access for those groups, associations, executive agencies, and individuals who had an interest in the policy. In contrast to the restrictive nature of deliberation over the informatics policy characteristics of the executive, the Congress offered the various protagonists in the debate an open arena where the various policy preferences, including those of the executive, were aired. The openness of the process and the accessibility of the institution not only brought to the arena different actors but, more importantly, generated new information, with significant policy concerns and implications.

Furthermore, it is important to notice that once the Congress was allowed to participate, it did not limit itself to the concerns of the executive, but managed to incorporate its own concerns in the final bill that was approved. For its support of the executive on certain policy issues, the Congress managed to extract many concessions it considered to be priorities. This ability to extract concessions in return for support is a very important feature of all legislative institutions, quite often neglected in the literature.

Even weak legislatures, such as the Congress in Brazil during the period under discussion, once they are able to maneuver as actors in the arena of public policy, manage to extract important concessions from the executive. By providing legitimacy for policy decisions, legislatures often compromise the legitimacy of other actors in the policy process, and bring their own, and very distinct, perspective into the policy that is finally decided on.

The case of the computer industry policy in Brazil represents an instance of the relationship between a legislature and a military regime that is different from the relations between the two branches of government in established constitutional and democratic polities. Even though Brazil has a presidential system (Hypothesis 1), the constitutional structure that was peculiar to Brazil's authoritarian-bureaucratic regime severely limited Congress' policy role. However, the relatively decentralized characteristic of Brazilian authoritarianism, with its institutional interest groups and several diffuse power centers, had a very important role in allowing for Congress' participation, for no agreement on the policy was reached inside the executive branch.

Even if we cannot consider the Figueiredo administration as "open," in reference to Hypothesis 2, executive agencies interacted with congressional committees to acquire and retain support and legitimation. Various interest groups (the domestic manufacturers, the users, the multinational corporations, the professionals) were active in the later phase of the policy-making process, mostly after 1983, and the policy issue stimulated the formation of new interest groups, such as coalition for the defense of national technology (Hypothesis 9). Parliamentary policy participation did increase as interest groups became functionally specific and homogeneous (Hypothesis 6) and strongly disagreed among themselves (Hypothesis 8).

It was a new rather than an old issue (Hypothesis 15), and became very visible, as the various interest groups put their cases to public opinion through the press. It directly affected only a relatively small group in Brazilian society, but this group, or groups, made it their goal to impress on the general public the notion that informatics would increasingly affect their lives, as the country moved into a modern industrial economy.

We have centered our analysis on the formulation rather than the implementation stage of this new policy (Hypothesis 16). Although the final version of the Informatics Law included a "National Informatics and Automation Plan" to be periodically submitted to Congress, and enhanced the legislature's policy activity in the implementation stage, in fact, the Congress was most active in the gestation and enactment of the computer policy. As we saw from the series of proposals made during the previous periods, congressmen also acted during the formulation period.

The hypotheses related to party organization and strength and its effect on the policy role of parliaments (Hypotheses 10, 11, and 12) were clearly shown to be valid. As the strength of the opposition increased after the 1982 election, the policy role of the Brazilian Congress increased dramatically in the policy under study. Besides, parliamentary parties were weakly organized and fragmented, with members of the government party (such as Senator Roberto Campos) leading the fight against the government's own bill. The same is true in reference to the candidate-centered electoral system (Hypothesis 4).

The committee structure of both houses in Brazil is permanent and parallel to the executive organization chart (Hypothesis 13). Therefore, the fight for the market reserve policy was spearheaded by the Chamber of Deputies' Committees on Communication and Science and Technology, while opposition to the policy was raised mainly in the Senate's Economics Committee (chaired by Senator Campos), which examined the policy from the viewpoint of economic policy as a whole, instead of examining it from the standpoint of communications or science and technology.

The opponents of the market reserve policy argued for the economic benefits that a higher degree of integration with the world economy would bring, while its supporters argued for a higher degree of technological independence. The issue was highly ideological, opposing economic nationalism against free trade, with an unusual (in the Brazilian case) coalition building capability. It pitted military leaders against some of their former supporters in the business community, while it put left-wing politicians and nationalistic military officers in the same trenches.

In Brazil, the institutionalization of Congress, its organizational capability to act, affected the extent of its involvement in the policy process. It was not, however, a totally limiting factor. For instance, the existing committee structure was inadequate, in terms of information, staff, and other resources, to produce policy alternatives. A capability nevertheless existed, including trained staff who were knowledgeable in computers, and a working computer department. So, once the Congress was recognized as a locus of policy by interest groups and the press, the policy alternatives were developed by these groups and presented to members, committees, and congressional staff.

Congressional actions in this policy area cannot be considered typical, nor can the high level of executive disagreement that characterized this policy. However, in other policy areas, such as wage and foreign debt, Congress, mostly in the third period (1981–85) did play an extremely important role, including refusing to accept austerity policies agreed upon by the executive and the International Monetary Fund, as part of the handling of Brazil's debt crisis.

Once the Congress was allowed to participate, it did not limit itself to the concerns of the executive, but managed to incorporate its own views in the final policy. For its support of the executive on certain policy issues, the Congress managed to extract concessions in its own priority areas. This ability to extract concessions in return for support is an important feature of all legislative institutions, even weak legislatures, once they are able to maneuver themselves as policy actors. By providing legitimacy for policy decisions, legislatures often compromise other actors' legitimacy and bring their own distinct perspective into the policy process.

Notes

1 The role of legislatures in comparative perspective has been analyzed in a series of books published by the Duke University Press. Among these books see, Michael L. Mezey, *Comparative Legislatures* (Durham, N.C.: Duke University Press, 1979) and Joel Smith and Lloyd D. Musolf, eds., *Legislatures in Development: Dynamics of Change in New and Old States* (Durham, N.C.: Duke University Press, 1979).
2 Brazil's informatics policy has been the subject of many scholarly works. For a review of how the policy was formulated and an evaluation of the problems it has faced and the success it has achieved see the following: Emanuel Adler, *The Power of Ideology: The Quest for Technological Autonomy in Argentina and Brazil* (Berkeley: University of California Press, 1987); Peter Evans, "State, capital, and the transformation of dependence: the Brazilian computer case," *World Development*, 14: 7 (1966); SEI, *Transborder Data Flows and Brazil: Brazilian Case Study* (New York: United Nations Center on Transnational Corporations, 1983).

The Portuguese sources include: Silvia Helena, "A industria de computadores: evolucao das decisoes governmentais," *Revista de Administracao Publica*, 14: 4 (1980); Benakouche Rabah, ed., *A Questao da Informatica no Brasil* (São Paulo: Brasiliense, 1985); *A Informatica e a Nova Republica* (São Paulo: HUCITEC, 1985); Gilberto Paim, *Computador Faz Politica* (Rio de Janeiro: APEC, 1985).
3 Emanuel Adler, "Ideological guerrillas and the quest for technological autonomy: development of a domestic computer industry in Brazil," *International Organization*, 40: 3 (1985), 675.
4 David Fleischer, "Brazil at the crossroads: the elections of 1982 and 1985," in Paul Drake and Eduardo Silva, eds., *Elections and Democratization in Latin America, 1980–85* (San Diego: University of California Press, 1986), pp. 299–327.
5 See Steven W. Hughes and Kenneth J. Mijeski, *Politics and Public Policy in Latin America* (Boulder, Co.: Westview Press, 1984), p. 57.
6 Robert Wessen and David Fleischer, *Brazil in Transition* (New York: Praeger Publishers, 1983), p. 30.
7 *Constituicao da Republica Federativa do Brasil* and *Regimento Interno*, Senado Federal and Camara dos Deputados.

8 Abdo I. Baaklini, "Legislative reforms in the Brazilian Chamber of Deputies," in Abdo I. Baaklini and James J. Heaphey, eds., *Comparative Legislative Reforms and Innovations* (Albany: State University of New York, 1977), p. 241.

9 For a detailed study of the role of the developmental ideology on the newly created military regime, see Peter McDonough, *Power and Ideology in Brazil* (Princeton: Princeton University Press, 1981), introduction and *passim*.

10 Adler, *The Power of Ideology*.

11 In *The Power of Ideology*, p. 211, Adler states that the roots of the policy go as far back as the 1968 Strategic Development Plan.

12 Paulo B. Tigre, *Technology and Competition in the Brazilian Computer Industry* (New York: St, Martin's Press, 1983), p. 65.

13 The First National Development Plan (1972–74) mentioned the importance of technology transfer as a "precondition" for economic development "associated with a strong internal technology development." Quoted by F. Biato and M. A. Figueiredo, *Transferencia de Tecnologia no Brasil* (Brasilia: IPEA) (Serie Estudos para o Planejamento, no. 4), 1973, p. 2.

14 Decreto no. 70370, of April 5, 1972, published in *Diario Official*, April 5, 1972, p. 11.

15 Tigre, *Technology and Competition*, p. 42.

16 The council was composed of representatives of SEPLAN, the National Council of Scientific and Technological Development (CNPq), the Armed Forces General Staff (EMFA), and of the Ministries of Communications, Education and Culture, Finance, and Industry and Commerce.

17 In his recorded vote, one of CAPRE's plenary members stated that this was a "policy retreat that meant the loss of an important market share to MNCs, diminishing the market for Brazilian computer manufacturers, which is crucial to our autonomy." Quoted by Cristina Tavares and Milton Seligman. *Informatica, A Batalha do Seculo XXI* (Rio de Janeiro: Paz e Terra, 1984), p. 67.

18 Cotrim himself was openly critical of CAPRE's policy role, as shown in an interview to *O Globo* (May 12, 1979). In it he charged that "there is no informatics policy, as there is no organization that is charged with policy making and policy implementation."

19 Quoted by Tavares and Seligman, *Informatica*, p. 69.

20 Decreto no. 84067, October 8, 1979, published in *Diario Official*, October 9, 1979, p. 23.

21 Tavares and Seligman, *Informatica*, p. 69.

22 Adler, *Power and Ideology*, pp. 214–15.

23 Tavares and Seligman, *Informatica*, p. 73.

24 *Diario Official*, March 6, 1981.

25 Projeto de Lei no 5332, de 1981, published in *Diario do Congresso Nacional* (Secao I), October 23, 1981, p. 11120.

26 Adler, *Power and Ideology*, p. 217.

27 Jornal da Tarde, March 15, 1984 and *Gazeta Mercantil*, March 17, 1984.

28 Adler pp. 266–70.

29 Projeto de Lei no. 406, de 1983, published in *Diario do Congresso Nacional* (Secao I), April 13, 1983, p. 1573.

30 Projeto de Lei no. 1384, de 1983, published in *Diario do Congresso Nacional* (Secao I), June 21, 1983, p. 5538.
31 Projeto de Lei do Senado no. 48, de 1984, published in *Diario do Congresso Nacional* (Secao II), April 5, 1984, p. 0485.
32 Projeto de Lei do Senado no. 93, de 1984, published in *Diario do Congresso Nacional* (Secao II), June 8, 1984, p. 1832.
33 The seminar was held in the Senate from June 14 to 16, 1983. A 352-page volume (*Seminario de Informatica do Senado Federal*, Brasilia: CEGRAF, 1983) with the verbatim conferences and debates was published that same year by the Senate's printing office.
34 *Diario do Congresso Nacional* (Secao II), March 23, 1983, pp. 0506 and 0508; May 20, 1983, p. 1861; June 16, 1983, p. 2464; June 18, 1983, p. 2548; August 5, 1983, 3156; August 6, 1983, p. 3196; March 22, 1984, p. 0243; April 10, 1984, p. 0620 and April 11, 1983, p. 3308.
35 The depositions and debates were published verbatim by *Diario do Congresso Nacional* (Secao II), from May until September, 1984. The first deposition was given by National Security Council Secretary General Danilo Venturini, on April 4, and published by *Diario do Congresso Nacional* (Secao II), May 9, 1984, p. 1100.
36 The bill (PLN 10/84) was sent to Congress by the message no. 77/84 (*Diario Oficial*, August 27, 1984), and it finally became Law no. 7232, October 29, 1984, published in *Diario Oficial*. October 29, 1984, p. 15842.
37 *Jornal do Brasil*, May 29, 1984.
38 The committee's report-writer, Senator Virgilio Tavora, has since published a two-volume, 1,422 page book on the informatics bill (*Politica Nacional de Informatica*, Senado Federal, 1985) that covers all the legislative life of Law 7232, from the initial executive message to the final text. It also prints all the hearings conducted by his committee.
39 The substitute bill and Senator Tavora's report were published in *Diario do Congresso Nacional*, September 29, 1984, p. 2287.
40 The Ministry of Science and Technology (MCT) was created by Decree no. 911466, of March 15, 1985, published in *Diario Oficial*, March 15, 1985, p. 4708. Article 2 put under the authority of the new Ministry CONIN, SEI, the Technology Center for Informatics (CTI), the Informatics Export Districts, and the Special Fund for Informatics and Automation, both instruments that were also created by law no. 7232. The only other major government organization included in MCT's jurisdication was CNPq, the National Council for Scientific and Technological Development, which was already in operation under the Secretary of Planning. A former Federal Deputy from Maranhao State, Renato Archer, was chosen by Tancredo Neves as the first Science and Technology Minister.
41 The new constitution, promulgated in October 1988, incorporated many of the policy recommendations suggested by the Congress in the areas of labor, oversight, and accountability, economic and scientific policies as permanent articles, defining Brazil's priorities and approaches in those areas.

7

Electronics policy and the Indian parliament

R. B. JAIN

This chapter examines the actions of the Indian parliament in policy relating to the electronics industry, in order to test some of the hypotheses raised in the opening chapter about the factors affecting legislative involvement in policy processes. India inherited the British parliamentary system upon its early postwar independence. In the world's most populous democracy, the prime minister is selected as the result of parliamentary elections in which the Congress Party usually holds a sizeable majority. As leader of the party of the government, the prime minister effectively controls parliament and manages the cabinet system. Having created the government, parliament reviews, questions, and debates the government and its policies. While parliament could unseat the government, it never has; while parliament could defeat a major government policy, it never has.

This chapter will examine what parliament has done over the years on the development and review of policy towards the electronics industry in India. As a parliamentary system within a Third World but rapidly developing country, India is particularly relevant to several of the hypotheses concerning the sources of parliamentary activity in the policy process. The impact of the parliamentary system itself is evident, as are the combined influences of a single party majority and the British style of non-specialized parliamentary committees. The Indian experience illustrates how a parliament can be intermittently active on a policy topic, mainly in the implementation rather than policy initiation stages.

This chapter will first review the policy process in India, and then turn to electronics policy. The development of an electronics policy over the years will be traced within the executive, and then we will consider the several ways by which parliament has examined and questioned those policies.

In a parliamentary form of government, as in India, the functions of the legislative body are primarily to legislate, advise, criticise, and ventilate public grievances. The executive, for the most part, proposes the legislation and policies necessary for the implementation of the societal objectives, and the parliament gives it its imprimatur, after deliberations and debates often suggesting modifications.

Within the parliament in India, legislative control over policy matters starts from the debate on the president's address, which generally outlines the policy proposals of the government of the day. Subsequently, through the use of question hour, debate over proposed legislation, budgeting procedures, and the various standing and permanent committees, parliament can and does exercise influence over policy activities of the government.

We will later examine the use of the floor in both debates and in question time on electronics policy, and then review actions by the three major financial committees of the parliament.

Public megapolicies generally begin with the political party which comes into power through its election manifestoes. The mandate that a party receives from the people at the polls is an endorsement of such policy perspectives. It is these policy objectives that the cabinet seeks to pursue through parliamentary approval. Government thus takes decisions on the basis of what "the party decides first".[1]

In the executive branch of government, policies are given concrete shape and direction by the prime minister and cabinet. They are assisted in this function by the various standing committees of the cabinet, and the prime minister's Secretariat of his personal advisors. Although the prime minister's Secretariat does not directly make any original proposals in policy matters, it has a great influence in moulding these by preparation of the briefs and analysis for the decision of the prime minister.

The interplay between the prime minister and his cabinet colleagues, the use of committee structure in the cabinet, and interaction between the staff of the cabinet Secretariat, prime minister's Secretariat and the ministerial Secretariat determines the final outcome of public policies through the executive branch of the government. This interplay depends to a great extent on the personal style of the prime minister and the political strength of his party.

Apart from these agencies, public policy development in India is also influenced by the policy planning cells established in several key ministries of the government, for example Agriculture and Foreign Affairs. In practice, these units have functioned more as research than as policy-making units as originally intended. In addition to these cells, the prime minister creates a number of non-governmental advisory committees from time to time to seek advice on national policy issues. The Economic Policy Advisory Committee, composed of some well-known economists in the country, is one of the most influential of such bodies. The prime minister is known to have sought advice from it as well as from various other industrial groups on many policy issues.

Other sources of major policy thought in the Indian political system are the various agencies of the bureaucracy, particularly the Planning Commission, which are engaged in a continuous process of discussion on micropolicy issues and the subsequent policy steps for their implementation.

In sum, the parliamentary system of India places policy initiative in the political party and cabinet, both under the leadership of the prime minister. The policy development process is confined to the ministries and cabinet, rather than being open to outside and parliamentary influences. Once a policy is presented to parliament, its party majority will support that proposal. Through floor debate and committee review, however, parliament is able to examine and question policy, especially in its implementation.

The experience of the Indian parliament in electronics policy illustrates hypotheses concerning the parliamentary system, the central direction of party and government, and the structure of parliamentary committees. This chapter will show that the activities of parliament were largely expressed in the implementation stage on an issue which combined technology with social benefits.

DEVELOPMENT OF ELECTRONICS POLICY: THE EXECUTIVE'S INITIATIVES

The growth of the electronics industry in India and the development of policy on this topic have been due largely to the initiatives taken by the executive. Parliamentary activity has largely been in reaction to executive-centered initiatives.

The Bhabha Commission

It was through a resolution of the Department of Atomic Energy, of August 12, 1963, that for the first time an electronics committee was appointed under the chairmanship of Homi J. Bhabha, chairman, Atomic Energy Commission. Its charge was to review the entire field of electronic components and equipment with regard to research, development, and production, and to advise the government on the quickest and most economical way of making the country self-sufficient in this field.[2] Since then, there have been various pronouncements on electronics industry and policy by the government until the latest liberalisation of electronics policy announced by the new prime minister, Rajiv Gandhi in March 1985.

As a part of Bhabha Committee implementation process, a National Conference on Electronics was held at Bombay from March 24 to 28, 1970. Reviewing the developments in the electronics industry since the publication of the Bhabha Committee Report in 1966, the conference observed that while the electronics industry in the entertainment field had developed substantially progress in other fields was quite small. In defence electronics, progress was even less than in communication electronics. Research, development, and production activities in the country were uncoordinated and widely dispersed under various agencies. In both defence electronics and communications there was still much dependence on foreign know-how and imports.

The conference noted that promotion of an industry in a ministerial government required committing substantial executive resources to securing effective inter-ministerial action. The conference, therefore, suggested that it would appear best to replace the Electronics Committee by a policy-making and implementing body set up under an act of parliament, or as a consequence of such an act.[3]

The Electronics Commission and The Department of Electronics

Recognizing the importance of developing an integrated and self-reliant electronics industry in the country, the Indian government created a separate Department of Electronics in 1970. In 1971, the government also formed the Electronics Commission, under the chairmanship of Professor M. G. K. Menon, who was then also the secretary of the Indian government in the Department of Electronics. Parliament has been involved mainly with these two bodies in discussions about electronics policy.

The Electronics Commission was charged with full responsibility to review the entire field of electronics with regard to research, development, and industrial operations. It had full authority to formulate policies in this field and to direct implementation, on sound technical and economic principles, of all measures, both promotional and regulatory, that is necessary for the country to attain self-reliance in the shortest possible time and in the best possible manner.[4]

Electronics policy strategies in 1985

The installation of Rajiv Gandhi's government in January 1985 ushered in a new era in the development of the electronics industry in India.

Immediately, the new prime minister told the Electronics Commission
that the government was determined to see that "India does not miss the
electronics revolution".[5] The government expected the Electronics
Commission to put India on the electronics map in the world with the
production of at least Rs 1,000,000 millions worth of electronics goods in
the next five years which is supposed to generate employment for 10
million people and offer an enormous potential for improving the quality
and skills of jobs all around.

To achieve these goals, the government on March 21, 1985 announced
a new electronics policy. The most important core measures of the new
policy are: first, the decision to throw open to large firms a number of
product lines, primarily in consumer electronics, which have hitherto been
reserved for the small and unorganised sector. The second is the extension
of exemption from the MRTP Act to cover more components and finished
systems. The third most important measure concerns the purchase of
equity in high-technology-based components and materials manufacture,
which is meant to attract know-how and capital to fields in which the
country has not been able to invest sufficiently in R & D. The fourth
measure, which did not receive universal acclaim, was the decision of the
government stipulating that the state would purchase video cassette
recorder/player technology as well as micro-ovens technology.

The liberalization of the electronics policy by the government had been
received with mixed reactions. While the big industrialists welcomed the
government policy, the small industrialists were disheartened since the
kind of protection that they had enjoyed so far had been withdrawn with
the announcement of this policy.[6]

The executive role in the formulation of policies in relation to a very
technical and strategically significant industry is almost total. It is the
executive, not the legislature, which exercises initiative in the development
of policies in such sophisticated technical areas. We will examine the
extent and the manner in which the parliament in India has been able to
influence the development of electronics policy within these limitations.

PARLIAMENT AND ELECTRONICS POLICY: DEBATES AND QUESTIONS

Parliament's interest in electronics policy is manifested through both
questions and debates concerning the Electronics Department and its
related organizations, and also by examining their demands for grants.
Parliament has also acted on the reports of three standing committees of

parliament, namely, the Estimates Committee, the Public Accounts Committee, and, most importantly, the Committee on Public Undertakings. Committee reports will be reviewed in the following section, while in this section, first the debates and then parliamentary questions on the floor will be considered.

Parliamentary debates

There have been a number of occasions when some of the issues concerning electronic policy have come under discussion on the floor of the parliament. We use a sample analysis of the debates in the Lok Sabha – the lower and popular house – between 1971 and 1976 and between 1980 and 1982 to assess the extent of deliberations by the legislators on the development of the electronic industry and electronic policy.

During the period between 1971 and 1976, most of the relevant debates in the Lok Sabha centered around the work of the Electronic Commission and the Electronic Corporation of India. Discussions centered on issues as wide and technical as the achievement of self-sufficiency in electronics, collaboration with foreign concerns, development of the electronic industry during the Fifth Plan period, import facilities, and the crisis in electronic industries in various states in India.[7]

In the Lok Sabha debates between 1980 and 1982, the concern of the legislators had moved from the mere production of electronic goods to the development of electronic technology in India. Legislators seemed to have become more concerned with the modern technological aspects of the electronic industry. The debates show the growing concern of the parliamentarians on the research and development of electronic technology, incentives to electronic industries, manufacture of highly sophisticated equipment, establishment of suitable institutional arrangements for electronic technology development, export promotion, and strategies for increasing productive capacity of the various electronic goods.

The legislators in general felt satisfied in leaving the details of policy development in a highly technologically complex field of electronic industry in the hands of the executive agencies. They were concerned only with prescribing or suggesting certain new policy directions while leaving them to be further developed and formulated by the executive agencies.

Thus it appears that in a high technologically complex issue, parliamentarians seem to vest great confidence in the technical executive agencies, which perhaps may be true in most other legislatures of the world as well. Many of the legislators, being laymen, are not competent to judge technical policy issues in all their ramifications and implications.

This observation leads to the suggestion that the policy activity of parliaments is low on questions of a technical and complex nature.[8]

Questions in the Lok Sabha

On the thousands of questions raised annually in the Lok Sabha, some 96 concerned electronics industry issues over the three-year period 1980–82 (Table 7.1). Of that total, 72 (or 75 percent) related to the policy issues in respect of the electronic industry, which is a good indicator of the members' concern about electronic policy development; while 25 percent of the questions related to the implementation and taxation aspects of the policy. The members' concern over policy issues in the electronic industry seems to have been exacerbated by the importance and fast development in electronic technology, which is felt practically in the every day life of the people. Members' questions may also be indicative of the pressures brought from indigenous industrialists on the members of the parliament seeking protection for their industrial establishments against competition by multinational corporations.

PARLIAMENTARY COMMITTEES AND ELECTRONICS POLICY

Electronics policy has at various times come under scrutiny by the three important financial committees of the Indian parliament, namely, the Estimates Committee, the Public Accounts Committee, and the Committee on Public Undertakings. These committees have given some very detailed suggestions affecting the development of the electronics industry in this country.

In keeping with its Westminster tradition, the Indian parliament has three major financially oriented committees which do not parallel the structure of administrative agencies, but which cover them all. Though each committee issues thirty to forty reports annually, it is not possible for the committees to review any one agency or any one policy topic very often. As a result, only four committee reports have examined electronics policy within the time period of this study. Furthermore, the committees are limited to questions of economy and efficiency, rather than encouraged to examine basic policy.

All three committees have members in proportion to party size in the chamber. Thus all three have a majority from the government party, though two of the three are chaired by opposition members.

Of these three finance and efficiency committees, the Committee on Public Undertakings is most directly concerned with the government's electronics policy because that policy is in part expressed through

Table 7.1 *Questions raised in parliament on electronics industry in India, 1980–1982*

Years	Total number of questions	Policy matters	Operation/ Functioning of electronic industry	Questions relating to taxation, import, export, etc.
1980	13	7	6	—
1981	35	25	4	6
1982	48	40	6	2
Total	96	72	16	8

Source: Lok Sabha Debates.

Table 7.2 *Government actions on recommendations of committees of Indian Lok Sabha on electronic policy*

Recommendations	Committee Reports		
	Estimates Committee 1973–74	CPU[a] Report 33 1981–82	CPU[a] Report 46 1982–83
Accepted by government	64	24	9
Dropped by Committee	5	2	—
No government reply	5	—	1
Government reply awaited	9	1	1
Total	83	27	11

[a] = Committee on Public Undertakings
Sources: India, Estimates Committee, *66th Report on Department of Electronics,* 5th Lok Sabha (1973–74); *Action Taken Report on Department of Electronics,* 5th Lok Sabha, 85th Report, 1975–76 (October 1975).

governmental corporations. Of these three committees, the Public Accounts Committee has examined electronics policy the least because its main attention is to whole ministries rather than to more specific activities.

Estimates Committee

The Estimates Committee of the Indian Lok Sabha examined the activities of the Department of Electronics during 1973–74 in its 66th Report of the 5th Lok Sabha on April 30, 1974. The committee made some very detailed analyses of the existing status of the electronics industry and the work of the Electronics Commission. Amongst the various recommendations made by the Estimates Committee, some related to the overall growth and development of the electronics industry.

In its report, the committee noted that there has been steady growth in the electronics industry in India since the Bhabha Committee made its recommendation in 1966 as discussed above. In view of the fact that the industry occupied a key position in the development of modern science and technology, the committee welcomed the constitution of the Electronic Commission and the Department of Electronics.

In a general survey, the committee recognized that developmental work had been carried out in public sector undertakings, such as Bharat Electronics Limited, Indian Telephone Industries, Satellite Communication etc., but felt that there had been an insufficient programme in defence electronics. It therefore recommended that it was of urgent importance that the next few years were devoted towards development and production of sophisticated instruments in this strategic field.

The committee also recommended that the government should review at the highest level the question of placing units responsible for manufacturing electronics under the Department of Electronics. The committee felt that for the electronics industry to develop in an integrated manner, it was essential to have system groups in every major user department like Defence, Atomic Energy, Space, Communications, and Steel, and Railways.

The committee also suggested that those who were entrusted with the responsibility of developing industrial electronics should publicise their achievement and availability of equipment to industrialists. The committee welcomed the proposal for setting up an Electronic Trade and Technology Development Corporation to ensure timely availability of the special grade material suitable for the electronics industry. The committee desired the government to consult with trade and industry while setting up this corporation, so as to have the benefit of their views and experience.

The committee was disappointed to note that India's position in world export trade in electronics was very low. In the total world export trade in electronics of US $5 billion in value, India's share was only about US $8 million. It was suggested that a working group should be established to watch for import and revenue bottlenecks, if any, in the achievement of export targets.[9]

The government furnished replies indicating the action it had taken on the recommendations contained in the report on January 6, 1975. The replies were then examined by Study Group 'F' of the Estimates

Committee at its sitting held on September 3, 1975, and the Draft Action Taken Report of the group was adopted by the committee on September 10, 1975.[10]

Out of 83 recommendations made in the original report, 64 recommendations, i.e., about 77 percent, were accepted by the government (see Table 7.2). The committee did not desire to pursue 5 out of the total recommendations made (i.e., about 6 percent), for the government's reply was satisfactory. The replies of the government to 5 recommendations, i.e. about 6 percent, were not accepted by the committee. Final replies of government in respect of 9 recommendations, i.e., 11 percent, were still awaited.

Most of the recommendations of the Estimates Committee accepted by the government concerned policy issues relating to the growth of the electronics industry. However, on some policy issues, the committee reiterated its earlier stand despite the government's reply.

For example, in its earlier report, the committee had stressed that particular emphasis had to be laid by the government on the development of backward areas outside the metropolitan and industrial cities. Incentives and concessions were needed for setting up industries particularly in small-scale sectors in those areas in order to narrow regional imbalances. The committee had also suggested that the government should take a positive initiative in the development of the electronics industry in such areas by setting up public sector units in electronics to encourage ancillary industries to grow around them.

In its Action Taken Report, the committee agreed with the observations for the department that providing incentives for the growth of industry in the backward areas in the country was a policy matter to be handled by the Ministry of Industrial Development in consultation with the Planning Commission and the Ministry of Finance and to be implemented through state governments. They also agreed that the location of public sector undertakings was to be determined largely by technoeconomic considerations.

However, reiterating the view expressed by the committee in its original report, it was for the Department of Electronics, as the nodal department in the field of electronics, to take a positive initiative in setting up public sector undertakings in such areas, subject, of course, to the minimum technology requirements in the setting up of such units.

The committee attached the greatest importance to the implementation of the recommendations accepted by the government. It urged the government to keep a close watch to insure expeditious implementation of the recommendations accepted by them. In cases where it was not possible to implement the recommendations in letter and spirit for any reason, it suggested that the matter should be reported in time with reasons for non-implementation.[11] The Estimates Committee has not considered matters relating to electronics policy again since then.

Public Accounts Committee

The Public Accounts Committee also once discussed certain aspects of electronics policy in its reports in 1975–76. However, its deliberations on electronic policy were only peripheral, for it was more concerned with the economic and social implications of computerization in government departments.

The committee's report noted the conflicting views regarding factors motivating the introduction of computers and other data processing equipment in various organizations. A reconciliation between these divergent views was perhaps a difficult task, particularly when the subject of computerization itself is a complex one, often even shrouded in an aura of supra-technological mystery.

In evaluating the need for computerization, the committee felt that it would be wrong to ignore the social cost of computerization; i.e., in an economy where the problem of unemployment is very large-scale and of serious proportions, the use of computers may not be always desirable and expedient.

The committee recommended that more precise policy and objective criteria for computerization in government departments be evolved soon by the Department of Electronics. The committee stressed that the government should issue clear guidelines to the effect that all future requirements for computers, data processing equipment, etc., should first be examined in the Department of Electronics with reference to the stipulated criteria.

The committee recommended that the government should draw a plan outlining the general strategy for Indian self-reliance in computers and in particular the manner in which it was proposed to meet the anticipated large requirements of mini-computers. It also urged the Department of Electronics to work out the requirements of technical personnel to watch the manufacturing programme envisaged for the computer industry during fifth and sixth plan periods.[12]

In its Action Taken Report on the 221st Report discussed above, the Public Accounts Committee appreciated the promptness with which the Department of Electronics has taken action on the various recommendations and objections made by the committee.

The committee felt satisfied that the Department of Electronics was by and large in agreement with the findings of the committee in regard to the loopholes which were prevalent in the system of hire, purchase, and utilization of computers and other data processing equipment.

While noting the steps taken by the government for creating the necessary infra-structure for the production of computers as also creating the right climate for the export of India-made computers, the committee urged that a White Paper outlining government policy and performance in the field of computerization should be presented to the parliament as early as possible.

The Public Accounts Committee did make some suggestions on policy, but it was left entirely to government initiative to incorporate those ideas in its overall policy development. Except for the review of the implementation of its own suggestions through the Action Taken Report, the committee could do little but to reiterate its stand, and urge the government to take whatever action was possible in promoting the growth of the electronics industry. The impact of the Public Accounts Committee has been at best a marginal one in the development of electronics policy.

Committee on Public Undertakings

The Committee on Public Undertakings (CPU) of the Indian parliament, which examines various public sector enterprises, has also been involved in the discussion of electronic policy while evaluating the functioning of the Electronics Corporation of India Ltd (1980–81), and the Electronics Trade and Technology Development Corporation Ltd (1981–82). The CPU not only considered and assessed the profits and losses of these agencies, but has also made recommendations relating to the revamping of unprofitable divisions and products, research and development, working capital management, production and sales, and pricing and control systems including the pricing policy of these agencies.

One of the specific features of the review by the CPU has been its analysis of the development of government policy towards the electronics industry. In this context, the committee discussed at length the licensing and import policy of the government in relation to industrial licensing of the manufacture of TV picture tubes, computers, import of "know-how" and foreign collaboration arrangements.[13] The committee emphasized the frequent uncertainty and indecisiveness of government policies with regard to the development of the electronics industry. For example, it noted:[14]

Frequent changes in policy and uncertainties can seriously hamper the progress of indigenous industry. The committee feel that the matter deserves immediate consideration... The committee are anxious to obviate any kind of hardship unwittingly caused to indigenous industry by the operation of economic and fiscal policies of government. In order that this may be ensured there should be a periodic and well-coordinated review of policies.

Similarly in respect of the performance of the Electronics Trade and Technology Development Corporation Ltd., the committee summarised its findings.[15]

The company has failed to achieve any significant growth in its 8 years of existence. Its organisation and management is weak and the management lacks cohesiveness... In the areas of exports and imports, it has at best projected an image of a poor middleman. Its financial management (especially cost, credit and inventory control) is unsatisfactory. The working results for the year 1980–81 have disclosed considerable losses. The committee trust that on the basis of this report the objectives and obligations of the company will be redefined and spelt out clearly, the policies and programmers reoriented and the management revamped so as to make the company an effective instrument of ensuring growth of electronics industry in the country.

Many of the detailed recommendations made by the CPU were accepted by the government. The acceptance ratio of recommendations in both these reports was 88.9 percent and 81.8 percent respectively (Table 7.2). Only in 3.7 percent and 9.1 percent of cases respectively, the government could not give any satisfactory reply, while only in 9.1 percent cases on the Action Taken Report of the ETTDC, there was a difference of opinion between the committee and the government, and, consequently, it did not feel satisfied with the explanation of the government on these few issues.

The above brief review of the three important parliamentary committees' involvement with electronics policy supports several of the hypotheses in chapter 1 concerning committees. Since the committees in India do not parallel the structure of administrative agencies but, rather, cross-cut the administrative structure, these committees are not able to keep a continuous watch over the agencies of the government concerned with any particular matter. Their evaluation of policies in any particular area is only *ad hoc* and intermittent.

THE INDIAN PARLIAMENT AND ELECTRONIC POLICY
DEVELOPMENT

This survey of the legislature's involvement in electronics policy indicates certain trends in executive accountability to the legislature in public policies, and provides a basis to test the hypotheses raised in chapter 1 in attempting to build a general model of legislative impact on policy development.

Stages of policy development

The foregoing analysis of the executive's initiative and the parliament's involvement in a particular policy indicates the specific role of the Indian parliament in the various stages of policy development.

In the gestation stage of policy the parliament as a whole has no discernible role in the preparation of policy-action proposals. The above survey of the executive's initiatives and role in the development of electronic policy clearly illustrates the dominance of political and administrative leadership of this topic. In a highly technical and sophisticated field, which is rapidly changing, it is always the voice of the experts that counts in policy development. Even when some of the plans formulated by specific administrative institutions come before the parliament, it is the "specialist" on the administrative staff who has the upper hand in defining potential future problems, rather than the members of the legislature. In the successive stages of policy formulation, however, the consensus on various policy issues is first achieved by the political parties in their own forums and is then vetted by the various cabinet committees assisted by the senior civil servants.

It is in the third stage, i.e., in policy deliberation and adoption, that the parliament as a whole and the members in their individual capacity can and do make significant contributions to the ultimate policy outcomes. The impact of such deliberation at times is only marginal, however, depending upon the ruling party's strength, the position of other parties, and the attitude of the leader of the house. The Indian parliament in this respect has been more or less moderate rather than either "strong" or "weak".

The Indian parliament's capacity to influence the implementation of public policy has been much more evident that in other stages of policy development. The various devices of parliamentary control existing in the Indian parliamentary system, such as the question hour and reviews by various committees, have favored an effective role of the parliament in the implementation of public policies.

The Indian parliament has hardly any noticeable role in the gestation of policy; it is more active at the stage of implementation. One possible explanation can be that the general public is more affected by the way policy is implemented. Therefore, members of parliament become more active and concerned, when the implementation of particular policies creates inequalities in the distribution of benefits or resources within the different segments of the population or affects particular interest groups in different ways. Members then have an opportunity to espouse regional or particular causes on the floor of the house, and to put the government on the defensive.

Electronics industry policy in India illustrates a technically complex issue, which discourages parliamentary activity, but one which also affects the distribution of benefits flowing to every region and constituency, and which stimulates parliamentary awareness and activity. Parliamentary concern for both policy and distribution of benefits has concentrated on the implementation of electronics policy, rather than on earlier stages of the policy cycle.

Institutionalization

The Indian parliament has been more active in criticising specific government policy issues than in framing new policy proposals. The existence of a single dominant party system in parliament has precluded detailed critical discussion on policy issues in the party forums within the parliament, consistent with the hypothesis. However, in the Indian context, the hypothesis that the policy activities of parliament are greater if the parliamentary parties are weakly organized or fragmented, is not supported. The policy activities of the parliament in India have not increased as a result of the weakness of the parties.

In the Indian parliament, the committees more than the parties have been active in all stages of policy development in electronics. While parties have been mainly active in the gestation stage of electronic policy by spelling out their respective stands in their election manifestoes, the committees of the Indian parliament, particularly the Estimates Committee and the Committee on Public Undertakings, have been quite active. The committees have questioned not only various aspects of the basic policy involving the growth of the electronics industry, but also the direction of its growth. However, it is questionable that these committees have made any real modification in the basic policy of the government in electronics.[16]

The Indian parliament is structured to create and support a government. That attribute discourages policy activity by parliament. Its committees, however, are structured to examine the implementation of policy. Consistent with the hypothesis, the cross-agency structure of the committees directs and limits their attention to implementation, and away from other stages of the policy cycle.

The environmental factors

The environmental factors in India seem to have a more important effect in conditioning parliament's involvement in policy-making. The hypothesis that the policy activities of legislatures is greater in presidential than in prime-ministerial systems is proved by the Indian experience.

In enforcing accountability, it is clear that, in India, parliament does possess the institutional capacity to make the executive answerable to it. Such a capacity of parliament, however, hinges upon various external circumstances including the position and personality of the chief executive, and the constitutional system. Within the constitutional framework, the various parliamentary procedures in India have been designed to give sufficient opportunities to the members of parliament not only to influence the processes of policy development, but at times also to initiate policy proposals.

However, the impact of all these processes is greatly hampered by certain extra-constitutional factors, chief among them being: (a) the absolute party majorities of the governments in the central legislature; (b) the gradual decline in the stature of men who constituted successive parliaments in comparison to those which followed after independence;[17] and (c) the attitude of the majority leader toward the opposition.[18] If the opposition is not able to rise above the level of rabble rousers, and is not behaving in a responsible manner, it is because of the constant denigration of the opposition by all the successive leaders of the ruling party after 1967.

Before that year, although the ruling party under Nehru had an overwhelming majority and the number of opposition members was much smaller, the opposition members took their role seriously and consequently raised the standard of debates in parliament and sufficiently influenced the policy processes. Nehru created an impression that the role of opposition was relevant. He was a serious parliamentarian who attended every session to the last minute and listened to every speech made in the house.[19] Dissidence even within the ruling party was recognised. There were many instances when ruling party members by their independent stand on various issues could embarrass even Nehru who nevertheless respected them for their honesty and courage. It is difficult to say how many of the ruling party members today have the courage to demand an explanation from the leader of the majority party about the failure of the government in any policy area.

The hypotheses that centralized direction by either party or government diminishes parliamentary policy activity are fully supported by the experience of the Indian parliament on electronics policy. India also suggests that factors of personal qualifications of members and the attitudes of the leadership are important in leading to centralized control over parliament.

Summary

The general conclusion that one can draw about the Indian parliament's capacity to influence public policy and hold the executive accountable is that given the environmental constraints, parliament's competence to make or initiate policy measures is extremely limited irrespective of the content of policy. While the capacity of the Indian parliament to influence defense in scientific and technical areas is very little indeed, it has also had only a marginal impact in most socioeconomic or domestic affairs.

While the Indian parliament has shown its capacity and willingness to modify various government policy proposals coming before it for discussion and approval, it has not been in a position to reject outright a policy proposal. Furthermore, it seems that the parliament in India has been most active in enforcing the executive's accountability to itself, despite the aberrations of an emergency (1975–77) and the continued existence of one-party rule in the legislature. In the final analysis, it thus seems more appropriate to suggest that in India the parliament has performed a more active role as "policy influencer" than either as "policy maker" or as "policy transformer".

Notes

1. See the Ruling of the Speaker, *Lok Sabha Debates*, 3rd Lok Sabha, September 12, 1963, col. 5793.
2. See Resolution No. 19/3/63 – Tech. II dated 12 August 1963 and consequent Report of the Bhabha Committee on Electronics, *Electronics in India* (Bombay: Electronics Commission, Government of India, 1966, p. 3.
3. For details see, Government of India, Electronics Commission, *Perspective Report on Electronics in India*, New Delhi, June 1975, pp. 21–33.
4. Ibid., pp. 39–42.
5. *The Hindustan Times*, February 6, 1985.
6. See *India Today*, April 15, 1985, pp. 122–23.
7. Taken from *Lok Sabha Debates* for years indicated in text.
8. Olson and Mezey, ch. 1, this vol.
9. India, Estimates Committee, *66th Report on Department of Electronics* , 5th Lok Sabha (1973–74).
10. As a follow-up of the implementation of its recommendations, the Estimates Committee constitutes various study groups from time to time to examine in depth the position of the government on those issues. The report of the study group is then considered by the committee as a whole.
11. India, Estimates Committee, *Action Taken Report on Department of Electronics*, 5th Lok Sabha, 85th Report, 1975–76 (October 1975), pp. 3–4.
12. India, Public Accounts Committee, *221st Report on Computerisation in Government Departments* (Department of Electronics), 5th Lok Sabha, New Delhi, Parliament Secretariat, 1975–76.
13. See India, Committee on Public Undertakings, *19th Report on Electronics Corporation of India Ltd.* Department of Atomic Energy, 7th Lok Sabha, CPU no. 428, New Delhi, Lok Sabha Secretariat, April 1985, pp. 40–59.
14. Ibid., p. 59.
15. Ibid.
16. Olson and Mezey, ch. 1, this vol.
17. For a detailed discussion of the impact of various parliamentary committees on the implementation of public policies, see R. B. Jain, *The Indian Parliament: Innovations, Reform and Development* (Calcutta: Minerva Associates, 1976).
18. For a detailed discussion of this aspect, see my paper on "Parliament, policy

and regime support in India: the impact of the crisis", a paper presented at the Duke–UNCG Conference on Parliaments, Policy, and Regime Support, Duke University, December 2–5, 1982.

19. A veteran parliamentarian, Madhu Limaye, has charged that the attitude of the then leadership of the ruling party has alternated between two sentiments of the former prime minister's (Mrs. Indira Gandhi) approach to parliament. "When the opposition is strong as in 1967–72, she is haunted and when it is weak, she has total contempt for parliament. While Nehru had greater respect for parliament and for the opposition, Mrs. Gandhi is paranoid." As quoted by P. P. Balachandran, "Indian parliament: the twilight era," in *Probe India*, December 1981, p. 10.

20. Ibid., pp. 11–12.

8

The Polish parliament and labor legislation during Solidarity[1]

DAVID S. MASON

Parliaments in communist party states are usually treated in Western literature as "rubber stamp" institutions that simply approve policies made elsewhere. As such, these bodies do not perform functions of interest articulation, representation, or policy-making that are characteristic of many Western legislatures. This assessment, however, oversimplifies the issue and obscures important differences in the legislatures of the various communist states. It also diverts attention from the dynamics of legislative authority in these states, and the extent to which the relationship between legislatures and other political institutions reflects broader aspects of the political system.

Even before 1980, the Polish parliament (Sejm) was, along with that of Yugoslavia, the most active and autonomous of East European legislatures. During the Solidarity era the role of the Sejm was enhanced even further. The period from August 1980 to December 1981 was the most open and fluid era in Poland's postwar history, and, during this time, virtually every political institution was reformed or revitalized. The Sejm was one of the few institutions that did not undergo substantial change in *composition*, since there were no new elections during this period, but it did take on a more active and, at times, obstreperous role.

This chapter examines the evolution of the Sejm from 1980 to 1983, focusing on the role of the Sejm in the critical area of labor legislation. During 1980 and 1981, a new trade union bill and legislation on enterprise self-management were two of the major issues that confronted both the regime and Solidarity. The Sejm came to play an important role in the evolution of these two pieces of legislation. The bill on self-management was enacted during this period, in October 1981, after considerable work by the Sejm. The new trade union legislation was not finally enacted until October 1982, almost a year into martial law. This was a very different environment, and the Sejm's role was much reduced over 1981. All of this will lead to a consideration of the role of the Sejm in the Polish political system, and a comparison of this role to those in other countries, East and West.

THE ROLE OF THE SEJM IN POLAND

The Sejm is a unicameral legislative body consisting of 460 deputies elected in direct elections every three to five years. Deputies of the ruling Polish United Workers' Party (the communist party, PUWP) have always constituted a majority of the assembly, typically holding about 55 percent of the seats. The remaining seats are divided among the PUWP's "satellite" parties, the United Peasant Party (113 seats in the 1980 elections) and the Democratic Party (37 seats), and some non-party members (49 in 1980; 74 in the 1985 elections). This last group includes representatives of three Catholic groups,[2] none of which, however, are supported or recognized by the hierarchy of the Catholic Church.

All of the Sejm deputies have permanent jobs elsewhere, and Sejm sessions are one to three-day affairs every month or two. Between parliamentary sessions, legislative authority is exercised by the Council of State, which is elected by the Sejm. Most legislation is introduced by the Council of State or by the Council of Ministers, the executive organ of the government, although since 1971 Sejm committees may also initiate legislation. All legislation passes through at least one of the twenty-five permanent committees, including the important Committee on Legislation (Komisja Prac Ustawodawczych), which reviews the technical and legal aspects of the bills. In recent years especially, two or more of the relevant committees will often constitute joint subcommittees to deliberate on a bill. Committees sometimes substantially revise legislation before it is presented to the plenary session for approval.[3]

After the introduction of martial law in December 1981, the regime constituted two "advisory" bodies that were attached to the Sejm, presumably in an effort to add legitimacy and credibility to that body. The Socio-Economic Council (Rada Społeczno-Gospodarcza) consists of ninety-five representatives of large enterprises and other official organizations. The Sejm Advisory Council (Zespół Doradców Sejmowych) consists of academic experts and other specialists. Both are empowered to offer advice and formal opinions on legislation and other matters before the Sejm.

Much of the Western literature on communist parliaments has simply dismissed them as "rubber stamps" that have no real legislative or representational functions, but rather serve only ceremonial or propagandistic functions. Only in the last decade have some area specialists gone beyond this formulation, sometimes arguing that legislatures in some communist countries are gaining in importance, and perhaps becoming more functional as articulators of popular interests or demands.[4] In the first book-length work on the role of communist legislatures, Dan Nelson (1982:8) suggests that while such legislatures may not provide representation in the Western sense of either "trustee" or "delegate," they may perform "a mediating function, connecting the citizenry to government." In the same volume, Stephen White identifies four main roles of communist legislatures: (1) to help legitimize the government; (2) to provide a means of societal integration and nation-building; (3) to play a "not negligible" role in the policy-making process (through refining and amending legislation); and (4) to monitor and supervise the work of government bodies. The first function is performed by all communist legislatures. The second pertains primarily to multinational states such as Yugoslavia and the Soviet Union. The third and fourth are performed to various degrees depending on the state. The Yugoslav legislature has been the most active in policy-making; the Polish in supervision.

Even in the policy-making category, the Polish Sejm has played a role. As Simon and Olson (1980: 212) have pointed out, the Sejm has "some standing" in the political system; its activity is particularly evident in the parliamentary committees, which have often revised, delayed, or amended legislation submitted to it by executive offices of the government. The role of the Sejm may change with changing political circumstances and, as such, may act as a kind of "barometer" of political life in Poland. In fact, this aspect of the role of the Sejm is recognized by Polish scholars as well, as indicated in the following passage:

The activity of the Sejm...is a kind of barometer of the general climate and pulse of political life. Just as an intensification of its activity and an expansion of its role in the system is an expression of accelerated social change and democratic development, so too a waning of the Sejm's activity and a diminution of its authority is a symptom of stagnation and setbacks in the development of social and political relations. (Jarosz, 1976: cited in Terry, 1981: 27)

Thus the role and activity of the Sejm has varied over time, and has been particularly synchronous with the cycle of political unrest in Poland. After the political upheavals (and leadership changes) of both 1956 and 1970, the role of the Sejm increased briefly, only to fall back to relative inactivity in subsequent years (Terry, 1981).

The potential for Sejm autonomy has always been circumscribed, however, by the lack of competitive elections, the limited number of plenary sessions (generally once a month for one day) and "the leading role of the Party." The Polish United Workers' Party (the communist party of Poland) holds about 55 percent of the seats of the Sejm and over 66 percent of the committee chairmanships, and its leading role insures that it exercises substantial control over the other seats as well. Almost all legislation is initiated either in government ministries and the Council of Ministers, both party controlled, or in the party itself.[5] During the 1970s, the regime allowed "informal consultations" between the initiating ministries and the corresponding Sejm committees, indicating the limited consultative role that the legislature played in those years (Terry, 1981).

On the other hand, the Sejm had some characteristics that often allowed it at least a limited role. The existence of the two satellite parties (the Democratic Party and the United Peasant Party) and three Catholic political associations in the Sejm "creates an arena in which there is considerable potential for interest articulation and aggregation, as well as political communication" (Simon and Olson, 1980: 213). Furthermore, while the plenary sessions themselves are mostly devoid of debate and policy-making, there is some such activity in the Sejm committees. Depending on the political character of a bill, party discipline (and therefore PUWP control) is not always exerted within Sejm *committees*; it is sometimes withheld until bills are ready for the plenary sessions. Thus, committee debates often cut across party lines (Olson and Simon, 1982). The number of committees has grown over the years, and the expertise of Sejm committee members had increased, adding to the potential role of the committees. Thus, even before 1980, Sejm committees occasionally made substantive changes to bills presented by the government.

In the most intensive recent study (in English) of the Sejm, Olson and Simon (1982) identify three factors indicating a growing capacity for action and independence by the Sejm: a qualitative improvement, in terms of training and education, of the membership of the Sejm; increased activity by the committees; and increased supervision and control over governmental administration. The result, according to the authors, is that the Sejm was moving from what Michael Mezey (1979) calls a "minimal parliament," which accepts government proposals quickly and without reservations, to a "marginal" one, which can delay and modify such proposals. Indeed, as we have seen, the Sejm did take on such characteristics even before 1980.

The Sejm during Solidarity

From the very beginning of the Solidarity period, the Sejm experienced a renaissance, as did virtually every other institution in Poland.[6] Even in the first plenary session of the Sejm after the Gdańsk Agreements, on September 5, deputies engaged in a lively and open debate on the problems facing the country. At first, criticism was focused largely on the past (Gierek) leadership, but during 1981 deputies often voiced open criticism of the current government as well. Such speeches were most often delivered by the non-PUWP deputies. At an October 1981 Sejm plenary session, for example, the non-party deputy Romuald Bukowski criticized the authorities for "exercising power neither by the will of the people nor on its behalf but rather through the implementation of various principles that were created in the past" (Radio Free Europe Research [hereafter RFER], November 11, 1981). This was surprisingly strong language, but was not unique for Sejm speeches during 1981. In its role as critic and sounding board for governmental policies, the Sejm came to resemble some Western parliaments. The party leadership apparently encouraged this autonomy, within limits. In 1981, for example, the PUWP relaxed party discipline in the Sejm on votes for personnel appointments (e.g., to ministries). This contributed to the appearance, at least, of autonomy and independence of the legislature.[7]

Statistical data also demonstrate the increased activity of the Sejm during this period. Several new committees were created in 1981 (continuing a longer-term trend), including permanent committees on Complaints and Suggestions and on Workers' Self-Management, and an extraordinary committee established to monitor fulfillment of the 1980 Agreements signed between the workers and the government. The frequency of committee meetings increased from about ten per committee per year before 1980 to eighteen per committee per year in 1980–82 (a trend which continued after 1982). Sejm deputies became more active on the floor of the legislature as well, as interpellations of government officials by deputies jumped from 26 in 1980 to 223 in 1981.[8] This activity frequently took up the bulk of the time of the Sejm's sessions. Popular expectations of the Sejm were shown in the number of letters and complaints sent to the Sejm, which increased from 7,786 in the last ten months of 1980 to 19,827 in 1981[9] (*Niektóre Dane Statystyczne*, 1985).

By the end of 1981, the Sejm was even able to resist pressure by the regime to pass an Extraordinary Powers Bill which, in restrospect, was an attempt to provide legal sanction for the eventual declaration of martial law. When the PUWP Central Committee ordered its Sejm deputies to push for such a bill, the non-PUWP deputies balked. They received encouragement from both the Church, when Primate Glemp urged deputies not to vote for the bill, and from Solidarity, when its Presidium threatened a general strike if the bill were passed. All of this was an extraordinary display of independence by the Sejm and, as T. G. Ash (1983: 242) observes, "another, important facet of the 'collapse of the system.'" The Jaruzelski regime was compelled to declare martial law without the bill, and did not achieve legal sanction of the act until after the fact.[10]

More importantly, the Polish parliament involved itself deeply in some of the many and important reform bills of the Solidarity era. The Sejm did not ever *initiate* these bills, but Sejm committees often played a major role in mediating between different groups with contending versions of reform legislation. The Sejm played a crucial role, for example, in bringing to fruition a revision of the Teachers' Charter, which addressed such issues as teachers' salaries and workloads, pedagogical techniques, and, probably most importantly, curricular content. A draft charter was initially put together by the Polish Teachers' Association (ZNP), but two more versions emerged from the government's Council of Ministers and then from the Teachers' Solidarity. By May 1981, "an acute impasse had appeared" (*Trybuna Ludu*, October 26, 1981) and the Sejm Committee on Education and Upbringing was brought in to mediate. All during the summer and fall, the committee arranged conferences with experts, teachers, representatives of the two unions and the Council of Ministers, and even sent deputies to the provinces for "fact-finding." As the chairman of the Sejm Committee wrote in October, "it is one of the committee's roles to reconcile positions, to try for a common consensus in proposing solutions, and in particularly difficult cases, to propose compromise solutions" (*Głos Nauczycielski*, October 25, 1981). A compromise version was finally achieved in early December and approved, with only minor revisions, by the full Sejm in early 1982 (after the declaration of martial law). The Sejm, and particularly Sejm committees, played a similar role in numerous other sensitive and difficult legislative issues.

Public opinion and the Sejm

During 1981, the Sejm was the most popular *official* political institution in Poland, perhaps because of the kind of open debate and autonomous activity described above. In polls on confidence in fourteen institutions, conducted in May by the government and in September by Solidarity, the Sejm ranked fourth, behind Solidarity, the Catholic Church, and the

Army. In the official poll, some 82 percent expressed trust in the Sejm; in the Solidarity poll, 50 percent.[11] These figures were much higher than for any other political institution, even for "the government" broadly considered. In another poll in the summer of 1981 on how well various institutions had done in helping alleviate the crisis, the Sejm ranked behind only the Church and Solidarity, receiving a positive assessment from half the sample (*Społeczeństwo polskie*).

The relative popularity and apparent viability of the Sejm led many Poles to focus on that institution as an object for political reform. In the summer of 1981, there was some discussion of a possible second chamber of the Sejm, to consist of deputies more genuinely representative of society. In Solidarity's Program, adopted at the union's October Congress, part of the program for establishing a "self-governing republic" consisted of the restoration of the authority of the Sejm and the amending of election rules to allow all political parties and organizations to nominate candidates. After free elections, the Sejm should then be "the supreme power in the state." By the end of 1981, over 70 percent of the population favored calling new elections to the Sejm and peoples' councils as one means of coping with the crisis (*Polacy* '81; cited in Mason, 1985: 174).

THE SEJM AND LABOR ISSUES IN 1980–81

A major issue that the Sejm, and indeed the country, had to face in 1981 was the new legislation on trade unions and on self-management. A new trade union bill became imperative from the very beginning, with the formation of the Independent Self-Government Trade Union, Solidarity. Legislation confirming the legality of the new situation was high on the agenda of Solidarity during the first half of 1981. Such legislation acquired urgency, from the regime's point of view as well, after some twenty of the old "branch" unions had withdrawn from the umbrella organization, the Central Council of Trade Unions, forcing the dissolution of the CCTU at the end of 1980. During the second half of the year, the major demand of Solidarity, and the most divisive issue between the union and the government, concerned the new legislation governing enterprise self-management.

As with the legislation on the Teachers' Charter, the Sejm was not involved in the early stages of either of these labor issues, but entered only later in a mediating role. In this case, as in others, the Sejm was ignored in the early stages. The legislature seemed to be caught in the middle; it was apparently viewed as potentially too independent by the authorities, and as potentially too compliant by the workers. The pattern with the new trade union legislation was typical: it began with the regime's appointment of a commission to revise the labor union laws.

In the Gdańsk Agreements, in the first point allowing the creation of independent trade unions, the government agreed to pursue a new trade unions' bill. The same day as the Agreements, Party leader Edward Gierek appointed a commission to develop such a bill, attached to the Central Council of Trade Unions. The composition of this commission was widely criticized, leading Gierek's successor, Stanisław Kania, to replace it in late September with a more representative group. This one consisted of seventeen lawyers and legal experts, twelve Solidarity representatives (including Lech Wałęsa), and five from the official unions. It was presided over by Sylwester Zawadzki, Chairman of the Sejm Legislative Committee (Sabat, 1981).

After seven months of work, the commission submitted a draft text of the law to the Council of State. Reflecting most of the demands of the workers, the document recognized both the right to strike and the principle of organizational pluralism. The Council of State, "taking note of the position of the Government Presidium" (which had reservations), forwarded it on to the Sejm at the end of May. There the two relevant committees (on Labor and Social Affairs and on Legislation) established a subcommittee to continue work on the legislation. As with the similar subcommittee formed to work on the Teachers' Charter, representatives of labor unions (including Wałęsa) frequently participated in the subcommittee's deliberations. There were continued disagreements between the government and Solidarity on some key issues, and even though the government had promised to have the bill by the end of the year, the debates continued right up until December 13. At the fateful and final meeting of Solidarity's national leadership in Radom on December 3, Solidarity demanded that the Sejm be presented with the Trade Union bill "in the version agreed to with representatives of Solidarity" (*Tygodnik Solidarność*, December 11, 1981). However, progress on this bill was interrupted with martial law, and was not resumed until February of 1982 (see below).

Self-management

The role of the Sejm was somewhat more evident and much more decisive on the self-management bill though, as with other cases, the Sejm was involved only quite late in the process. Self-management was not one of the issues raised during the dockyard strikes in the summer of 1980 and did not become an element in Solidarity's program until the summer of 1981. The initiatives for enterprise self-management came not from the

Solidarity leadership, but from an unofficial "Network" of self-management initiatives among Solidarity activists, and from the government, whose January 1981 economic reform guidelines suggested broadening the role of workers' self-management.

By the summer of 1981, Solidarity had officially adopted the demand for self-management, based largely on the "Network" proposals. By then, the government had also introduced its draft Bill on Workers' Self-Management. There were numerous differences in the two versions, but the most important centered on the hiring and firing of factory directors. Solidarity wanted the workers to hire and fire the director, and the director simply to carry out decisions of the self-management council. The government bill provided only that the workers would be consulted on management appointments, and that the ultimate power to hire or fire would remain with the party (Ash 1983).

The conflict over this issue reached a high pitch during Solidarity's national congress in September. Numerous delegates spoke out against the government bill. In the two-week interim between the first and second sessions of the Congress, Solidarity representatives met with the Sejm committees working on the bill and reached a compromise (*Tygodnik Solidarność*, October 2, 1981). Wałęsa managed to persuade Solidarity's Presidium to accept the compromise bill, but the next day Party First Secretary Kania informed the PUWP deputies to the Sejm that the compromise was not acceptable. That evening, representatives of the non-PUWP Sejm deputies told Prime Minister Jaruzelski that they would not vote for the Party version of the bill.

Paradoxically, the regime's customary desire to achieve unanimity in the Sejm plenary sessions gives the small non-PUWP factions a disproportionate voice. The government in this case could easily have won victory without their votes. But in an effort to avoid a split vote, the government allowed further modifications of the bill. The Sejm committees thus returned to the bill, worked intensively on it for two more days, and finally achieved a bill close to the one the Solidarity Presidium had approved. It was passed in the Sejm on September 25, the day before the opening of the second session of Solidarity's Congress.

This was not the end of the matter, since deputies at the reconvened Solidarity Congress were incensed at Wałęsa's perceived authoritarian behavior in reaching the compromise, and at the nature of the compromise itself. They passed one resolution censoring Solidarity's Presidium for its methods, and another calling on individual enterprises to hold referenda on whether they would abide by the compromise formula. The issue of self-management remained a divisive one through the end of the year.

This issue, like others, showed the difficult position the Sejm was in. In this case, the Sejm was too independent from the regime's point of view, and too compliant for many Solidarity activists. Nevertheless, the ability of the Sejm to challenge the regime, and to pressure both Solidarity and the government to compromise, was unprecedented. As the British journalist T. G. Ash (1983: 214) later wrote:

the behavior of the Sejm was without precedent in the history of Poland since 1947. For the first time, infected with democracy after a year of revolution, the deputies had directly and publicly rejected the communist Party whip.

Even apart from this dramatic episode, the Sejm had defined a new and more expanded role for itself during 1981. With the Teachers' Charter, the Bill on Trade Unions, and the Bill on Self-Management, the Sejm was able to act as mediator in helping to achieve a compromise between different interests and positions. This was accomplished largely through the committees (and unofficial meetings of some of their chairmen), which were able to meet more frequently, and with less publicity, than the plenary sessions of the Sejm. Such meetings allowed a freer exchange of views and, probably because of the lack of publicity, a greater willingness on each side to compromise. The Sejm was in a unique position to carry out this role. In a society that distrusted almost everything official, the Sejm managed to maintain some degree of integrity and popular acceptance, as an *institution*. On the other hand, the Sejm of 1981 had been elected in early 1980, before Solidarity, and therefore consisted largely of people acceptable to the regime. From the regime's point of view, then, the *membership* of the Sejm, at least, could probably be trusted not to go too far toward accommodating Solidarity.

THE SEJM UNDER MARTIAL LAW

The role of the Sejm after the declaration of martial law was, of course, greatly reduced, but even then did not return entirely to the "rubber stamp" role of earlier years. Partially because of Jaruzelski's inability to win the Sejm's approval for the Extraordinary Powers Bill in late 1981, martial law was invoked without formal legal sanction. Only after the fact was martial law formally established by the State Council. At the first Sejm session under martial law, on January 25–26, the legislature retroactively accepted the martial law decree, with only six abstaining votes and one opposing. All of these were from non-party or Catholic (Polish Catholic Social Association) delegates, some of whom voiced muted criticism of official policies on the floor of the Sejm.

This seemed to be the pattern of Sejm behavior in the first year of martial law: the legislature was not able to block legislation, or force major changes in it, but some deputies continued to criticize the government and its policies, and to abstain on or oppose unpopular legislation. Indeed, the Sejm passed a record number of bills (57) in 1982, many of them contributing to the enhanced power of the state (*Rocznik Polityczny i Gospodarczy 1981–1983*). But there were critics, such as Romuald Bukowski, the non-party deputy who had voted against the martial law legislation, who continued to speak out on major issues. In a July 5 (1982) Sejm speech Bukowski called for a general amnesty, lifting of the ban on suspended organizations (of which Solidarity was one), a restoration of civil liberties, and the lifting of martial law (RFER, July 12, 1982). The Sejm's usual practice of unanimous voting was also broken frequently. When the Sejm passed an "anti-parasitism" bill requiring most men to work, 22 deputies abstained and 12 opposed the bill. In an even blunter form of protest, 9 members voted no and 55 abstained when Stanisław Ciosek was named Minister of Labor Affairs in March 1984. Ciosek, as Minister without portfolio in charge of trade union affairs, had been the government's main point of contact with Solidarity before and after martial law.

New trade union legislation

After 1981, the most crucial piece of legislation facing the government, the workers, and the Sejm was the trade unions bill. As seen above, work on this legislation had continued through most of 1981, but key issues were still unresolved at the end of the year. Martial law changed the situation dramatically, and the process was practically begun anew when in February 1982 the Council of Ministers' Committee on Trade Unions published its "Proposals on the Trade Union Movement" (*Rzeczpospolita*, February 22, 1982). This proposal contained mostly general considerations about the nature of the future trade union movement. The trade unions should be self-governing and independent of state and administrative agencies, but they should support socialist democracy, and should have the right to strike only as a last resort, and not for political purposes.

Initially, at least, it appeared that the regime had not ruled out the possible reactivation of Solidarity, although in a more restricted form. Discussions on the government's "Proposals" in the press and in the Party often included this possibility as one alternative (RFER, April 26, 1982). But by the time the Sejm was charged with working out the details of the new legislation in July, the government's parameters for change seemed to exclude any possible role for Solidarity.

This time, unlike 1981, the Sejm had no real mediating role, in that there was no legal alternative to the government proposal. The Sejm was meant to use the "discussions" of the government proposals as a resource for developing its legislation, but its task was largely restricted to working out the details within the parameters set by the authorities. According to the underground leadership of Solidarity, the law that finally emerged had little relationship to the 1981 draft, having been thoroughly revised by the Council of State "without any negotiations or consultations with Polish society." Of the seventy-five articles of the December 1981 draft, fifty-five had been significantly changed (Bujak, 1983). Even the Sejm's Socio-economic Council, set up by the martial law authorities to discuss pending legislation, was not consulted on the bill.

According to the new statutes (Bienek, 1983), the new unions were to be "independent of the administrative and economic organs of the state"; on the other hand, they were to be grounded on the principle of the social ownership of the means of production, to recognize the constitutional principle of the leading role of the Party, and to respect the constitutional bases of the foreign policy of Poland (meaning Poland's alliance with the Soviet Union). The new unions were to be organized on the "branch" basis (rather than the regional one of Solidarity) and could be organized only at the factory level until 1984. Until 1985, only one trade union would be allowed in any one enterprise.

The new unions were extremely controversial. The law that created the new structure had also banned Solidarity, so carried negative connotations for that reason. Furthermore, the Solidarity underground called for a boycott of the new unions and demanded "trade union pluralism" at the enterprise level. By the middle of 1983, the official press began to suggest the "pluralism" could be a blind for "counterrevolutionary activity" and by the summer of 1984, government spokesmen were rejecting the notion of pluralism out of hand.

Despite the Solidarity boycott, enough people joined the new unions so that by the end of 1984, there were some 5 million members. This was only half the number that had belonged to Solidarity; but according to several different academic surveys,[12] about a third of the members of the new unions had also been in Solidarity. As one might expect, there was much bitterness and division over the issue of the new unions: between members and non-members and especially between Solidarity members who joined and those who did not. Non-members overwhelmingly thought people joined the unions for the material benefits only. Members, however, gave a variety of reasons, including a belief (by some 21 percent) in the possibility of defending workers' interests through the new unions

("Lublin 83"). Of union members 65 percent strongly support the new unions; among non-unionists, 50 percent are not interested in them, and another 14 percent considered themselves "opponents" of the new structures (*Związkowiec*, 1985).

Despite the importance and controversy associated with the new unions (or perhaps because of it), Poland's legislature seems to have been only marginally involved in the development of the new legislation after martial law, or in the various modifications and emendations of the legislation that followed in 1983 and afterwards.[13] The important role of mediator that the Sejm had played in 1981 was no longer necessary in the absence of opposing groups and opposing policies. In developing the trade union legislation of 1982, the regime did attempt to "consult" with society and with experts, and to elicit public comments. But these efforts were circumscribed both by the authorities and by the tense environment of martial law. Poland was no longer the forum for the kind of open and free-wheeling debate that requires mediation. The general pattern for the new trade union bill was determined by the Council of Ministers, the State Council, and, presumably, the Politburo. The Sejm, and even the advisory Socio-economic Council attached to it and appointed by the martial law authorities, was excluded from the process.

HYPOTHESES: THE SEJM AND POLITICAL PARTICIPATION

The changed nature of the political environment in Poland in the period 1980–82 allows the testing of some of Olson and Mezey's hypotheses (chapter 1) about the nature of parliamentary activity.

Policy attributes

In the Polish case, it seems to be true (Hypothesis 15) that the activity of the parliament is greater on issues which are new and controversial and which involve diverse publics. One might add also that such activity increases in new *situations*, since in this case it was the newness of the situation that generated the controversy, the saliency, and the multiplication of publics. In normal times, the Sejm's role has been much more limited, and is restricted to relatively routine matters. A European commentator only slightly overstates the case in arguing that "the entire activity of the [East European] parliaments consists of either approving acts and decrees of the state council, or routinely adopting the national plan and budget" (Hazan: 38).

During 1981, many more of the issues that came to the Sejm were new and controversial, and therefore attracted the attention and energy of the parliament. This was especially true of labor issues, which were central elements in the whole process or "renewal." Of course the Sejm did address other more routine matters as well during 1981, such as the reorganization and renaming of a number of government ministries. These matters, however, were more bureaucratic than political, therefore less controversial and involved less input from the Sejm.

By 1982, the trade union and self-management issues were still controversial, but they were no longer new, many people had turned away from political issues, and some of the most important groups in society were not allowed an official role in the debate. The role of the Sejm was correspondingly reduced.

With regard to Hypothesis 16, the role of the Sejm was the greatest during the intermediate stages of legislative development. Neither in 1981 nor earlier did the Sejm play a major role in initiating legislation. Both the trade union legislation and the self-management proposals originated outside of parliament, occasionally with competing versions being developed by the government (in the Council of Ministers) or extra-governmental groups (like Solidarity). On these two issues, as with others, the primary role of the Sejm was a mediating role, attempting to find a middle ground in the legislation that was acceptable to both sides. A possible role for the Sejm in the implementation stage was truncated by martial law, before these two acts could be effectively implemented.

Internal influences

Normally, the role of legislatures in communist countries is weak because of the domination of the communist party (Hypothesis 10), the centralized nature of the party (11), and the control of the parliamentary party by the executive agencies of the party (12). While all of these remained true in Poland, in all three cases the role of the Polish United Workers' Party diminished during 1981, contributing to the enhanced role of the legislature. In Poland, there were other parties and factions in the Sejm, but these typically had not played an independent role. During 1981, the "satellite" parties, the Catholic factions, and the non-party candidates all assumed a stronger role, occasionally even forcing the government to compromise on issues to avoid a split vote in the legislature. Furthermore, the PUWP itself became divided and demoralized during 1981, and this was reflected in its parliamentary faction as well, which did not always blindly follow the party whip.

Most of the activity of the Polish parliament occurred within its committees. While the reasons for this locus of activity are many, as discussed below, their effectiveness during 1981 was enhanced by the fact that they are permanent and largely parallel the structure of the government's ministries[14] (Hypothesis 13). This enabled members of the committees to work directly with their counterparts in the relevant government ministries, and to bring in their own experts who could, in turn, have influence on the ministerial officials.

Indeed, the gradual development of the committee system in the Sejm was a major factor allowing the Sejm to take advantage of its own opportunities when the external conditions changed with the birth of Solidarity. The gradual growth in the number of parliamentary committees over the years, the increasing sophistication of the structure and functioning of the committee system, and the increasing relevance of committees' jurisdictions all contributed to the Sejm's ability to act with dispatch and efficiency in what was otherwise an unstable, even chaotic, environment. Without the committee system, and the careful procedures developed to coordinate the committees, the Solidarity events could well have produced chaos inside the Sejm and immobilized it.[15]

External influences

In the Polish case, the environment, broadly considered, is by far the most important determinant of the role of the Sejm. Both in the past, and in recent years, the Sejm's role has increased during periods of popular unrest and leadership instability. To some extent, the political elite allows greater latitude at such times in an effort to restore regime legitimacy and social order. But, to an even greater extent, the more active role of the Sejm in 1981 (as after the 1956 and 1970 events) was due to the more open atmosphere that allowed the formation of new interest groups (Hypothesis 9), especially Solidarity. With the emergence of genuine political conflict between Solidarity and the government (Hypothesis 7), a forum for compromise and mediation was required, and the Sejm was one of the organizations that played such a role. In our rather limited case study, the role of the Sejm was greatest on the Teachers' Charter bill, where a functionally specialized interest group (the Polish Teachers' Association) was involved (Hypothesis 6) and where this group disagreed with Teachers' Solidarity (Hypothesis 8). Perhaps the role of the legislature would have been even greater if there had been more such specialized groups. At the time, the broad-based and heterogeneous Solidarity claimed to speak for most groups in society, and was jealous of this role. In many cases, the Solidarity leadership wanted to deal directly with the appropriate government ministers or party officials, leaving the Sejm on the sidelines.

Hypothesis 2 also holds in the Polish case. In general, the role of the Sejm has not been very great precisely because the "executive branch" (including the party) is closed, centralized, and hegemonic. During 1981, however, the governmental ministries became more "open," in their willingness to discuss and negotiate with Solidarity and other groups; and the party became more decentralized, as grass-roots reformism swept through the organization and transformed its leadership. All of this was reversed with a vengeance after December 1981, once again reducing the Sejm's room for maneuver. For the Polish parliament, the environmental factors loom large indeed.

Both before and after the Solidarity experience, with a more monolithic political system, there was no need for a mediator among groups and positions, as had been the function of the Sejm in 1981. As we have seen before, the role of the Sejm in "normal" times is largely a passive one, approving and sometimes revising legislation that is born and developed elsewhere. The Sejm may be "consulted" by the government, but the role of the Sejm is largely defined by the executive authorities of the government and the party. During 1981, however, with the proliferation of independent and autonomous interest groups and their interaction with government agencies (itself a reflection of the increased openness of the government), the Sejm was able somewhat to define its own role, and to leap into this more pluralistic environment.

CONCLUSION

The pattern of participation and activity by the Sejm in recent years conforms to that described in the Introduction: the Sejm is a kind of barometer that reflects what else is happening in the society and the political system. In times of upheaval, when the regime is forced to allow a somewhat more open political environment, the Sejm can also develop somewhat more autonomy. The Solidarity era was the most open in recent Polish history, and the Sejm played its most active and important role in the postwar period. Even so, its field for maneuver was limited by both "internal" and "external" constraints (Blondel, 1973). Internally, the parliament was constrained by its members, who had all been elected in the pre-Solidarity period. As an institution then, the Sejm was not as much part of the "renewal" that swept Polish society in 1981 as were most other institutions, including the party, which underwent considerable turnover from bottom to top. Party members retained a majority in the Sejm, and it was the same Party members who were elected before Gdańsk. Externally, the Sejm was constrained both by the constitutional principle of the leading role of the party, and by the continued (though weakened) dominance of the executive agencies of both the party and the state and, as 1981 progressed, the army.

Despite these constraints, the Sejm was involved in a major way on major pieces of legislation, including the critical bills on self-management and on trade unions. It was able to do this in two ways: through mediation, and through its constitutional prerogatives for approving all legislation. The Sejm, and particularly its committees, was able to mediate between Solidarity and the government (and sometimes with third parties) by virtue of its relatively autonomous and neutral position in the political system. The committees were particularly appropriate for this mediating role because of the informality and relative secrecy of their sessions and their ability to meet more frequently than the plenum. The Sejm committees were never entirely trusted by either the government or by Solidarity, but neither were they entirely distrusted. They were able, therefore, to play this limited mediating role.

The second factor is the constitutional requirement that the Sejm pass all legislation. In some communist states, the parliament is often bypassed on important policy issues, and this has been true to some extent in Poland. But, in Poland, the Sejm has existed as an institution for over 400 years, and its formal constitutional powers have been respected *de jure* if not always *de facto*. Thus, all the major reform bills of 1981 were sent through the Sejm. In practice, of course, the majority position of the Polish United Workers' Party in the parliament would have allowed easy control of the legislative process. Somewhat paradoxically, however, as we saw in the case of the self-management bill, the regime's desire to achieve unanimity in the Sejm plenary sessions gave the minority factions a disproportionate voice. When this group threatened not to vote for the government's self-management bill, the government allowed further modifications of the bill. In this sense, this minority group achieved a role similar to that of a small third party holding the swing votes in a parliament closely divided between two larger parties.

During 1981, the Sejm seems to have moved from what Blondel (1973) calls a "truncated" legislature with only limited influence on a limited number of issues, to the next most active type, which he calls "inhibited." As he describes such legislatures (p. 139), they have "fairly considerable influence in immediate matters but very little influence, even in the long run, on general matters. They have some effective power in constraining executive legislation, but even this has its limits; they have very little power to initiate new ideas, and their initiative remains concentrated on intermediate questions." Certainly, though, the 1981 Sejm would be at the low end of this category, in which Blondel places both the French and the Indian legislatures.

The Sejm, like most other institutions in Poland, became more active and independent during 1981. Unlike Solidarity, other trade unions, and most cultural and academic institutions, however, the growing independence of the Sejm was restrained by the party and state leadership, and may even have been engineered by the authorities to convey the impression of vitality and "renewal" within the government. In the process, the Sejm did become more active, contributing to the very real democratization that was occurring throughout Polish society. From the regime's point of view, this began to undermine the ultimate constitutional (and geopolitical) requirement of the leading role of the Party. With martial law, all independent political activity was banned, most independent institutions were abolished or restructured, and the Sejm returned to its more passive role of a truncated legislature.

Notes

1 This chapter was written before the momentous changes in Poland in the summer and fall of 1989, including the establishment of a second parliamentary chamber, the Senate; the holding of parliamentary elections in June, which were fully contested in the Senate and partially contested in the Sejm; Solidarity's capture of virtually every seat available to it in both chambers; the defection of the communist party's "satellite" parties to Solidarity; and the subsequent formation of a Solidarity-led government under Prime Minister Tadeusz Mazowiecki. These changes herald the emergence in Poland of a genuinely democratic and functional legislature, and indeed of parliamentary democracy.

2 The three Catholic political associations are Pax, the Christian Social Association and the Polish Catholic Social Union.

3 For further treatment of the role and functioning of the Sejm, see Simon and Olson (1980), Terry (1981), and Hazan (1985), pp. 33–56.

4 For a review of the literature on communist legislatures, see Nelson (1982).

5 Of the 173 bills passed between October 1980 and February 1985, 150 were initiated by the Council of State or the government, and 23 by Sejm deputies, either in groups or through committees (*Niektóre Dane Statystyczne*, 1985).

6 For the changes that affected even the Polish United Workers' Party, see Mason (1984).

7 This policy on voting for appointments continued even after the imposition of martial law.

8 This figure declined steadily after 1981 to 120 in 1982, 70 in 1983, and 59 in 1984.

9 This figure declined to about 10,000 per year after 1981.

10 This version of events has been challenged by some members of the Sejm (in discussions with the authors), who contend that there was no real conflict in the Sejm on this issue. Some Solidarity supporters, on the other hand, believe the Extraordinary Powers Bill was a smokescreen put up by a government that had planned martial law months before.

11 For the full results of these surveys, by the government's OBOP and Solidarity's OBS, see Mason (1985), p. 118. A national representative sample in 1984 showed 60.5 percent still expressing trust in the Sejm.

12 For example, an unpublished pilot survey conducted in July 1983 by the

197

198 DAVID S. MASON

University of Warsaw of 697 employees in the city of Lublin; and a second unpublished national representative sample of adults conducted in the spring of 1984.

13 Some members of the Sejm's leadership have strongly disagreed with this point, contending that the role of the Sejm, at least in legislative matters, was more substantial after martial law than before, and pointing to the high number of bills passed in 1982 and 1983 as evidence of such influence and activity.

14 As part of Gierek's efforts to strengthen the role of the Sejm in 1971, committee jurisdictions were redrawn to better correspond to ministerial divisions, and the ministries were instructed to consult with the relevant Sejm committees in drafting legislation (Terry: 33–4).

15 The author is indebted to David Olson for the ideas in this paragraph.

References

Ash, Timothy Garton (1983) *The Polish Revolution: Solidarity* (New York: Scribner's).

Bienek, Gerard, Jan Brol, and Zbigniew Salwa (1983) *Ustawa o związkach zawodowych* (Warsaw: Kziåżka i Wiedza).

Blondel, Jean (1973) *Comparative Legislatures* (Englewood Cliffs, New Jersey: Prentice-Hall).

Bujak, Zbigniew, *et al.* (1983) "Report on the situation of trade unions in the Polish People's Republic," translated and published by the Committee in Support of Solidarity, New York.

Głos Nauczycielski. Periodical.

Hazan, Baruch A. (1985) *The Eastern European Political System: Instruments of Power* (Boulder: Westview).

Jarosz, Zdzisław (1976) "Niektóre nowe elementy w organizacji o formach działania Sejmu VI kadencji," *Państwo i Prawo* (August–September). Cited in Terry (1981).

"Lublin 83." A pilot survey of 697 employees in the city of Lublin, conducted in July 1983 by the Institute of Sociology of the University of Warsaw.

Mason, David S. (1984) "The Polish Party in crisis," *Slavic Review*, 42: 30–45.

—— (1985) *Public Opinion and Political Change in Poland. 1980–1982* (Cambridge: Cambridge University Press).

Mezey, Michael L. (1979) *Comparative Legislatures* (Durham: Duke University Press).

Nelson, Daniel (1982) "Communist legislatures and communist politics," in Nelson and White (1982), pp. 1–13.

Nelson, Daniel, and Stephen White (1982) *Communist Legislatures in Comparative Perspective* (Albany: State University of New York Press).

Niektóre Dane Statystyczne o Pracy Sejmu i Jego Organów (Some Statistical Data about the Work of the Sejm and its Organs) (1985) (Warsaw).

Olson, David and Maurice Simon (1982) "The institutional development of a minimal parliament: the case of the Polish Sejm" in Nelson and White (1982), pp. 47–84.

Polacy '81. Authors: W. Adamski, I. Bialecki, J. Simorska, L. Beskid, E. Skotnicka-Illasiewicz, E. Wnuk-Lipinski, K. Jasiewicz, A. Mokrzyszewski,

L. Kolarska, A. Rychard, A. Titkow (Warsaw: Polska Akademia Nauk, Instytut Filozofii i Socjologii).

Radio Free Europe Research, *Background Reports*. Periodical.

Rocznik Polityczny i Gospodarczy 1981–1983 (1984) (Warsaw: Państwowe Wydawnictwo Ekonomiczne).

Rzeczpospolita. Daily newspaper.

Sabat, Anna (1981) "The basic tenets of the Polish Labor Union law are published," Radio Free Europe Research, Background Report, 76 (17 March 1981).

Sadowski, Christine (1984) "Bread and freedom: workers' self-government schemes in Poland," in Jack Bielasiak and Maurice Simon, eds., *Polish Politics: Edge of the Abyss* (New York: Praeger), pp. 96–117.

Simon, Maurice and David M. Olson (1980) "Evolution of a minimal parliament," *Legislative Studies Quarterly*, 5: 211–32.

Społeczeństwo polskie przed IX zjazdem PZPR (1981) (Kraków: Press Research Center), cited in James P. McGregor, "Polish public opinion in a time of crisis," *Comparative Politics* (October 1984), p. 28.

Terry, Sarah M. (1981) "The Sejm as symbol," in Maurice Simon and Roger Kanet, eds., *Background to Crisis: Policy and Politics in Gierek's Poland* (Boulder: Westview), pp. 27–64.

Trybuna Ludu. Party daily newspaper.

Tygodnik Solidarność. Solidarity weekly newspaper.

White, Stephen (1982) "Conclusions," in Nelson and White (1982), pp. 191–5.

Związkowiec, January 27, 1985. This trade union monthly presents the results of a 1984 survey of workers in large industries.

PART IV
CONCLUSION

9

Parliaments and public policy: an assessment

MICHAEL L. MEZEY

The several chapters in this volume have provided us with a wealth of data not just on legislatures but on the nations themselves and on the manner in which their political institutions struggle to deal with some of the major policy questions of the day. These chapters demonstrate once again that each political system is to some extent unique and to that same extent its legislature and the policy-making role that it assumes also will be unique.

None the less, it is still important to know how far or how little the data of these chapters have advanced us toward a better understanding of the variables that can offer a cross-national explanation for the salience of legislative institutions in the policy-making process generally and, more specifically, in economic policy-making. With these data, gathered from such a diverse set of national contexts, we can return to the hypotheses with which we began this volume to see if they are supported or weakened by what our several authors have taught us about their respective legislative institutions. We will then conclude with some suggestions about what the next step in our inquiries should be.

EXTERNAL INFLUENCES ON THE LEGISLATURES' POLICY-MAKING ROLE

Hypothesis 1. The policy activity of the legislature will be greater in presidential than in prime ministerial systems.

The distinctly American bias of this hypothesis is suggested by the fact that its strongest support comes from the three studies that involve the American Congress. Ippolito attributes the high level of congressional activity on credit policy in part to the constitutional separation between the president and the Congress. LeLoup and Woolley find that legislative

involvement in monetary policy is greater in the United States than in
Great Britain, West Germany, and France in part because of the
constitutional authority that the Congress derives from a presidential
system. Olson *et al.* note that the role of the Congress in regard to
industrial policy is made possible by the independence of the Congress
from the president, and certainly the comparatively lower level of British
parliamentary activity in this area must be attributed in part to its
parliamentary system.

These papers, however, do offer two qualifications to the hypothesis.
Baaklini and do Rego note that even though Brazil has a presidential
system, an active role for the Congress is discouraged by the strong
military support that the executive enjoys. This observation should
reinforce the traditional caution against focusing too closely on
constitutional paper rather than on actual distributions of power and
argue that under some circumstances the policy-making role of a
constitutionally autonomous legislature may not differ from one that is
constitutionally subordinate.

The second qualification comes from the observation of Olson *et al.*
that while congressional activity on the trade dimension of industrial
policy was encouraged by the constitutional independence of the Congress,
little ultimately happened because of the president's refusal to go along.
This serves as a reminder that legislatures usually need the executive to
make public policy and that while constitutional separation may produce
legislative activity, such activity may culminate in policy-making
stalemate.

A final point worth noting is the probable utility of examining
Hypothesis 1 in light of Hypothesis 16 dealing with policy-making stages.
That is, the relative activity of the legislature and the executive in both
presidential and parliamentary systems may vary with the policy-making
stage. In the former, presidents may dominate the implementation stage
while Congress dominates the deliberation stage. In parliamentary
systems, the role of the legislature will increase markedly at the
implementation stage.

Hypothesis 2 .The policy activity of legislatures will be greater if the
executive branch is more "open" than "closed," and decentralized rather
than centralized.

Support for this hypothesis comes from the two studies that described
the greatest enhancement of the legislature's policy-making role. In
Poland, these changes coincided with a greater openness (although not
decentralization) of the executive. In Brazil, the executive did not become
more open but did become somewhat more decentralized, thereby

permitting greater scope for legislative action. Among those systems in which significant change was not observed, one can still array legislatures according to their influence and observe a relationship between that array and the openness and decentralization of the executive. Certainly, in those legislatures that LeLoup and Woolley say had the least impact on monetary policy (West Germany and France) the executive has a tradition of both greater centralization and less openness than in Great Britain and the United States, where legislative activity in this area is somewhat greater. Similarly, the greater activity of the United States Congress in industrial policy and credit policy compared with that of the Indian Lok Sabha on electronics policy is partially explained by a more open and decentralized executive branch in the United States than in India.

Hypothesis 3. The policy activity of legislatures will increase as issues are handled by operating agencies rather than by high level executives.

Operating agencies tend to be more involved in policy at the implementation stage and often that is where legislatures are most active. Thus, British MPs, according to Wood, avoid public forums in favor of working directly with agencies on the specifics of regional economics policies. Similarly, the influence of the Indian Parliament on the nature of electronics policy was most apparent at the implementation stage when the policy was in the hands of the Department of Electronics.

However, this hypothesis presumes a basis for legislative access to the agencies. Thus, while monetary policy is in the hands of operating agencies, the tradition by which these agencies are insulated from "political" influence inhibits legislative, and often executive, involvement in this area. It is also important to note with Olson *et al.* that in situations in which multiple agencies are involved in policy implementation, legislative involvement may be frustrated.

Hypothesis 4. Legislative policy activity will be greater in decentralized and candidate-centered electoral systems than in party centralized electoral campaigns.

Candidate-centered electoral systems are correlates of highly decentralized party systems. When candidates depend upon local constituencies for their election and when the electoral role of political party organizations is minimized, legislators are likely to seek ways to respond to perceived electoral needs through participation in the policy process. The decentralized nature of American congressional elections has been consistently cited as an explanation for congressional policy-making behavior (Mayhew, 1974). Olson *et al.* note that congressional interest in industrial policy, particularly its trade components, was spurred by the anticipated role of the issue in future elections. Similarly, in Brazil, the nascent parties are not particularly important in election campaigns, and Baaklini and do Rego suggest that this has contributed to greater legislative concern about constituency policy preferences. With monetary policy, in contrast, LeLoup and Woolley note that the relatively low level of congressional concern is explained by the absence of any perceived tie between that issue and constituency concerns.

While parties continue to play an important electoral role in Great Britain, the growing importance of candidate variables in the outcome of elections has encouraged greater interest and activity on the part of MPs in regard to the shape of economic development legislation. On the other hand, in situations where parties continue to dominate the process of parliamentary recruitment (India, Poland, France, Germany), the scope of legislative policy-making activity continues to be restricted.

Hypothesis 5. The clearer the policy preferences of the electorate and the more they disagree with the chief executive, the greater the policy activity of legislatures.

Electoral constituencies are likely to develop clear policy preferences in regard to economic policies that have an immediate and unambiguous local impact, and it is in those instances that legislators will find themselves subject to the greatest pressures for action. Thus, Wood connects parliamentary activity and influence in regard to industrial policy to the territorial impact of such policies and to the emerging role of the MP as a buffer between the center and the periphery. LeLoup and Woolley agree that legislative activity in regard to monetary policy occurs only when there is a clear impact on electoral constituencies.

What seems to happen, as well, is that legislative deliberations center on those aspects of a complex policy that have the most obvious constituency implications. Thus, it has been the trade aspect of industrial policy that has been of greatest concern to members of the American Congress while in Brazil the trade and privacy dimensions of informatics policy has been the focus of legislative concern. In the United States, congressional activity in regard to credit policy, according to Ippolito, was motivated by a view of credit policy as a distributive and therefore a constituency issue rather than as a fiscal and therefore a non-constituency issue. Put this way, Hypothesis 5 becomes a variant of Hypothesis 16 which predicts a relationship between legislative activity and issue type.

Hypothesis 6. Parliamentary policy participation will increase as interest groups are functionally specialized and homogeneous in composition.

This hypothesis appears to evoke near unanimous support from our case studies. In nearly every country discussed, legislative activity was associated with specific interest group concerns. Sejm activity in Poland in regard to the Teachers' Charter Bill was linked with the involvement of teachers groups, and the Brazilian Congress' interest in computer industry policy was depicted as responsive to the demands of industrial groups. In India, back-bench MPs sought to influence electronics policy through the question period and Jain suggests that many questions were encouraged by affected interest groups. In the United States, Ippolito attributes the proliferation of credit programs to the activity of highly specialized groups that benefitted from such approaches while LeLoup and Woolley argue that Congress' involvement in monetary policy frequently takes place at the behest of bankers. In Great Britain, Wood says that local firms in need of help in regard to government economic development schemes contact their MPs, particularly Conservatives, who then act on behalf of these interests.

Hypothesis 7. Parliamentary policy activity will increase as interest groups disagree with operating bureaus.

There is evidence from some of these chapters that legislatures often provide a means for interest groups to gain leverage in their disputes with the bureaucracy. The role of the Sejm increased, for example, as Solidarity and the Polish bureaucracy came into more frequent and intense conflict. As interest groups concerned with computer policy came into conflict with the Special Secretariat for Informatics, the Brazilian Congress' role increased as it came under pressure from both the interest groups and the bureaucracy. In the United States, those who view themselves as aggrieved by the activities of the Federal Reserve Board frequently seek congressional intervention or at least pressure on their behalf. And in Great Britain, as noted, local business interests who are disappointed by bureaucratic decisions regularly seek intervention from their MP. But, the real question here, answered only partially by our case studies, is whether parliamentary activity leads to policy action or whether the bureaus in question are so insulated from legislative influence that parliamentary pressures are ineffectual.

Hypothesis 8. Parliamentary policy activity will increase as interest groups disagree among themselves.

One of the traditional roles of the legislature is to provide an arena in which conflicting groups can articulate their views. Thus, the legislature should have a more visible role when groups conflict than in instances of group harmony. In legislatures as diverse as the Polish Sejm, the Brazilian Congress, and the American Congress, conflict among interest groups seemed to be associated with increased levels of legislative activity. In Poland, disputes between two different teachers' groups, according to

Mason, increased the Sejm's role in regard to the Teachers' Charter Bill. In Brazil, strong disagreement among interest groups concerned with computer policy was associated with an enhanced legislative role. In the United States, the multiple and conflicting interest groups concerned with industrial policy stimulated a great deal of legislative activity although, as we have noted, little in the way of legislative action.

Hypothesis 9. Policy participation by legislatures will increase as new interest groups become active on policy matters.

Again, the evidence on this point comes from the two studies that described the greatest change in the legislative policy-making role: Poland and Brazil. In both instances, the emergence of new interest groups was associated with increased legislative policy participation. Rather than positing a causal connection between the two phenomena however, it is more reasonable to presume that the same conditions lead to the emergence of both. That is, the conditions that make it possible for an enhanced parliamentary role in a formerly more authoritarian system are also those that make it possible for new, more active, and, as suggested in Hypothesis 8, more conflictual interest group environments to form. This is a point that we will address in greater detail in the concluding remarks at the end of this chapter.

INTERNAL CHARACTERISTICS OF PARLIAMENTS

Hypothesis 10. The policy activity of parliaments will be greater in party systems in which parties are numerous and in which no one party or coalition is dominant, rather than in a system in which there are few parties and in which one party or coalition is dominant.

There seems little doubt from these studies that a movement away from hegemonic party control is connected with enhanced legislative policy-making activity. Mason associates the increased policy-making activity of the Sejm with the diminished influence of the United Workers Party and the greater activity of the other parties in the Polish system, and in Brazil the rise of an opposition party also coincided with an increase in congressional influence. In both countries, the legislature was less active during periods when the government was less hospitable toward opposition parties. In the United States, Congress seems to assume a more central role during periods in which one party controls the Congress but the other controls the presidency. As Olson *et al.* suggest, the 1981–86 situation of divided party control both within Congress and between Congress and the president created ideal conditions for congressional action in regard to industrial policy.

However, a linear relationship between the number of parties and the strength of the legislature does not necessarily obtain. When a party system is extremely fragmented, the role of the legislature may be just as restricted as it is when it is dominated by a single party. As Mezey (1975) shows in regard to Thailand, legislatures in such systems are usually dominated by military elites. An alternative hypothesis suggesting a curvilinear relationship between legislative policy-making activity and party dominance may be more appropriate. Such an hypothesis would associate less active parliaments with one-party systems, but also with no-party systems and highly fragmented multi-party systems, while more active legislatures are associated with non-fragmented competitive party systems.

Hypothesis 11. The policy activity of parliaments will be greater if the parliamentary parties are weakly organized or fragmented, rather than hierarchically organized and cohesive.

In the United States, the autonomy of the modern Congress and its members has been connected with the highly decentralized nature of the American party system and the resulting inability of legislative party leaders to discipline their members. In contrast, the comparative weakness of legislatures in Marxist political systems as well as in European parliamentary systems has usually been traced to the capacity of party leaders to enforce discipline. There is little in these studies that would lead one to question this conventional wisdom. When parliamentary parties become more decentralized, as has happened in the United Kingdom, the policy-making role of the Parliament has been enhanced. Across nations, as LeLoup and Woolley demonstrate, there is a direct relationship between the interest and involvement that their four legislatures display in monetary policy and the strength of party discipline in those systems.

A minor dissent here comes from Jain who says that the decentralization of the Indian Congress Party had no noticeable impact on the Lok Sabha's involvement with electronics policy. A more important quali-fication is entered by Olson *et al.* who note that when parties are too decentralized, as is often said to be the case in the American Congress (Sundquist, 1981: 161–2), conditions may be ripe for activity without action because the same party decentralization which makes for legislative autonomy also deprives the legislature of its primary mechanism for bringing a majority together behind a particular policy option.

One additional point that these studies suggest is the need to keep our assessments of the strength of particular governing parties current. Wood makes the point that those who still think of the British parliamentary parties as tightly disciplined highly unified organizations probably have not been paying close attention to British politics for the last ten or fifteen years, and Mason's discussion of the decentralization of the United Workers' Party may well be surprising to those who do not follow East European politics closely.

Finally, it is important to note that party discipline may vary according to issues. As Jewell and Patterson (1977: 401) note, in the United States Congress "partisan alignments and cohesion are much stronger on some social and economic issues than on others," and in other political systems it seems reasonable to assume that party discipline will be more apparent on those issues central to the concerns of party leaders rather than on other more peripheral issues. This suggests a possibly interactive relationship between issue type and party cohesion as they mutually influence levels of legislative activity.

Hypothesis 12. The policy activity of parliaments will be greater if the parliamentary parties are autonomous from external units, rather than subordinate to either governmental executives or external national headquarters.

This hypothesis, like the preceding two, has long been a staple of the comparative political parties literature (Duverger, 1954) and is supported by these studies as well. Wood argues that parliamentary involvement in industrial policy is related to the success of the Parliamentary Labour Party in regaining a degree of autonomy from the national party organization. In the case of Poland, the relaxation of central control over the United Workers' Party's legislators lead directly to a more active policy-making role for the Sejm. In contrast, the continued strength of external party organizations in France and West Germany as well as in India worked to restrict legislative policy involvement in those nations.

Hypothesis 13. The policy activity of parliaments will be greater if committees are permanent and parallel the structure of administrative agencies, rather than *ad hoc* and cross-cut the administrative structure.

As with the connection between parliamentary party autonomy and the legislative policy-making role, the connection between the strength of the committee system and the strength of the legislature's policy-making role has been well-documented (Shaw, 1979). At the extremes, Olson *et al.* confirm the frequently made point that the Congress' policy-making role is dependent upon its strong committee system, while weak committee systems are almost always associated with weak legislatures. In between these extreme cases, some subtleties do emerge. In some legislatures that do not seem to be very active in regard to policy-making, more may be happening in the less visible committee arenas than on the floor of the legislature. Mason's observations about the importance of Sejm committees in Poland reflects earlier findings of significant committee activity there and in other East European legislatures (Olson and Simon, 1982). Even in more active legislatures, the committees may be the crucial arena. LeLoup and Woolley find that in the British parliament and the United States Congress activity in regard to monetary policy is more likely to take place in committee than on the floor.

Again, Olson *et al.* indicate the disadvantages of strong autonomous committees when they suggest that in the American Congress action on industrial policy was inhibited by the fact that no one committee had exclusive jurisdiction in this area. Therefore, different committees with different agendas and constituencies all got a piece of the legislation, thereby reducing rather than enhancing the chances for action. This suggests a caveat to Hypothesis 13 in the sense that committees that cross-cut the administrative structure might deal more effectively with issues such as industrial policy than committees that parallel the administrative structure and thereby reify conventional policy categories. An additional caution is suggested by the case of the West German Bundestag where a strong committee system that parallels the bureaucratic structure does not seem to be associated with significant levels of parliamentary activity because of the decisive role of political parties in the German political system (Loewenberg, 1967: 143ff; Johnson, 1979).

POLICY ATTRIBUTES

Hypothesis 14. The policy activity of parliaments will be greater on issues of societal regulations and benefits, and on propagation of values, than on questions of security and finance.

The data from these chapters tend to support this hypothesis. The Brazilian Congress became increasingly involved in legislation on the development of an informatics industry as issues of nationalism and privacy rather than technology began to dominate the debate. In India, in contrast, these non-technological issues never seemed to enter the computer industry debate and the Lok Sabha was only marginally involved. In the United States and Western Europe, legislative activity in complex financial issues such as credit and monetary policy increased when the distributive and redistributive implications of these policies became more salient. Similarly, in the United States and Great Britain, as the distributional and redistributional implications of industrial policy became clear, legislative interest and activity picked up, particularly among those legislators who viewed their constituencies and regions as either potential winners or potential losers in the process.

These findings, while consonant with Hypothesis 14, also suggest a cautionary note, for its wording implies that policies can be readily classified as involving, for example, societal benefits rather than finance. However, nearly every economic policy area has both fiscal and societal aspects, and the degree of legislative involvement may depend on which dimension of the issue becomes salient in the debate. Rather than characterizing a policy area, it may be more useful to conceive of every policy area as providing several potential "handles" for legislative activity. As credit policy becomes perceived as an aid to education issue, or as industrial policy and monetary policy become perceived as employment issues, or as computers become perceived as raising privacy or employment issues, it is hypothesized that legislative interest will increase. To the extent that these issues are perceived as technical, international, or obscure, less legislative activity is hypothesized. This rephrasing of Hypothesis 14 focuses attention on how a policy issue is framed and perceived rather than on how it would be classified based on an objective evaluation of its content.

Hypothesis 15. The policy activity of parliaments will be greater on issues which are new rather than old, salient rather than quiet, and which activate diverse and numerous publics rather than a small and homogeneous public.

The findings in regard to Hypothesis 15 are somewhat mixed. In Poland, the labor issue was new, as was computer industry policy in Brazil, and in both countries parliamentary activity was, apparently, higher on these than on other issues. On the other hand, computer industry policy also was a new issue in India and there the Parliament was not especially active. In regard to economic policies, the specifics of issues such as industrial strategies, monetary decisions, and credit policies are not at all well understood by or salient to mass publics although the consequences of decisions in these areas may be quite salient. The catalyst for legislative involvement in these cases is probably the diversity of the publics that are activated by these perceived consequences. One reason why legislative activity was high on labor issues in Poland was that this issue seemed to activate wider publics than more technical budgetary policies.

While these findings seem to support Hypothesis 15, a somewhat contrary view comes from Ippolito's finding that the relative *invisibility* of credit policy *encouraged* Congress to act in this area because the consequences of its action were so little understood. This suggests that legislatures may be able to act more quickly on narrower and less salient issues because the diverse publics that are activated by broader and more salient issues may lead in those cases to policy stalemate. It is worth noting in this context that while Olson *et al.* found a great deal of legislative *activity* on industrial policy they found little in the way of congressional *action*.

These contradictory conclusions are indicative of the substantial issues of definition and measurement that must be dealt with before Hypothesis 15 can be rigorously tested. How can we determine if an issue is old or new? Can budgetary policy ever be new? How can the salience of an issue or the diversity of the publics that it activates be estimated?

Hypothesis 16. The policy activity of parliaments will be most extensive at the implementation stage, intermediate at the stages of gestation and deliberation and decision, and least in proposal formulation.

As with Hypothesis 15, the findings in regard to Hypothesis 16 are mixed. LeLoup and Woolley detect legislative involvement in monetary policy only at the implementation stage. This is what Jain finds in regard to electronics policy in India, and Wood indicates that it is at the implementation stage that back-bench MPs are able to exercise some influence on behalf of their constituencies in regard to industrial policy. In contrast, Baaklini and do Rego find legislative involvement in the gestation and enactment of computer policies in Brazil while Olson finds intense congressional involvement in the development of industrial policy, in part because of executive opposition to the entire concept. Mason notes that the Sejm was mostly involved in the enactment stage of labor legislation and that it had nothing to do with its gestation or, because of martial law, with its implementation.

These findings suggest that detecting the precise stage at which the legislature becomes involved may be difficult. Wood says that in Great Britain the cumulative impact of back-bench activity at the implementation stage may result in executive decisions to introduce new legislation. In Brazil, legislators introduced bills that had little chance for passage, but helped shape the policy proposals ultimately formulated by the executive. In other words, while policy may appear at first glance to originate from the executive, the executive may have been encouraged to act by prior but less apparent legislative activity. This is exactly the finding of various studies of where policy originates in the American political system. While the tendency has been to view the president as the source of major policy initiatives, more often than not the original idea has come from the Congress (Chamberlain, 1946; Moe and Teel, 1971; Orfield, 1975).

CONCLUSION

As one goes through these hypothesized bivariate relationships between an enhanced parliamentary policy-making role on the one hand and the presence of party opposition, interest groups, and a more open executive on the other, one is tempted to preface each hypothesis with the qualifying phrase "all things being equal." Obviously, there are other factors at work besides those identified in these hypotheses and the effects of these exogenous factors need to be specified. For example, a movement toward liberalization of a political system, whether in Brazil or in Poland, has consequences for parties, interest groups, and the legislature. The primary question should be what caused this liberalization; how it altered the relationship among the parties, interest groups, and the legislature should be the next question.

What this suggests is that the summary of the specific data bearing on our bivariate hypotheses should not obscure the rich and more general contextual data contained in the individual chapters in this volume. These data provide a systemic perspective from which to explain the presence or absence or enhancement or diminuition of the policy-making role of individual legislatures.

Also, as we plan future research efforts, it may be useful to seek comparisons within more narrowly defined categories. The utility of broad comparisons diminishes when the United States Congress at its least active level is more active than the Polish Sejm at its most. What looks like a dramatic increase in the policy involvement of the Brazilian Congress may, from the perspective of the United States or Western Europe, appear to be only marginal change.

While such an approach sacrifices generalizations that can be reached only with data from the entire span of political systems, we may be able to specify more precisely the nature of our several bivariate relationships as well as the patterns of interaction among the several independent variables by using narrower categories that have the effect of controlling for system variance.

We also need to sort out those variables that explain a great deal of the variance in legislative activity or performance from those that explain only marginal variance. Certainly, in Poland, the strength and hegemony of the governing party is the most important variable from which all others follow, while in Brazil, the nature of executive power and particularly the role of the military, is most important. As an hypothesis, we might say that the policy-making role of a nation's legislature varies directly with the hegemony and cohesion of its executive centred elites. By "executive-

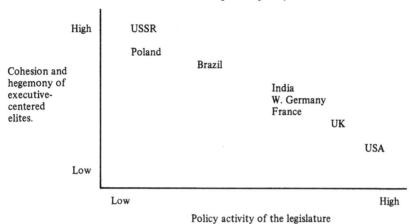

Figure 9.1   Policy activity of the legislature and executive-centered elites

centered elites" we mean that complex of military and civilian bureaucracies, the president, and the governing party that in some combination is present in every modern state. The hypothesized relationship is shown in Figure 9.1.

At the extreme, in the Soviet Union executive centered elites are drawn together into a relatively cohesive whole that dominates the political system. At the other extreme, in the United States such elites are divided and autonomous. This model suggests that the openness and decentralization of the executive has the strongest impact on the activity of the legislature and that other external variables as well as those variables associated with issue type and internal structure, are of secondary importance.

Finally, one normative question raised by Ippolito needs to be addressed. He asks whether or not the legislature performs its policy-making activities effectively. He suggests that in regard to congressional activity on credit policy we have "a constitutional invitation to act along with an institutional capacity to do so. What is missing are the incentives to make the activity worthwhile." Most of the chapters in this volume have worked from the unexamined premise that an increase in the legislature's prerogatives and therefore of legislative policy-making activity is worthwhile.

The question is whether this is so, whether Congress specifically and legislatures more generally use their policy-making prerogatives in an effective manner (see Mezey, 1986). While clearly the definition of "effective" is open to debate, unless one can answer the question affirmatively, the arguments for the enhancement and maintenance of a central role for the legislature in the area of economic policy-making must rely heavily if not solely on appeals to democratic theory.

While democratic theory provides a potent and in the view of many a sufficient justification for legislative autonomy, the recent history of the legislature's policy-making role suggests that its prerogatives need to be justified in practical as well as philosophical terms. When legislatures act because they have the right to do so but act incompetently and ineffectively, then their prospects for being able to act in the future diminish. If it becomes clear that the subordination of the legislature to the executive increases the likelihood of effective public policy action, then arguments for legislative autonomy will not succeed in the long term no matter how eloquently they are ground in democratic precepts. Therefore, the next issue on the research agenda of those interested in comparative legislative behavior must be assessments of the consequences of legislative ability.

References

Chamberlain, Laurence (1946) *The President, Congress and Legislation* (New York: Columbia University Press).

Duverger, Maurice (1954) *Political Parties: Their Organization and Activity in the Modern State* (New York: Wiley).

Jewell, Malcolm and Samuel C. Patterson. (1977) *The Legislative Process in the United States*, 3rd edn (New York: Random House).

Johnson, Nevil (1979) "Committees in the West German Bundestag," in John D. Lees and Malcolm Shaw, eds., *Committees in Legislatures: A Comparative Analysis* (Durham: Duke University Press).

Loewenberg, Gerhard (1967) *Parliament in the German Political System* (Ithaca: Cornell University Press).

Kuyhew, David E. (1974) *Congress: The Electoral Connection* (New Haven: Yale University Press).

Mezey, Michael L. (1975) "Legislative development and political parties: the case of Thailand," in Chong Lim Kim and G. Robert Boynton, eds., *Legislative Systems in Developing Countries* (Durham: Duke University Press).

Mezey, Michael L. (1986) "The legislature, the executive and public policy: the futile quest for congressional power," *Congress and The Presidency* 13:1 (Spring), pp. 1–20.

Moe, Richard and S. Teel (1971) "Congress as policy-maker: a necessary reappraisal," in R. C. Moe, ed., *Congress and the President: Allies and Adversaries* (Pacific Palisades, Cal: Goodyear Press).

Olson, David and Maurice Simon (1982) "The institutional development of a minimal parliament: the case of the Polish Sejm," in Daniel Nelson and Stephen White, eds. (1982) *Communist Legislatures in Comparative Perspective* (Albany: State University of New York Press).

Orfield, Gary (1975) *Congressional Power: Congress and Social Change* (New York: Harcourt, Brace Jovanovich).

Shaw, Malcolm (1979) "Committees in legislatures," in John Lees and Malcolm Shaw, eds., *Comparative Committees* (Durham: Duke University Press).

Sundquist, James L. (1981) *The Decline and Resurgence of Congress* (Washington, D.C.: The Brookings Institution).

Name index

Adler, Emanuel, 131, 132
Ash, Timothy Garton, 186, 187

Baaklini, Abdo, 202, 204, 211
Beer, Samuel, 105
Bienek, Gerard, 189
Blondel, Jean, 2, 194, 195
Bonker, Rep. Don (US), 82
Brady, David, 12
Braunthal, Gerard, 8
Brizida, Joubert (Brazil), 139, 142, 147
Bujak, Zbigniew, 189
Bukowski, Romuald (Poland Deputy),
  182, 188
Bullock, Charles, 12
Bulpitt, Jim, 106, 107, 108
Burns, Arthur (US), 34, 37

Cain, Bruce E., 105, 109
Campbell, Colin, 9
Campos, Sen. Roberto (Brazil), 139, 146,
  147, 155
Chamberlain, Lawrence, 211
Ciosek, Stanislaw (Poland), 188–89
Cobb, Roger, 96
Converse, Philip, 116
Coombes, David, 103
Cotrim, Paulo (Brazil), 137
Cox, Andrew, 107
Crick, Bernard, 39, 42
Curtice, John, 105

Davidson, Roger, 96
d'Estaing, Giscard (France), 47–48
do Rego, Antonio, 201, 203, 210
Dunleavy, Patrick, 119
Duverger, Maurice, 13, 208
Dyson, Kenneth, 107

Dytz, Edson, 139, 142, 148

Eagleton, Sen. Thomas (US), 89
Elder, Charles D., 96
Epstein, Leon, 13
Evans, Barbara, 41

Ferejohn, John, 105
Figueiredo, Pres. Joao (Brazil), 135, 140
Fiorina, Morris, 2, 105
Franklin, Grace, 75, 92, 96

Gandhi, Rajiv, Prime Minister (India),
  164
Garrand, Ted, 8
Gennari, Octavio (Brazil), 138, 139, 146
Gierek, Edward (Poland), 182, 185
Grant, Wyn, 104, 113

Hagger, Mark, 120
Hazan, Baruch A., 191
Heclo, Hugh, 93
Heinz, Sen. John (US), 82
Herman, Valentine, 2
Hibbing, John, 104
Huntington, Samuel P., 5
Husbands, Christopher, 119

Ippolito, Dennis, 201, 202, 205, 210, 212

Jacoby, William G., 119
Jain, Randihir, B., 205, 207, 211
Jarosz, Zdzislaw, 181
Jaruzelski, W., Prime Minister (Poland),
  183, 187, 188
Jewell, Malcolm, 208
Johnson, Nevil, 2–7
Jones, Charles, 95, 96

217

General index

219

For EU product safety concerns, contact us at Calle de José Abascal, 56–1°,
28003 Madrid, Spain or eugpsr@cambridge.org.